WOMEN IN AGRICULTURE IN THE MIDDLE EAST

Perspectives on Rural Policy and Planning

Series Editors:
Andrew Gilg
University of Exeter, UK
Keith Hoggart
King's College, London, UK
Henry Buller
University of Exeter, UK
Owen Furuseth
University of North Carolina, USA
Mark Lapping
University of South Maine, USA

Other titles in the series

Winning and Losing
Edited by Doris Schmied
ISBN 0 7546 4101 5

Critical Studies in Rural Gender Issues
Edited by Jo Little and Carol Morris
ISBN 0 7546 3517 1

Contesting Rurality
Michael Woods
ISBN 0 7546 3025 0

Women in the European Countryside
Edited by Henry Buller and Keith Hoggart
ISBN 0 7546 3946 0

Equity, Diversity and Interdependence
Michael Murray and Brendan Murtagh
ISBN 0 7546 3521 X

Mapping the Rural Problem in the Baltic Countryside
Edited Ilkka Alanen
ISBN 0 7546 3434 5

Women in Agriculture in the Middle East

Edited by

PNINA MOTZAFI-HALLER
Ben Gurion University, Israel

Routledge
Taylor & Francis Group

LONDON AND NEW YORK

First published 2005 by Ashgate Publishing

Published 2016 by Routledge
2 Park Square, Milton Park, Abingdon, Oxfordshire OX14 4RN
711 Third Avenue, New York, NY 10017, USA

First issued in paperback 2016

Routledge is an imprint of the Taylor & Francis Group, an informa business

British Library Cataloguing in Publication Data
Women in agriculture in the Middle East. - (Perspectives on
   rural policy and planning)
   1. Women in agriculture - Middle East 2. Women in agriculture
   - Egypt 3. Women - Middle East - Economic conditions - 20th
   century 4. Women - Egypt - Economic conditions - 20th
   century 5. Women - Middle East - Economic conditions - 20th
   century 6. Women - Egypt - Social conditions - 20th century
   7. Sex role - Middle East 8. Sex role - Egypt
   I. Motzafi-Haller, Pnina
   630.8'2'0956

Library of Congress Cataloging-in-Publication Data
Women in agriculture in the Middle East / edited by Pnina Motzafi-Haller.
      p. cm. -- (Perspectives on rural policy and planning)
   Includes bibliographical references and index.
   ISBN 0-7546-1920-6
      1. Women in agriculture--Middle East. 2. Women agricultural laborers--Middle East.
   I. Motzafi-Haller, Pnina. II. Series.

HD6077.2.M628W66 2005
331.4'83'0956--dc22

2005007434

ISBN 13: 978-1-138-27743-4 (pbk)
ISBN 13: 978-0-7546-1920-8 (hbk)

Contents

List of Acronyms   *vii*
Acknowledgments   *ix*

1   Introducing Gender into a Regional Agricultural
Development Project in the Middle East: Professional and
Political Challenges   1
Pnina Motzafi-Haller

2   Women in Agriculture in Jordan   13
Laith Al-Rousan

3   Women in Agricultural Production in the Palestinian Authority   47
Rema Hammami

4   A Critical Assessment of Research on Gender in the Israeli
Rural Sector   93
Pnina Motzafi-Haller

5   Gender and Agriculture in Egypt   115
Zeinab El-Tobshy

6   An Annotated Bibliography on Women and Development
in Egypt   141
Zeinab El-Tobshy

7   Conclusions: The Politics of Producing Knowledge in Development –
Gender in Rural Production   165
Pnina Motzafi-Haller

Index   *171*

List of Acronyms

ARCATF	Agriculture Relief Committees and Arab Thought Forum, Palestine
ARIJ	Applied Research Institute Jerusalem
BPWC	Business and Professional Women's Club, Jordan
BZU	Birzeit University
CAPMAS	Egyptian Central Agency for Public Mobilization and Statistics
CCA	Community Centers, Jordan
CEDAW	Center for the Elimination of Discrimination Against Women, Jordan
Danida	The Danish International Development Assistance
DAWN	Development Alternatives with Women for a New Era
DHS	Department of Statistics, Jordan
FAO	Food and Agriculture Organization
GDP	Gross Domestic Product
GFJW	General Federation of Jordanian Women
GNI	Gross National Income
GUYS	General Union of Voluntary Societies, Jordan
IDF	Israel Defense Forces
IFAD	The International Fund for Agricultural Development
JD	Jordanian Dinar
JNCW	Jordanian National Committee for Women
JNFW	Jordanian National Forum for Women
JOHUD	Jordanian Hashemite Fund for Human Development
JRF	Jordan River Foundation
JWU	Jordanian Women's Union
MENA	Middle East News Agency
MOA	Ministry of Agriculture
MOALR	Ministry of Agriculture and Land Reclamation
MOL	Ministry of Labor
MOPIC	National Team for Combating Poverty, Palestine
NCRFW	National Commission on the Role of Filipino Women
NEF	The Near East Foundation
NGO	Non-Governmental Organization
NHF	Noor Al-Hussein Foundation
NIS	New Israel Shekels
PA	Palestinian Authority
PBDAC	Principal Bank for Development and Agricultural Credit, Egypt

PCUWA	The Policy and Coordination Unit for Women in Agriculture, Egypt
PENGON	The Palestinian Environmental NGOs Network
PIALES	Palestinian Institute for Arid Land and Environmental Studies
QAF	Queen Ai'a Fund for Social Development
RPAWANE	The Regional Plan of Action for Women in Agriculture in the Near East
SFD	Social Fund for Development, Egypt
UNDP	United Nations Development Program
UNICEF	United Nations Children's Fund
UNIFEM	United Nations Development Fund for Women
USAID	United States Agency for International Development
WB	World Bank
WBGS	The West Bank and Gaza Strip
WCARRD	World Conference on Agrarian Reform and Rural Development
WID	Women in Development
YMWA	Young Muslim Women's Association
YWCA	Young Women's Christian Association
ZENID	Queen Zein Al Sharaf Institute for Development, Jordan

Acknowledgments

The essays included in this book are based on reports commissioned by the Regional Agricultural Program. I wish to thank the Regional Program, coordinated by Danida, the Danish International Development Assistance Agency, for their financial support and for encouraging me to work with my Palestinian, Jordanian and Egyptian colleagues on transforming the original reports to chapters in this book.

Each of the contributors to the book has enjoyed the research assistance of many dedicated people who are all named and thanked for their work in the individual chapters. On my part, I wish to thank my student and research assistant Ms. Sigal Nagar Ron for her help in collecting the necessary data for my chapter on Israel. I also wish to thank Ms. Miriam Bar-Lev who invited me into this project and was a dear friend as much as an able and patient administrator.

My work, as editor, was made easier because of the excellent academic facilities I had at my disposal at the Blaustein Institute for Desert Research located at Sede Boqer, Israel. I wish to thank my students Ben Okyere and Asmini Bwebwe for their hard work in making this manuscript ready for publication. I am also deeply grateful to the people in Ashgate Press who were willing to wait for years until this book came to light and for their professional and prompt handling of the manuscript when it was ready.

While each of the chapter authors is responsible for his or her essay, none of them, nor any of the organizations who supported the original reports, are responsible for the views and analysis I offer, as editor, in the introduction and conclusion of this book. All the faults and mistakes, misunderstandings and views articulated in these two chapters are my sole responsibility.

In memory of my mother

Farha Shabbtai Motzafi

Born 1920, in Basra, Iraq
Died 1998, in Rehovot, Israel

She was, like many of the women who stand at the center of this book,
an illiterate yet an admirably resourceful Middle Eastern woman

Chapter 1

Introducing Gender into a Regional Agricultural Development Project in the Middle East: Professional and Political Challenges

Pnina Motzafi-Haller

This book is about the place of women and gender relations of production in agriculture in the Middle East. It contains detailed explorations of the position of women in the national economies of Jordan, Egypt, and the Palestinian Authority. Each country-based case study follows a similar pattern of exposition, moving from a more general review of existing research about women in the national economy and society to a more focused examination of data and research results documenting the role of women in the rural sectors of these national economies and, more specifically, in the agricultural production systems within each of these economies. The main goal is to provide an updated overview of the position of women in the agricultural production systems in these four Middle Eastern settings. The Egyptian case material was rich enough to necessitate two distinct chapters. The first offers a general review of data on gender and agriculture in Egypt, while the second presents a detailed annotated bibliography that documents the wealth of research carried out in Egypt on this topic.

The fact that this volume is structured the way it is cannot be justified only in academic terms. It must be explained by outlining the story behind the production of this volume. This background is a complex and intriguing tale that links the way knowledge is produced to the critical social and political settings within which it is produced. The work presented in this book is a result of rare collaboration among Egyptian, Jordanian, Palestinian, and Israeli scholars during a brief and shifting moment of grace in the conflict-ridden history of the Middle East. It is my feeling, as the editor of this volume that the complex professional and political circumstances within which this book was produced must not be treated as a mere background relegated to the memories of those who participated in it. I believe that some of the more significant lessons that may be drawn from this volume are to be found in a critical reflexive examination of the very process that led to the production of this book. The complex political context within which this book was produced has shaped its unique nature and structured both its strength and its admitted weaknesses.

The book can thus be read on two distinct levels. For the reader who is interested in learning about the reality of gender relations of production in the Middle East, the detailed work presented in the following chapters will provide a useful and much needed overview of the issue of gender and agriculture in the Middle East. Each chapter presents an updated review of current research based on a close reading of published and unpublished data. Much of this data on gender and agricultural production is scattered in internal reports and in policy-oriented publications that often are not easily accessible. Many of these reports are available only in Arabic or Hebrew. Taken together, the four detailed "country-reports" presented in this book provide a useful synthesis of such scattered and inaccessible data basis. Each chapter points to significant gaps in the distinct data bases it reviews in order to lay the grounds for a more directed future research on the subject. Three of the chapters also offer detailed policy recommendations designed to improve the reality of gender inequality that they describe.

But the book can also be read as a fascinating story of the way gender is introduced into settings where "development work" is done. A brief outline of the settings that have led to this book is necessary before one begins to explore the questions that link politics, academic analysis, and development work.

This book is based on original reports commissioned by The Regional Agricultural Program, a six million dollar regional Middle Eastern project of agricultural cooperation initiated by the Danish Government in 1997. The Regional Agricultural Program was to be one of the early signs of peaceful cooperation in the Middle East among four specific "partners" – Egyptians, Jordanians, Palestinians, and Israelis. Development, and particularly rural development, stood at the center of this vision of a new era of peace and of the new effort to initiate regional collaboration in the Middle East. The language of planning such cooperative project was technical: "The most important principle of the cooperation is to develop a transfer of technology, genetic material, and managerial experiences, all in relation to arid and semi-arid agricultural development" (The Danish International Development Assistance, Danida 1997: 1). One of the earlier documents produced by a planning workshop held in Alexandria, Egypt, in November 1997 identified a "common denominator" which could serve as a basis for such peaceful cooperation:

> There was a full understanding that such activities should promote sustainable development. The trust of the discussions was mainly on arid and semi-arid zone development, recognizing this as the common denominator to the four partners.

The document speaks about the "integration of research, development, extension training and project implementation" and it begins by outlining four major fields upon which future programs should focus – soil and water management, integrated practices for rain-fed dryland crop improvement, small ruminant production, and post-harvesting techniques and marketing approaches. Although the question of gender and the role of women in agricultural production were not cited as a distinct field in this original overall program, it was introduced in the planning process from its outset. It was never clear, however, how is gender to be included in the larger agenda of the regional project. A special working group was formed in Cairo in November 1998 in order to discuss the ways in which women could be integrated into the project. In its turn, the working group called for the formation of a research team of four scholars, "experts on gender", that should prepare an overall review of the existing database on gender issues in agriculture in the Palestinian Authority, Jordan, Israel, and Egypt (Danida, 1999). This "preliminary assessment of existing data on agriculture for gender specific data" (Danida 1999: 2) was to form the first step in a three-step larger plan. It was expected that the assessment of data on gender and agriculture would point to specific "gaps in our knowledge" about the subject in the respective national settings. Based on this preliminary "stocktaking" of existing databases, the nominated research team of "gender specialists" was expected to propose "a set of criteria" for selecting future comparative regional studies, (quantitative, as well as qualitative). The third and final step in the process envisioned by the original "working group" was that the team of "gender experts" prepare a set of recommendations about the ways in which gender could be integrated into the larger regional project, or in the words of the paper produced in Cairo: [the team is expected to prepare] "an implementation strategy – how, when, and who" (Danida, 1999).

The four original reports submitted to the Steering Committee of the Regional Agricultural Program, and the comparative analysis produced by the four "gender-specialist" scholars in a joint workshop held in Amman in December 1999, form the core of this book. Yet the process that led from the production of the original consultancy reports to this book has been long and complex. As expected, a lot of work had to be done to make the structure and style of the reports comparable. Long sections were cut out from some reports, while other sections had to be expanded and revised in order to get a more uniform coverage by all chapters. Eventually, all the essays had to be updated in order to include data that was not available at the time when the original reports were written. The Palestinian report was thoroughly revised and updated by a Palestinian scholar, Dr. Rima Hammami, who was not part of the original team.

This necessary editorial work was carried out in extremely difficult circumstances that presented logistical, as well as political and deeply moral, dilemmas. As hostilities and tensions in the region mounted, it became extremely difficult to maintain on-going communication necessary for producing this joint project. Towards the end of 2000, and after the outbreak of the second Palestinian

Intifada, it was virtually impossible to get in touch with the contributors to this volume. For long months and years, it was not clear if the project will be published at all. It became the center for several heated discussions by the central Steering Committee, composed of official representatives from each participating country together with the Danish facilitators. For as it turned out, this book project became the only tangible, completed part of the larger regional cooperative project. All other project components, including our proposals for further comparative research and for the establishment of training workshops on gender awareness (see chapter 7) had never been implemented. At the time of this writing, it seems that all other applied segments of the agricultural project were postponed indefinitely.

What can we learn from these less than conventional circumstances about the difficulties of working as consultants in development programs and, more specifically, about the ways of introducing gender into research and policy? I wish to briefly reflect here on three sets of interrelated issues that shaped the production of this book. I shall begin by exploring the ways in which feminist concerns enter development discourse and practice. I will then speak about the inherent tensions between academic and applied development work, and I will end with a brief comment about the limits of an apolitical perspective common to this and many other similar settings where development, research and consultancy work are integrated.

Regional Peace, Gender, and Development Work

In her review of contemporary scholarship on women in the Middle East, Deniz Kandiyoti (1996) identifies three main phases, or waves in such scholarly work. The first wave is associated with studies that have explored the links between feminism and nationalism in the Middle East. One of the key questions that stood at the center of this body of work has been the compatibility of Islam with women's emancipation. Western feminist discourses were challenged by local scholars who questioned the universality of such "imported" models and argued for alternative, "indigenous" feminist models based on Islamic teachings. During the second phase, the position of women in Middle Eastern societies was directly related to development concerns. Critical of earlier assumptions that considered women's equal participation in society to be a simple outcome of national consolidation and economic modernization processes, these feminist writings (that came to be known as the WID literature, or the Women in Development school) argued that development processes are always gendered, and that research and analyses must thus assess the impact of development projects on women and attempt to get government and nongovernmental agencies to include women as recipients of development benefits. The third phase Kandiyoti outlines is characterized by an expansion of these more limited, earlier, liberal feminist and anti-orientalist discourses as Middle Eastern feminists enter into more sophisticated dialogues with Western and postcolonial feminists.

Given its stated goals and the history of its production, this book is a classical product of the WID (Women in Development) discourse, and it thus falls squarely within the second phase of research and scholarship outlined by Kandiyoti. In fact, it suggests that the WID liberal modernist model never fell by the wayside, as the more recent critical feminists might have wished (cf. Sen and Grown 1987, Kandiyoti, 1996; Marchand and Parpart 1995). It is a very powerful perspective that is stubbornly held by development practitioners who are often ignorant or uninterested in the fierce critique leveled against their modernist assumptions in the critical postmodernist academic literature. A closer look into the way gender was dealt with in this Middle Eastern Regional Agricultural Project, might suggest some of the reasons for the persistence and adaptability of the WID discourse. How relevant is the critical postmodernist discourse on gender to applied projects in the Middle East or elsewhere? What are the limits and the strengths of a modernist liberal feminist framework that has informed projects similar to the one that stands at the center of this book? In considering these questions I would like to examine the logic that shaped our work and the way in which the modernist WID model structured the actual outcome of the larger project that this publication is only a part of.

It must be made clear from the outset that the concern with gender or with what was termed "the role of women in agriculture" was introduced into the larger program of regional development by the Danes, who initiated, and contributed most of the funding for, the regional project. It did not emerge as an initiative of any of the four Middle Eastern "partners" of the project. In fact, attention to gender was an explicit guideline built into all projects initiated or supported by Danida, the Danish International Development Assistance body, a part of the Danish Foreign Ministry. A 1996 official publication of the Danish Ministry of Foreign Affairs (distributed to participants in the Cairo 1998 workshop) outlines the principles of such official policy. The book-long document titled *Agriculture: Danida Sector Policies* states that gender equality is one of Danida's four major policy objectives for the year 2000, along with poverty reduction, environmental sustainability, and democracy and decentralization. The document includes a brief paragraph that is worth quoting in full (1996: 4):

> Danida considers that measures to alleviate the time constraints on women and improve their limited access to agricultural development resources in general and to land ownership/tenure rights and credit extension advice in particular, must have high priority. Danida will promote gender-specific analyses in agricultural research, prioritize support to education and the employment of female degree-holders and extension officers, and encourage the formation of women's groups as focal points for extension advice and credit delivery. In Danida's support to the development of rural financial services, efforts will be made to identify and promote credit delivery systems that facilitate women's access to credit.

The logic for such a strong policy directive is drawn from research and insights adopted by other international aid agencies and are not unique to the Danish international development agency. It is based on the idea, established by WID researchers and practitioners since the late 1970s that members of rural households do not share the same interests and that they are often affected in diverse ways by intervention intended to increase the rural household income. For example, the Danida 1996 official document argues that "Generally, the wife controls only a small share of the household income, but tends to spend a larger part of her income on food for the family than the husband does." Or that "the woman often spends more hours than the man on agricultural activities although she alone has responsibility for taking care of the children, collecting fuel wood and water, and feeding the family" (p. 41) Based on such classical WID analytical model assumptions, the policy paper concludes that "agricultural research and other interventions have to be based on gender-disaggregated data, and that policies and interventions have to be developed from a sound understanding of the different roles, objectives, potentials and constraints of men and women in the rural household" (p. 42).

In order to implement this specific "Danida's policies on women in agriculture" all Danida-supported projects are instructed to enter into a "dialogue with governments" and with other donor agencies "with a view to promoting women's access to land ownership and property rights" and, in general, work to promote "gender-specific data, analyses and approaches" (1996: 42).

This official Danida document was made available to the members of the original working group that met in 1997 to set the agenda for the "gender specialist" team. Later, the four of us consulted it when we developed our workshops and laid out the outline for our respective synthetic reports. From the outset, the model advocated by the Danida policy directives seemed very useful and convincing and it inspired our individual work of culling gender-specific data from official national disaggregated statistics and from micro-level studies. We all felt that we worked against what El-Tobshy had described in her contribution as "the general lack of awareness of gender issues at all levels of society." Indeed, the challenge, taken up in this volume, has been to expose the specific trajectories of the ways in which women were excluded from resources in the respective settings examined and to document the systematic failure of past policies and projects to rectify this situation. Based on such synthetic analysis the essays presented in this volume make the critical argument that integrating women into mainstream society and economy is not simply a matter of good will. It should be thought through and followed by specific policies for social change. The long lists of policy recommendations that close most of the chapters in this volume attest to this reformist urge and the assumed link between research, knowledge, and directed change.

But the classical shortcomings of the modernist WID model are all too evident in these analytical works. The idea common to all the proposed policy recommendations is essentially reformist. "Mainstreaming gender" is the key term.

Underlying this notion of reform is a blunt modernist model that blames the problem on timeless "traditions" but one that seeks to transform existing patterns of gender discrimination mainly in economic life. In the introduction to chapter 3 Rema Hammami phrases it in explicit WID terms: "mainstreaming women in development process is not simply a justice issue, but also one of efficiency and economic sustainability." This binary model that poses the "non-efficient" "traditional" versus the "economic sustainability" of the "modern" aspired society is shared both by Danida officials and the contributors to this volume, although the "gender specialists" vary with respect to the way they impose this model on their findings and conclusions. A Danida official document from 1997 has this to say about traditions and the problem of gender inequality in the Middle East:

> In the traditional farming communities in the Middle East inadequate participation of women in the decision making process on the farms due to tradition and custom is a major problem for accelerated and sustainable economic development. (Danida 1997: 6)

Al-Rousan echoes this perception when he places the blame for the marginalized position of Jordanian women on the traditional paternalistic system that "we in Jordan have inherited from our ancestors". Similarly, El-Tobshy speaks about "overcoming traditional barriers" as a key factor in her analysis of the place of Egyptian women in society and economy. Hammami and Motzafi-Haller are more critical about this model and present it as a model that exist in the lives of the people themselves (e.g., the Palestinians who credit agricultural production with greater value to their lives because it reminds them of a by-gone past) or because such binary model continues to structure policy and research attention. Thus, Motzafi-Haller shows how Israeli national statistics and the attention of academic research were focused on those women who were considered more "modern" and westernized, while paying little attention to those "traditional" women, Jewish and non-Jewish, who did not fit into that model of modernist progress. The contributors grapple with the implications of their proposed reforms and with the tensions these might produce in specific settings in the Middle East. Al Rousan states: "our challenge is to achieve a compromise between our best-cherished Arab traditions on the one hand, and the requirement of modern concepts of progress and development on the other."

Academic and Applied Research

Working on this book created for me, as editor, a strong sense of schizophrenia on two levels. The first level had to do with the growing sense of rupture between the collaborative work that provided scholarly and professional meeting grounds for likeminded participants from around the region on the one hand, and a rapidly deteriorating political reality that stood in the way and often disrupted such collaboration on the other hand. We were all committed to use our academic and research skills in a project that sought to improve the conditions of life for men and women in the region. From the range of our disciplinary backgrounds, we contributed to a project that signified all that a real peace in the region could bring: shared work on issues that concerned the development of arid and semi-arid lands, building institutional settings that will bring together professionals and scholars, and strengthening existing organizations in order to provide the basis for a greater gender equality. Yet these goals seemed more remote and unrealistic as hostilities in the region increased and the prospects for peace seemed less attainable.

My deep sense of frustrations went beyond these particularly difficult political circumstances and touched upon the more prosaic tensions embedded in the dual role I played in this project as both an academic anthropologist and as a consultant on gender issues in a project of rural development. In intriguing ways, my very involvement in this regional project led me into exciting academic discourses on feminism in the Arab world that I have not been familiar with. Following my repeated visits to Cairo, to Amman, and to Jericho, and my meetings in these places with Arab feminist women, I began to read the feminist literature that had discussed the question of gender in Arab societies. What I learned form this rich literature was much more complex than the simplified model that stood at the basis of all deliberations of the working groups on gender that I took part in during the past four to five years of the project work. I summarized some of my insights and discussed their relevance to my own understanding of the Israeli feminist discourse in an academic essay published in 2001. At the same time, I also began to read quite extensively in the growing body of critical academic writing about development. As I edited version after version of this book and continued to take part in workshops in Cairo, Amman, and Jericho, I felt the need to bring the questions that were raised in this critical academic work to bear on my consultancy experience. Yet the more I read in these two bodies of academic writing (the one focused on debates about the meaning of feminism in the Middle East and the second dealing with critical thinking on development and gender) and the more familiar I became with the debates and issues it raised, the more conflicted I became about the possibility of bridging these two worlds of knowledge and praxis.

Boutheina Cheriet, an Algerian professor of comparative education, commented on this inherent tension when she cautioned in a conference held in Cairo in 1997 that "linking gender and women's studies to policy formulation should be handled with suspicion" (1997: 94). Cheriet calls for a complete rupture between feminist social research and the positivist tradition that stands at the center of the development ideology of regional and global institutions that professed a concern with the effect of development policies on women. It is necessary, Cheriet argues forcefully (1997: 96), to break away from the technocratic thinking with its hopes for a smooth transition from traditional society to modern society that typifies development institutions because, she insists, what they produce is "paternalist feminism." Such paternalism, Cheriet maintains, positions women as objects in projects imposed from above or from outside and stifles public debate necessary to allow women to become active social actors in the process of transforming their lives. Cheriet's powerful conclusions are based on her familiarity with the Algerian experience of "development". Failure of many projects in Algeria, Cheriet asserts, stems from a repeated pattern in which women are asked to "participate" in already intellectualized and preformulated projects. Development projects carried out in this paternalistic model, she concludes, have adverse, rather than positive, impact on women's lives.

I find Cheriet's feminist critique very disturbing particularly because I had been involved in this Middle Eastern collaborative project for as long as I had. I had talked to rural women in Jordan and in Egypt and I worked during long days with Muslim, Christian and Jewish professional women who worked in a range of government and non-government organizations. It is precisely such on-going direct experience with this project that convinces me that such a call to denounce all development-centered modernist practice and discourse is not very helpful. The proposed disengagement between critical academics like Cheriet (see also Harding, 2000; Kandiyoti, 1996; Marchand and Parpart, 1995) and the development practice and its institutional settings will not help to dismantle paternalistic feminism. It will only increase the impenetrable wall that effectively sets apart academic and development-centered discourses. Academics will continue to produce their, at times undecipherable, theoretical writings and the practitioners in the field will be left with their well-intentioned, if at times paternalistic, work of "mainstreaming" women into existing projects. The critical feminist academics might feel nobler, less "defiled" by the complex daily realities of sexism and gendered inequality while unhindered project managers and policy planners will continue to recreate sexist relationships that exclude and denigrate women. I do not think this state of affairs is very productive. Instead of this stand-still, I propose that more academic feminists who level the radical critique of modernist models take a greater active role in development institutions and projects. By being part of the process they might have greater effect on development discourse and practice, limited as it may seem to be in the first blush. They might be able to have some impact on the kind of work carried out in such institutions. My view here is not original, nor novel. It was widely discussed and explored in the excellent book *Development, Crises and Alternative Visions: Third World Women's Perspectives* written by Gita Sen and Caren Grown in 1987 and by the more recent thought-provoking *Whose Development? An Ethnography of Aid* written by Emma Crewe and Elizabeth Harrison (2000). These two books were written in the aftermath of what was known in the academic literature as the "development crisis" articulated in critical books such as *Encountering Development* (1995) by Arturo Escobar or in James Ferguson's *The Anti-Politics Machine* (1990). My position that academics, and particularly, critical feminist academics, can and should be engaged in the on-going process of development work is inspired by such "post-crisis" insights. Not only do critical academic feminists have much to contribute to development discourse and practice (as Crewe and Harrison admirably show in detailed case studies), but, and this is based on my own experience with this project, such engagement in "real life" processes may also prove to be a productive way to stimulate, challenge, and enrich their own theoretical thinking. Critical feminist academics might realize, as I had, that speaking about the need to respect indigenous knowledge or the noble call to allow poor rural women to set their own agenda is often an unaffordable luxury in the reality of life of most poor women; or that often gender oppression is so pervasive that any effort to empower women and encourage their direct participation in projects is a much more difficult task than it may sound from the critical academic Ivory Tower. Critical academic feminists might discover, as I had during my long engagement in this Middle Eastern comparative case study, that combating sexist attitudes that inform official policies and daily practice may very well be the only *possible* first step in the ultimate agenda of transforming gender oppression. In other words, critical academic feminists would do well to check their ideas and theories against the daily realities of women's struggles for survival and do so from the uncomfortable position of working from within development institutional settings.

The dialogue between academic and applied discourses must remain open in order to enrich both development and academic discourses. Some of the more recent writing and new thinking that articulated under the label of DAWN (Development Alternatives with Women for a New Era) is one such interesting direction. The development alternatives advocated by the DAWN model focuses on the vantage point provided by an analysis that rests on poor women's lives and experiences. Sen and Grown (1987: 20) insist that: "it is from the perspective of the most oppressed, i.e., women who suffer on account of class, race and nationality, that we can most clearly grasp the nature of the links in the chain of oppression and explore the kinds of actions that we must take." I think the DAWN focus on the experience of women as the basis for generating ideas about the kind of action taken to improve their lot is an important insight that could challenge the WID-inspired development practice that tends to rely on "specialists" or "experts" as the sole source for such policy directives. The comparative project proposed as a future research goal by the contributors to this volume was a step in that direction – a step that was never taken due to larger structures of power and regional politics. It is to the stubborn insistence not to address the politics of this development project that we now turn.

An Apolitical Discourse in a Very Political Setting

In his now classical book entitled *The Anti-politics Machine,* James Ferguson (1990) shows that many donor countries chose to limit their development projects and their social reformist agenda to issues and concerns that would not unsettle existing power structures within which they work. Despite the oppressive complex relationship between apartheid South Africa and the small, landlocked nation of Lesotho, argues Ferguson, international aid agencies preferred to define the problem of poverty and underdevelopment in apolitical terms and focus on agricultural development. This apolitical approach is shared by most mainstream donor agencies that shy away from entering the sensitive area of what they define as internal or local politics and thus limit their projects to reforms that stay within the given social and political status quo. The situation in the Middle East program that stands at the center of this volume is a classical case of an apolitical discourse and practice. The project began, as in the case of Lesotho reported by Ferguson, by paying attention to agriculture and to the "development of arid lands" as the most neutral, apolitical common concern to the four members who were to participate in the project. Considerable energy was expended in all written and oral discussions to speak about "partners" and avoid the use of the term "countries" or "nations," given the volatile position of the fledgling entity of the Palestinian Authority. Planners and the Danish facilitators made all efforts to emphasize the *collaborative* nature of the project. Detailed attention was paid to assuring a balanced representation of participants from all the four "partners" in committees, meetings and workshops and that such meetings will convene in all sites. No one spoke about the vast differences in the size and nature of these presumably equal units of comparative research. No mention was made in our comparative chapter, commissioned by the project planners, to take account and consider the interconnections that pertain among these partners' economies and societies. Such discussions might have to raise the very political question of the absolute dependency of the Palestinian economy on the Israeli economy, or of the fragile nature of the peace between Israel and Egypt or Jordan. The choice was to avoid dealing with such issues. When speaking about gender equity, the possibility of transforming gender role definition in society or challenging existing patterns of gendered division of labor that shaped such inequity was never directly raised. The recommendations remained on the level of "mainstreaming" women and of "closing gender gaps." The language of the Danish practitioners, as well as that of the local "specialist" interlocutors, never challenged existing power structures within each national boundary.

The book, as I suggested above, can be mined for such silenced issues. It can serve as a useful source for an overall view of our existing knowledge about gender and agricultural production in the Middle East, but it also can serve as a case study for what is not said, for what one can read between the lines. It is presented to enable both kinds of readings.

References

Cheriet, B., "Gender, Development and Policy Formation," in Cynthia, N. and Altorki, S. (eds.), *Arab Regional Women's Studies Workshop. Cairo Papers in Social Science*, 1997, 20, 3: 68–94.

Crewe, E. and Harrison, E., *Whose Development? An Ethnography of Aid*. London and New York: Zed Books, 2000.

Danida, *Agriculture: Danida Sector Policies*. Copenhagen: The Danish Ministry of Foreign Affairs, 1996.

------- "Seminar on Regional Agricultural Cooperation in the Middle East: Report and Findings," Alexandria, Egypt: Internal mimeo, 1997.

------- "Women in Agriculture Core Group Meeting in Cairo," Cairo, Egypt: Internal mimeo, 1999.

Escobar, A., *Encountering Development: The Making and Unmaking of the Third World*. Princeton, New Jersey: Princeton University Press, 1995.

Ferguson, J., *The Anti-Politics Machine*. Cambridge: Cambridge University Press, 1990.

Harding, S., "Gender, Development, and Post-Enlightenment Philosophies of Science," in Narayan, Uma and Harding, Sandra (eds.), *Decentering the Center: Philosophy for a Multicultural, Postcolonial, and Feminist World*. Bloomington and Indianapolis: Indiana University Press, 2000: 240–262.

Kandiyoti, D. (ed.), "Contemporary feminist Scholarship and Middle East Studies" in *Gendering the Middle East: Emerging Perspectives*. Syracuse, NY: Syracuse University Press, 1996: 1–29.

Marchand M. and Parpart J. (eds.), *Feminism, Postmodernism, Development*. London and New York: Routledge, 1995.

Motzafi-Haller, P., "Reading Arab Feminist Discourses: A Postcolonial Challenge to Israeli Feminism," *Hagar: International Social Studies Review*, 2001, 2: 63–89.

Sen, G. and Grown, C., *Development, Crises, and Alternative Visions: Third World Women's Perspectives*. New York: Monthly Review Press, 1987.

Chapter 2

Women in Agriculture in Jordan

Laith Al-Rousan

Although there are many similarities in the situation of women all over the world, every society enjoys its own particularity, and Jordan is no exception. We in Jordan have inherited a strict paternalistic system from our ancestors, which seeks "with the best of intentions" to overprotect woman. The result is that over the years women have been marginalized to the point of being excluded from most decision-making processes, both inside and outside their homes. This state of affairs has resulted in creating a totally dependent woman; she must refer to her male guardian with regard to even the simplest of matters – those relating to her own life and that of her children. Our challenge is to achieve a compromise between our best-cherished Arab traditions, on one hand, and the requirements of modern concepts of progress and development, on the other.

In Jordan, as in many less-developed countries all over the world, rural women are responsible for rearing small livestock and handling large livestock not raised on free ranges, for gathering food, fodder and fuel wood, and for drawing water and managing the domestic water supply. Rural women often provide most of the labor and make decisions about a wide range of post-harvest operations, including storage, handling and marketing. They are also predominant in off-farm food processing activities, either working in micro enterprises or as wage laborers in agro-industries. However, women's work in agriculture has often been invisible, and their role in promoting food security both at the household and national levels has long been underestimated. This is partly due to their 'invisibility' in national statistics, as well as their lack of access to decision making structures at farm and policy levels. As shown in recent studies, this situation is not unique to Jordan.

The problem is more general: development policies and programs often fail to view women as agricultural producers in their own right. For example, an IFAD study carried out in 114 developing countries in 1988 reported that the wage-earning status of women in the agricultural sector was 68% of men's wages. In 2003, women's monthly wage increased to 85.7%. Recently, the government set a minimum wage to benefit women working in the private sector.

This and more recent studies have also noted that rural women often lack access to land, which could enable them to stabilize or enhance their production systems. In 2003, Jordan national statistics indicated that only 3%

of women were landholders and that men owned the majority of animal flocks
(97.1% of cows, 78.5% of goats, sheep and 97.1% of poultry). Women's
income-generating projects led to a higher percentage of female ownership of
goats and sheep. Efforts to increase the women's secure access to resources
(land, credit, equipment and technology, education, and training, etc.) proved
to be not only a positive step towards more general agricultural growth in the
society, but also a way to increase food production and better nutrition security
for all.

Table 2.1   Demographic indicators

Indicator	
Female percentage of total population[1]	47.8%
Life expectancy at birth (years) [2]	80.69 (2004)
Percentage of households headed by females [6]	19%
Average number of children ever-born per woman 40-49 years [3]	5.9
Average age at first marriage (years) [3]	26.8
Maternal mortality rate (MMR per 100,000 live births)[4]	41.4
Infant mortality rate (IMR per 1,000 live births) [3]	22
Deliveries assisted by modern health workers [3]	97%
Contraceptive prevalence rate (for married women) [5]	58%
Female illiteracy rate (15+ years) [6]	15.8% (2001)
Primary school net enrollment [7]	95%
Secondary school net enrollment [7]	72%
Female enrollment in tertiary education [8]	47%
Female enrollment in science and technology faculties [8]	39%
Female labor force participation rate (for females 15+) [9]	14.7%
Female employment in the public sector [10]	44% (2001)
Female workers who are self-employed [9]	5.5%
Female wage workers [6]	16.4% (2001)
Unemployment (female) [11]	20.8% (2003)
Female parliamentarians (Upper & Lower Houses) [12]	3.3% (2002)
Women occupying top rank in the civil services [10]	7.43% (2001)
Percentage of females in the Judiciary [13]	2.8% (2003)
Professional unions [14]	21.2% (2001)
Labor unions [15]	22% (2002)
NGOs [16]	25% (2000)
Municipal and rural councils [12]	27% (2003)
Women's participation in political parties (founding members) [12]	8% (2002)

The main goal of this chapter is to explore the current status of rural Jordanian women and examine their role in agriculture. The review will progress from an assessment of the place of women in Jordanian society in general, to the more specific place of rural women and finally, to their particular role in agricultural production. Data are drawn from official statistics published by a range of government ministries in Jordan, as well as from a few regional surveys, with more focused research carried out by international development agencies working in Jordan, as well as academic research.

Current Status of Jordanian Women

Demographics

Jordan is a small developing country located in the Middle East. It has a population of 5.6 million (2004), which is growing at a natural rate of 2.67% per year. Women constitute 47.8% of the population. Almost half of the female population (48.3%) is women of childbearing age, 42.4% are less than 15 years old, and only 9.5% of women are beyond their reproductive cycle. Table 2.1 draws on a range of national statistical databases summarize several critical demographic indicators of women in Jordan. It shows that most women in Jordan live in households headed by males; females head only 19% of Jordanian households. While more than half of the married women in Jordan use contraceptives (58%), the average number of children per woman is still quite high, 5.9 (2000). The illiteracy rate for childbearing-age women is 20%, and their participation in the labor force stands at 14.6% (2001). Most women who enter the labor force find their position in the public sector; very few are self-employed. Table 2.1 also presents the low-level of female participation in elected political bodies. Only 3.3% (2002) of the parliamentarians in Jordan are women, and only 2.8% (2003) of the judiciary is female.

Women in Education

A closer look at the educational level of women as compared to men in Jordan is offered in Table 2.2a and 2.2b. The data presented show that there is a direct correlation between the level of formal education and gender – the higher the educational level, the lower the percentage of women who have attained that level. For example, among the illiterate, more than 70% are female, while less than 10% of Ph.D. holders are female. However, in 2001, the percentage of women Ph.D.s increased to 24.7%. The difference at the B.A. disappeared in 2002, with 50.7% female and 49.3% male B.A. graduates. The gender gap is smaller within the category of elementary and secondary school education in 1994.

Women in Agriculture in the Middle East

Academic qualifications are critical for securing a job in the public sector, where most women are employed. The academic qualifications of women searching for work in the government sector in 1996 were the following: Secondary Certificate, 43%, Community College, 68.7%; B.A., B.Sc., and postgraduate studies, 41.2%. Table 2.3 records data that document the importance of vocational training for entry into the labor market. It shows that no women enter the industrial sector, while more women than men can be found in the administration and finance sectors.

Table 2.2a   Level of education by gender in 1994

Academic level	Male %	Female %
Illiterate	22.4	72.6
Read & write	56.4	43.6
Elementary	53.2	44.8
Preparatory	54.2	45.8
Secondary	51.9	48.1
Intermediate diploma	44.5	55.5
Bachelor	67.6	32.4
High diploma	76.2	23.8
Master	82.2	17.8
Ph.D.	90.1	9.9
Unspecified	46.0	54.0

Table 2.2b   Percentage distribution of Jordanians aged 15+ by educational level and gender, 2003

Educational level	Female %	Male %	Total %
Illiterate	14.9	5.1	9.9
Less than Secondary	50.1	59.2	54.8
Secondary	18.2	17.4	17.8
Intermediate Diploma	9.8	6.5	8.1
Bachelor and above	7.0	11.8	9.4
Total	100.0	100.0	100.0

The Vocational Training Corporation (VTC) was established in Jordan in 1976, providing the following tracks: Craftsman Training Programs, Skilled Worker Training Programs and Semi-Skilled Worker Training Programs. An example of other organizations that also provide training is the Anwar Al Huda Islamic Charity to foster women's development – culturally, socially and health-wise – by providing financial support for female students and vocational training for girls.

Table 2.3 Vocational training and distribution of students accepted, 1996–97 academic year

Type	Male %	Female %
Industrial	49.9	-
Administration and finance	32.0	43.2
Agricultural	5.6	0.6
Hotel	8.9	-
Nursing	3.2	13.0
Home cottage industries	-	43.2
Total	100.0	100.0

Women's Economic Participation in Jordan

The pattern of women's employment in Jordan is irregular and unstable. It seems that most women are interested in working while in their twenties until their thirties. In other words, they seek employment outside their home before marriage, but afterwards, leave their jobs to have children. This limits their experience and development in public life. In the developing world, millions of women work in the informal economy: agricultural workers, home-workers, domestic employees, the self-employed, unpaid family workers, and workers in unregistered enterprises. The informal economy makes up significant proportions of the total workforce in these countries, especially if agriculture is included, and more women are employed in this sector than men.

Women comprised 11% of the total labor force in 1994, 16.6% in urban areas and 12.1 % in rural areas. In 2000, their participation remained low, only 13.6%. The highest concentration of the female labor force was in government offices and defense. Table 2.4 summarizes female participation in four economic sectors in 2003.

Table 2.4   Distribution of the economically-active population by sector in 2003

Sector	Women % (2003)
Agriculture	2.1
Manufacturing	10.7
Petty trade, restaurants, hotels, food and beverages	0.8
Community, social, personal services	4.9

There is a growing awareness of the vital role working women play in family welfare and survival. Many governments are now taking measures to overcome traditional, cultural and other forms of discrimination that bar women from access to equal opportunities at work. Similarly, some private companies in both developed and developing countries are instituting programs that promote the welfare, advancement and retention of their female workers, since they realize that women's skills and talent can be key for success. Despite this change in attitude, the unemployment rate among women is still high.

According to the 1994 Census, the unemployment rate among females (18 years and above) reached 32.3%. The 1996 unemployment and income survey showed that unemployment for the total population above the age of 15 years reached 12%. Among the recorded unemployed, 21.1% were female and 10.6% were males. The difference in the two surveys cannot be completely explained by the two years gap between the time the two surveys were carried out. Probably different criteria for defining "female unemployment" played a major role in the significant difference in the statistical record. In 2003, female unemployment was 20.8%. However, at present, there is an increasing trend towards participation of women in the labor force. This contributes to the empowerment of women and strengthens their participation in public life in general.

Women in Positions of Leadership and Decision-Making

Women in positions of leadership and decision making can be defined at different levels, starting with senior positions in government, the executive, legislature, judiciary, as well as leadership positions in the local community, civil society and other in institutions. It is important that women participate in decision-making and policy formulation and that they have their own views and opinions. They must be aware of these policies' existence and how they affect their own lives. The following is a review of developments in positions held by women in important decision-making bodies during 1980–2003.

Participation in Parliament

Although the government had issued an amendment to the law in 1974, permitting women to be elected to parliament, no woman entered the parliament until 1993. In 1993, one of the three women candidates was elected to the 80-member Lower House, as the only female member, and one woman was appointed to the 40-member Upper House (Senate). She continues to serve. In 1997, 17 women were candidates for parliament, but none were elected. Three women were appointed to the Senate in the same year. In 2003, women composed 5.5% of the Lower House and 12.7% of the

Senate. During that year, Jordan enacted a quota system insuring six seats for women. The quota was instituted to encourage women's participation in politics, and it modified some laws concerning women rights.

Participation in Government

In 1979, the first woman occupied a ministerial post (as Minister of Social Development) in the 32-member cabinet. In 1984, another woman became Minister of Information in a 25-member Cabinet. During the period 1985–1992, in which six successive governments were formed, no woman was appointed to a ministerial post. In 1993, a woman was appointed Minister of Industry and Trade. In January 1995, the same woman became Minister of Planning and another woman was appointed to be the Minister of Social Development. Jordan's first female judge was appointed in May 1996. In 1996-1998 there was a female Minister of Planning. In 1999, a woman played the role of Deputy Prime Minister.

Participation in Foreign Affairs

Only one woman was appointed ambassador in 1970.

Participation in Local Councils

From 1980 through 1986, one woman was appointed to the Amman and greater Amman Mayoral Councils and in 1990, nine women and later eight women were appointed members of Local Consultative Councils. In 1995, ten women were elected to Municipal Councils. One woman was elected Head of Municipal Council. In other councils, one woman was a member of the Higher Council for Health, one in the Higher Council for Education, and one on the Executive Board of the University of Jordan. In 1999, eight women were elected in municipal elections, but Jordan's first woman Mayor lost her seat.

Women in the Field of Administration

The percentage of women senior administrators and professional legislators is very low, representing 5.1% of the total number of those serving in such professions in 1991. Women as employers represented only 1.5% of the total number of employers in 1991.

Organizations Involved With Women's Development

Over the past few years, Jordanian national organizations concerned with the advancement of women in society made real efforts to secure the participation of women in both government and non-government institutions.

Governmental Organizations (GOs)

In the early 1970, Governments and development agencies viewed women mainly in their capacity as housewives, mothers and discussed them as a vulnerable sector of society. By the 1980s, and increasingly by the 1990s there was a shift into encouraging women to take a larger role in development. The following organizations contributed to this move in Jordan:

1. The Ministry of Education: Female participation in vocational training courses was encouraged. Women formed just 20% of the total number of students in vocational training schools in 1999.
2. The Ministry of Social Development: This ministry played a particularly important role in supporting the education and training of rural men and women. It provided loans for small projects planned in cooperation with local voluntary associations. In 2002, 40% of these loans were given to women who took advantage of such programs.
3. The Ministry of Health and Health Care: In addition to its on-going service to the population and its particular focus on providing preventive and treatment services for women and children, this Ministry also provided loans to support small projects to decrease poverty. Other Ministries that also had their share in supporting the women growing role in society include the Ministry of Youth, the Ministry of Justice, the Ministry of Information, the Ministry of Labor (that funds production projects to encourage individual self-employment, 19.7% of funds was used for agricultural projects in 2000.)
4. The Ministry of Municipal and Rural Affairs and the Environment, the Jordan Institute for Public Administration, the Ministry of Agriculture: the Vocational Training Corporation, the Development and Employment Fund, Department of Statistics, Agricultural Credit Corporation (in cooperation with the Ministry of Agriculture and Non-governmental organizations, provides a low interest loans, 6–8.5%, for small farmers. Women composed 12% of farmers who took loans in 2002). Several academic institutes were also important in this process. These include, Al Al-Bayt University, Mu'tah University, Yarmouk University, Jordan University of Science and Technology, The Hashimate University.

NGOs that Promote Women's Issues in Jordan

NGOs are important actors for change. These non-profitable organizations address and promote many issues that support the development of a modern society. The first women's organization in Jordan was the *Women s Solidarity Society,* formed in 1944. This organization played a prominent role in relief work for Palestinian refugees. The *Women's Federation Society,* founded in 1945, aimed at improving the cultural and social status of women, but also focused on health, childcare, and programs for poor citizens. In 1949, both societies merged into the Jordanian Hashemite Women's Society

Jordanian Women's Union (JWU) is a non- profit organization established in 1945. Its main objective is to promote women's rights by organizing and unifying their efforts to improve the status of Jordanian women and enhance equal opportunities for them, including access to land ownership, investment, income, credit and training.

The *Young Women's Christian Association* (YWCA) was established in 1950 to serve women and the community without social, religious, or racial discrimination to promote women's cultural, economic, and social roles, and to train women in leadership skills. The YWCA operates four branch offices, runs a hostel for women, several vocational training and employment centers, nurseries for children of working mothers, and social, cultural, and educational programs for mothers.

In 1952 the *League to Defend Women's Rights* was founded to raise the Jordanian women's awareness of their political role and the need to defend their social and economic rights. This laid the groundwork for the establishment of the *Jordanian Women s Union* (JWU), which has been in operation, with some interruptions, since 1953. It deals with women's rights, the elimination of all forms of discrimination against women, and the promotion of equal opportunities. At present, the Union's work focuses on the eradication of illiteracy, provision of legal counseling services, counseling for victims of family violence and abuse, legal reforms for the benefit of women, and studies and research. Currently, the Jordanian Women's Union has around 5,000 members and operates branches in seven governorates of the Kingdom.

The *General Union of Voluntary Societies* (GUYS), established in 1959, comprised today of more than 600 charitable societies, provides substantial educational and social services to women, children, the poor, and the disabled.

The *Young Muslim Women's Association* (YMWA) was set up in 1972, under the patronage of Her Royal Highness Princess Sarvath al Hassan. The YMWA offers education and employment for the disabled and runs a hostel and a community college for women.

The *Business and Professional Women*'s *Club* (BPWC), whose honorary president is Her Majesty Queen Noor, was established in 1976, and has four offices, the largest one is in Amman. Its members are mostly businesswomen and women professionals. The BPWC has initiated small business counseling that offer business advice and financial support for women entrepreneurs. The club also runs a legal counseling office for women, a hotline which offers personal and legal counseling, information and documentation center for women's studies, and a business 'incubator' service. Career counseling has become one of BPWA's new favorites – the demand for mentors and career counselors is very high among women who seek support from BPWA.

The *Community Centers* (CCA), founded in 1977, as an NGO that comprises today eight independent centers in various poor urban and rural areas in central and south Jordan. Originally an offshoot of a course on social development and organization of the Sociology Department of the University of Jordan, the Community Centers pursue a strong participatory and need-oriented approach to community development. It focuses on raining community members in how to conduct research on sensitive topics that affect their daily lives. The centers also offer vocational training courses for women and help create small income-generating projects. They also conduct educational, health, legal, and leadership programs for women and educational programs for children.

The *Queen Ai'a Fund for Social Development* (QAF) was established in 1977 and is chaired by Her Royal Highness Princess Basma Bint Talal. The organization operates approximately 50 community centers. Each addresses the particular needs of the community it serves, aiming at helping people to help themselves. QAF centers offer technical training and support for the establishment of small local enterprises, but also preschool education for children, as well as health, educational, and legal programs for women. QAF strongly promotes women's involvement in community development pro-cesses. Today it is known as the *Jordanian Hashemite Fund for Human Development (JOHUD)*.

Her Majesty Queen Noor is the honorary president of the *General Federation of Jordanian Women* (GFJW), established in 1981 as an umbrella organization for grassroots women's associations and societies. The GFJW now includes around 80 societies and committees, has offices in each of the twelve governorates, and runs 25 countrywide multipurpose centers for women and children. The Federation offers educational opportunities and guidance in family welfare and health, advocates legislative reform favoring women and promotes income-generating programs. The Federation also supports women's efforts to play an effective role in political decision-making.

The *Noor Al-Hussein Foundation,* established in 1985, runs a wide range of development activities in the field of the family health and development, children's welfare, promotion of culture and heritage, and educational development. The Foundation has also set up a program to train women in management and leadership skills. Projects promote community and individual self-reliance, participation in decision-making and project implementation with a focus on women empowerment.

The *Jordanian National Committee for Women* (JNCW) was established in 1992 and is headed by Her Royal Highness Princess Basma Bint Talal. The committee aims at optimizing women's participation in economic, political, and social life. The members of this semi-governmental policy forum are appointed and comprise of public and private bodies concerned with women's issues. The JNCW coordinates the development of the Jordanian national strategy for women and oversees its implementation. Its membership consists of the highest level of authority in government and civil society – representatives of NGOs, academic, research and professional institutions. JNCW pronounced the first National Strategy for Women adopted by the government in 1993. The National Strategy for Women is the product of an intensive effort by a large number of women and men researchers, experts and activists in the fields of women's rights and empowerment. In 2000, it presented the Committee on the *Elimination of Discrimination Against Women* (CEDAW) report to the United Nations CEDAW Committee. In 2001, JNCW formed a committee to plan and coordinate all activities regarding women participation projected for the2002 parliamentary elections.

The *Queen Zein Al Sharaf Institute for Development (ZENID)* is a local social training provider established in 1994 that supports voluntary groups, governmental agencies, women's organizations and youth activities by providing information, training and consultation.

The *Jordanian National Forum for Women* (JNFW) another organization chaired by Her Royalty Highness Princess Basma Bint Talal, was founded in 1995. It aims at training women in basic life skills, promoting legal literacy and increasing women's involvement in the country's development process, in general, and political decision-making, in particular. The JNFW has 24 main committees in the country's 12 governorates and around 12,000 members in branch committees throughout the Kingdom. JNFW also lobbies for positive perceptions and beliefs in order to change negative attitudes towards women.

Jordan River Foundation (JRF) runs socio-economic traditional income generating projects since 1995 and works on supporting the *National Child Safety Center.*

The NGOs Coordinating Committee was established in 1996. It is an executive arm of JNCW, through which all NGOs active in the women's domain coordinate their efforts and set their priorities at the national level. It also serves as a focal point between JNCW and the respective public organizations. In addition it works with the JNCW in translating the National Strategy for Women into practical programs.

The *Jordanian Committee for Women's NGOs,* founded in 1996 and chaired by Her Royalty Highness Princess Basma Bint Talal aims at establishing a mechanism of coordination among the efforts of all NGOs that work for the advancement of women in Jordan.

The *Princess Basma Women's Resource Center* was also established in 1996 and is a support body for policymakers and women's groups. The center acts as a focal point linking the Jordanian National Community for Women and various women's organizations. It provides services through its three departments: the research and studies department which generates information relevant to women's problems, the media and public awareness department, which is responsible for the dissemination of information, publications, etc., and a meeting center, which can be used by women's groups.

Other NGOs Include:

1. Al-Aqsa Welfare Society/Madaba
2. Arab Women Organization of Jordan
3. Young Women's Christian Association (Y.W.C.A.)/Madaba
4. Eidoun Women's Society
5. Al-Fuheis Working Women's Society
6. National Association for the Mentally Handicapped
7. Housewives' Society/Zarqa
8. Women's Association for Eradication of Illiteracy
9. Marj Al-Hamam Women Society
10. Human Forum for Women's Rights
11. Saqr Quraish Charity Society
12. Circassian Charitable Society
13. Al-Nahda Women Society/Souf
14. The Jordanian Psychiatric Rehabilitation Society
15. Society for the Development and Rehabilitation of the Rural Women
16. Um Al-Qura Association for Social Development
17. General Federation of Jordanian Women/Jarash Branch
18. Wadi Al-Urdon Women's Society
19. Jerash Women's Society
20. Jordanian Women's Development Society

This overview of the various activities carried out in a range of women centered organizations demonstrates that there has been an ongoing concern with women's welfare in Jordan and that due to the activities of such organizations, considerable progress for women has been achieved throughout the last decades. However, today Jordanian women's organizations face the following three challenges:

*   To remain useful tools for individual women from all walks of life by helping them to solve their pressing problems and to reach equality with men in all spheres of life.
*   To start/intensify an open and respectful dialogue among the organizations themselves, and improve coordination and cooperation where needed.

- To formulate and pursue culturally sensitive responses to the developments of the international women's movement.

Rural Women

Women living in rural areas deserve special attention since their living conditions differ substantially from those of urban women. Jordan is a highly urbanized country – only 22% of the total population lives in rural areas. The living standard of rural families is lower than those in urban areas. The workload for women in poorer families is particularly heavy. In Jordan, as in many other parts of the Arab world, rural women and their families have less access to clean water, electricity, sanitation, and sewage disposal than urban families.

Although women in Jordan have achieved progress in the field of education and substantial efforts have been made towards reducing the illiteracy rate, illiteracy among women is still very high, especially in the rural areas. 30.3% of rural women are still illiterate, as compared to 17.8% of women living in urban settlements. Women's illiteracy rate correlates with the size of the household. For women with households that have ten and more members, illiteracy reaches 91%. Although their rate of participation in the elementary education cycle does not differ significantly, more urbanized women acquire secondary school, as well as post-high-school education. This situation is partly due to the general lack of secondary schools and colleges outside the main cities, but it is greatly exacerbated by the fact that the facilities that do exist, cater first and foremost to male students. Employment opportunities for rural women are very restricted since few have intermediate diplomas, university degrees, or higher studies.

In general, far fewer rural women have made use of maternity and contraceptive health care services than urban women, and they have preferred the traditional, less safe contraceptive methods. The 2003 fertility survey indicates that the current use of contraceptives (both modern and traditional) stands at 58% (59% of urban women and 55% of rural women). The use of modern contraceptives is estimated at 40% (41% for urban and 37% for rural). Women living in Jordan's central region have the highest rate of modern contraceptive use (41.5%), while in the north, the use rate is 36.3%.

The percentage of anemic women varies between regions, but is often significantly higher in rural than in urban areas. Biomarker data collected in the 2002 JPFHS indicated that 26% of women in Jordan have some degree of anemia, and 34% of children under the age of five years were shown to have anemia. Severe anemia is not a serious health problem in Jordan.

In comparison to poor urban women, poor rural women suffer much more frequently from headaches, back pain, respiratory problems, oral and dental problems, urinary tract infections, fatigue, and exhaustion. They also complain

much more often about having too many social obligations, worry more about the
health of their family members and their own health, and more frequently indicate
that they have problems with their children.

The Role of Women in Agriculture

In many countries rural women play a significant role in agricultural activities.
These activities include production of food for the household, planting and
weeding, harvesting and post-harvest activities, livestock care, as well as
commercial farming. Specific tasks and activities in some societies are regarded as
predominately female work. They are generally tedious and time-consuming and
are considered to be household duties rather than 'work'. A women's use of time
and her mobility are constrained by multiple domestic, reproductive, and
agricultural roles. Moreover, there are more barriers preventing women, as
compared to men, from improving their productivity.

According to FAO's 1989 global survey, rural women have a reduced access to
agricultural extension services worldwide in comparison to men, and technology is
rarely designed specifically to address their gender-based needs. In Africa as a
whole, only 7% of all agricultural extension resources were allocated to women
farmers, and home economic extension received only 1% of these resources. In the
Sudan, for example, in the Gezira irrigation scheme, only 11% of 120,000 farmers
targeted by the agricultural extension services were women.

A field survey carried out in 2003 recorded that 78% of households reported
receiving agricultural extension services, with Aghwar – 85%, Ajloun – 56.6%
and Badia – 90% of total households in each. This agricultural extension was
offered by: men (46.2%), women (38.5%) or both (15.4%). Women offered
85.2% of the services in Badia while men offered 73.5% of the services in
Aghwar. In Ajloun, the pattern is different: 41.2% by men and another 41.2% by
both men and women.

Extension programs are provided in the following fields: agricultural
production (60.3%) the food industry (16.7%), animal production and health
(14.1%). The Ministry of Agriculture designs the majority of programs (60.3%),
and it designs another 24% in conjunction with the private sector. The MOA
extension service account for more than 92% in Ajloun and Badia while the private
sector, NHF, JOHUD, Cooperation Organization and charitable organizations play
a significant role in Aghwar.

Extension programs are accessed mainly through seminars and lectures
(38.5%), followed by field visits (24.4%). However, the majority of extension
services to women are accessed through seminars and lectures (80%).

The average amount of time and resources allocated to women farmers
worldwide by extension organization in 1989 was 5% of the total, ranging in
specific areas from 1%–9%. The lowest percentage was observed in North
America, and highest percentage was found in the Near East region.

Studies of Jordanian agriculture have focused on labor use and the division of labor on farms. Several studies documented that Arab rural women provided up to 70% of the agricultural labor in many Arab countries, either as owners of land or as hired laborers. (Abid-Alhamid, 1997).

According to the Labor Force Sample Survey (2001) in Jordan, the economic activity rate is estimated to be 11.7% for women and 65.5% for men. Female economic activity is only 9% in rural areas. The lowest economic activity rate is in Zarqa (8.3%), while the highest is found in Karak (15.9%). Only 4.1% of the total employed population (15+ years of age) works in agriculture, hunting and forestry (4.2% male and 2.9% female). According to the field survey (2003), the percentage of working females in agriculture is around 25% of the number of male workers. The highest rate is found in Ajloun (31%), followed by Aghwar (30%) and Badia (17%). Al-Saraf (1996) suggested that the main constraints facing women working in agriculture are:

1. Norms and traditions that stop women from working outside the family farm unit.
2. National statistics neglect to record the role of working women in the family.
3. Lack of job opportunities for women, as compared to men.

A survey carried out by Hammad (1980) in Deir-Alla in the Jordan Valley found that women's contribution to agricultural work was highest in plant and milk processing (80% of work), caring for domestic animals, and harvesting (70%). Medium contribution was observed in weeding (60%) and storing crops. Low contribution was observed in planting (30%), and there was only a minor contribution in land preparation (10%), pruning trees (5%), and marketing (10%).

In another early study carried out by the Queen Alia Fund (QAF) in 1981, a survey in the Karak Governorate was conducted on the contribution of women to rain-fed agriculture in five villages and to irrigated agriculture in one village. The results of this survey showed that more than one-third of the women (37.5%) participated in all agricultural operations in dry farming areas. It was also found that about one-third of the women (36%) in all villages kept a small number of animals, and two-thirds of these women were fully responsible for all farming activities, which included feeding, cleaning, milking, and processing the produce. In general, although women did share in decision--making, the level of participation in marketing farm products was low (about 22%).

In 1985, Malhas reviewed other studies undertaken in the Jordan Valley in the early 1980s. She indicated that the role of women was greater in home gardens and domestic food processing. The absence of the males expanded the radius of activities for women and enhanced their role in managing the farms. The women interviewed considered their contribution as vital to the survival of their households. The workload in domestic, agricultural, and nonagricultural productive activities were so heavy that most women were not acquainted with the concept of free or leisure time.

A field survey carried out in Jordan in 2003 demonstrates the following patterns of gendered division of labor in agriculture:

1. Preparation of land for planting (hoeing and plowing) is usually done by men (52.3%), followed by both men and women (29.1%), and finally by women alone (18.6%).
2. Weeding appears to be women's work (52.3%), followed by both men and women (31.4%).
3. Planting is often the responsibility of men (46.5%).
4. Fertilization is carried out mainly by men (51.4%) and to a lesser extent by both men and women (25.7%).
5. Irrigation is also largely a man's responsibility (46.5%); only 27.5% of the cases surveyed reported that both men and women are engaged in irrigation.
6. Pesticide spraying – the same work-sharing pattern as in irrigation.
7. Harvesting is a cooperative activity, with women shouldering most 50% of the work load.
8. Packing produce is also a cooperative activity. 50% of the sampled household reported that both men and women are responsible for this work; only 29% of the sampled households reported that packing is carried out by women only.
9. Marketing of agricultural products – men, 67.9%; women, 24.7%.
10. Women are mainly responsible for animal husbandry (53%).
11. Feeding of animals is usually carried out by women (74.3%).
12. Watering animals is 75.3% the responsibility of women.
13. Milking is carried out by women (90.3%).
14. Care of animals is largely done by women, 85%.
15. Supervising calving – women, 82.3%.
16. Shearing – women, 51%; men, 32%.
17. Marketing of animals is split almost evenly: 40% by men, 38% by women and 22% by both.

The interest by international organizations, such as the UN and the USAID, in documenting women's place in rural society produced several interesting studies in the 1990s. More attention was paid to regional differences within Jordan and more studies began to use interviews rather than simple surveys as the main tool of research. One of the first fruits of this new focus was 'Alkudauri's work in the early 1990s. Al-kudauri (1993) conducted a study in two villages: 300 women in Raymon were interviewed and 284 women in Al-Hashemiya. She concluded that 80% of the women were married before the age of 20, and that the average family size was eight persons in Raymon and nine in Al-Hashemiya. More than 50% of the women had not had miscarriages. The illiteracy rate was quite low in Raymon (31.3%) and higher in Al-Hashemiya (49.6%). Traditions and values have played a vital role in discouraging women from pursuing their education. The study reveals that the level of women's participation in the wage labor force is very low, and most women's work is in the informal sector, for which they receive little or no income because their skills are considered as "traditional", i.e., are taken for granted. With regard to the husbands' professions and income, the study revealed that most men in the study areas worked in the military services, and their monthly income was around 148 JD in Raymon and 118 JD in Al-Hashemiya (between 130-160 US $).

A more recent study published in 1998 by Al-qussous set out to determine the training needs for rural women in the Zarka region. Al-qussous concluded that 38% of those in the sample expressed a strong interest in training designed to develop women's skills. Furthermore, the study showed that there were differences between the degree of the training offered and demographic characteristics. Not surprisingly, all the women interviewed in the study asked for more social services (education and health) and expressed their wish that their rural infrastructure facilities would be improved (water, sewerage and transport). Many noted interest in specific training programs that might increase their earning capabilities, with priority for sewing. An interesting observation made in this interview-based research was that more than 50% of the women interviewed were unaware of existing development projects in their areas. It was thus concluded that existing development projects in the study areas were, in fact, incompatible with the women's basic needs. The research findings raise a critical question that has implications beyond the study objectives. The questions to be asked are "How are development projects chosen? Why? Who is the target group?" As this study demonstrates, when asked, rural women can express their needs but their needs are often ignored. Thus planning of future rural development projects should consider these findings.

How does one explain then the field survey of 2003 results that found that the number of women who received agricultural training was higher than that of men: 48.5%, as compared to 36.4%? The 2003 reported that in Aghwar, men accounted for 64.3% of trainees, while in Ajloun the gender division of trainees was almost even. In Badia, women formed 85.2% of the trainees. The particularly high rate of training received by women is unique and was due, in part, to the fact that the areas selected for the field study is the hub of several recent income projects funded by international donors. Another factor that might explain this unique case is that in the region studied both men and women provided agricultural training. Specifically, men provided 75% of training in Aghwar, women provided 85.2% of training in Badia. Both men and women accounted for 54.5% of training in Ajloun.

Another important aspect of research carried out in Jordan since the 1990s has been its greater attention to regional variation. The category "rural women" was thus questioned, and regional variations of ethnic, economic, and social diversity among regions within the country began to be considered. One of the best examples of such an approach can be found in the studies carried out by The Near East Foundation (NEF) in 1993. The focus of research was the role of women in agriculture in two regions. One study focused on agro forestry and farming activities in one village in Jerash Governorate (Soul) and in one village in Ajloun Governorate (Koufrangeh). The second study focused on the use of pesticides. The women interviewed in the agro-forestry study (50 women) were classified into three categories: family farm laborers (65%), farm managers (30%), and wage laborers (5%). Fifty-six percent of the women were illiterate. Farm income represented 88% of a family's total income. The main farming activities were fruit tree planting (olives, grapes, and almonds). Vegetables and cereals were grown on a limited scale. Goats, cows, chickens, and donkeys were the main livestock owned in the two villages. The main technical problems were directly linked to protection of the plants and to marketing. Food processing within the farm household was centered on dairy products, pickling (mainly olives), and fruit processing (mainly, drying grapes and figs).

Women farmers who acted as family laborers accounted for two-thirds of the respondents. Women wage laborers were day workers, working outside the household compound. They performed their work under the supervision of the farm managers. Thus, they were not expected to make decisions or to have special skills. Typical activities included planting, weeding, picking, and harvesting. The income of this wage labor is vital for low-income families. Thus, lack of resources and sources of income has pushed the women to work as wage laborers outside of the household. These women were found to contribute to most farming activities, but they had limited agricultural skills. Their work was typically unpaid and their main incentive for hiring themselves out for farm work was stated to be their intention to improve the family's standard of living. In the families of these hired female farm laborers, it was found that although males were the decision-makers, women were often consulted.

In considering this hired labor by women it is also important to examine the rate paid for such labor. According to a labor force survey carried out in 2001, the majority of women working in the agricultural sector (75% of the total of female workers) received a salary of less than 100 JD per month, as compared to only 40% of working males who received this low salary. Thus, most females were employed at the very low levels of the occupation structure intensifying the relative poverty of women in the rural areas. Moreover, rural female unemployment rate stands at 22.4%. Most of the unemployed were young, educated and first entrants into the labor market. If the unemployed female is the head of her household, the poverty of the household is particularly harsh.

Women farmers who assumed a managing role represented less than one-third of the total sample. They were often widows, divorced women, or women who managed the land due to the absence of men. Twenty-two percent of the women in the research sample acted as head of household. They managed all farm activities except for marketing farm produce, which was delegated to close male relatives. Women in this category were found to have strong personalities and more significant technical experience, as compared to other women in the sample. Land ownership has given these women the opportunity to assume a decision-making role, while the absence of women's control over land resources (prevalent in the other two categories of women in the research sample – family laborers, and wage laborers) has relegated those women to a consulting role, at best.

The sample in the second study undertaken by NEF in 1993 consisted of 100 women farmers. In this study, women were also classified into three categories: farm managers, family laborers, and wage laborers. Most women in this study were in the category of family laborers. These women farmers were found to be involved in identification of pest and disease problems, preparation of pesticides for application, and application or supervision of the application process in the absence of men. Women were also found to be reluctant to be involved in spraying due to possible harmful effects. Female wage laborers were not involved in pesticide application. This is partly explained by the low-level skills of women hired. The few women who were engaged in pesticide application did not use protective wear and, like the men, refrained from following proper technical procedures for pesticide application

Decision-Making in Agriculture

In terms of decision-making in the agricultural production process, the 2003 field survey records the following: 65% of agricultural decisions are taken by men, as compared to 22% taken by women and 13% by both. When men own land, men make 81% of the decisions. When land is owned by women, women make 76.5% of the decisions.

Decisions concerning animals and animal products are made by men in 55% of the cases and in 36.5% by women, with 8.5% by both. This pattern changes with ownership, when men own the animals, they make 95% of decisions. When women own the animals, they make 100% of decisions.

The role of women in agricultural decisions has increased to 33.3% where agricultural land is either rented or owned. In Badia, the men make 100% for the decisions.

The differences between these two studies can be attributed to their respective focus – one is more concerned with general agricultural production, the other more specifically with pesticide application. It might also be attributed to the variation in the regional population. This observation was also made by Himour in 1994. In a survey carried out in the Al-Azraq area in the Zarqa Governorate, Himour (1994) found that the contribution of women to agricultural work was restricted to home gardening. Growing vegetables and fruit trees were the main type of household agricultural activities. Ninety-two percent of the sample raised some animals (about 20 birds, 1–3 sheep or goats per household) and some women had two cows. Thirty percent worked as wage laborers outside the household. Thirteen percent owned the land and 9% had taken independent decisions with regard to agricultural work. No women used any machinery. Seventy-one percent spent 1–2 hours/day in farm work. Only 20% of the women in the research sample received credit from commercial banks used by their husbands, and in all cases, these monetary inputs were secured through male relatives, most often the women's husbands.

The contribution of women was the highest in caring for domestic animals (75%), but some also shepherded and sheared sheep, weeded, harvested, and worked in transportation and storage. A medium contribution was observed in planting (45%) and marketing (40%). The lowest contribution was observed in pesticide application (20%), with a minor contribution in pruning trees (5%). Food processing (using traditional methods) was found to be exclusively female work, such as baking bread for sale, pickling, making tomato paste and dairy products, and drying vegetables. It was concluded that extension services should be enhanced for home gardening and home economics.

Focusing his research in north of Jordan in Irbid, Karablieh (1990) found that the farm household contributed 19% of the total labor requirement for growing cereals and legumes under rain-fed conditions. In this region, the contribution of females to agricultural production was quite limited; it was only 3% of the total labor, but represented 16.7% of the household labor. The female contribution was relatively high in planting and fertilizing; medium in threshing and manual harvesting, and low in weeding, cleaning and transport. Weeding was the most important activity of women in cereal production (56% of married women's work, planting (23%), and manual harvesting (13%). Weeding was the most important activity of women in legume production (54% of total wives' work), manual harvesting (36%), and transport (7%). Contribution of hired female labor was more significant in cereal production than legumes (17%, as against 0.4%). The highest contribution of female labor in cereals was in winnowing and cleaning, threshing, and manual harvesting, while their contribution in legume production was limited to winnowing and cleaning (26% of the total labor of this activity).

One explanation for the limited contribution of women to this regional agricultural production was the introduction of mechanical harvesting and the adoption of herbicides. These new technologies have effectively displaced women from agricultural work. Another reason was related to social considerations – farmers do not want their wives or daughters to do farm work outside the boundaries of the homestead. Another explanation for the recorded minimal rate of female participation in agricultural production in the region might be the source of the data: male farmers were interviewed and they tended to minimize the importance of farm work carried out by female family members.

The rate of female participation in agricultural production was also recorded by Al-Rimawi (1991), who carried out a comparative study in the Jordan Valley and in the eastern region. Al-Rimawi found that 36% of her sample of 194 farming households involved the labor of female farm family members, most of them wives of the head of the household. Fifty-six percent of these wives were involved in farming activities. Forty-three percent of the wives were involved in farming activities for less than one month, and 20% for more than six months. The involvement of wives and other female members of the rural household in the agricultural production carried out within the family farm was linked to the size of the rural household, farm size, the number of dependent youngsters (i.e., under the age of 15), and to the availability of water for irrigation, as well as vegetable production and farm income. Women's involvement with tending fruit trees in the rain fed areas was high, but normally lasted only a few weeks. Shepherding and looking after animals was almost exclusively a female job.

Eighty-one percent of the rural households in Al-Rimawi's sample had at least one member involved in off-farm employment. They were employed mainly in the rain-fed areas, in salaried or wage labor and regular jobs, outside the agricultural sector and in the tertiary sector. Public administration was a major employer for all households' members; self-employment and business ranked second for operators, and farm-related jobs ranked third.

Brockhaus (1996) carried out a survey in the Karak Governorate at Wadi Ibn Hammad on the role of women on sheep and goat farms in Jordan. The survey showed that efforts to expand the spheres of women's activities beyond the domestic role could lead to a pattern that deviated from the expected behavior of women and, in the long run, help transform elements in the gender structure of local value system, in which religion plays very prominent role. Brockhaus convincingly argued that local traditions are not necessarily based on religion. On the contrary, some traditions may be in direct conflict with religion, i.e., preventing women from inheriting land. Thus, traditions can be altered and gender hierarchies transformed.

Specifically, Brockhaus documented that women in Wadi Ibn Hammad are involved in many activities in animal production (milking, feeding, and processing, etc.). The average number of sheep and goats per household was found to be 60 animals; about 80% of the households had less than 50 animals. Forty-four percent of farm households were landless or owned less than four dunums, and 70% owned less than 50 dunums. Widowed women farmers were responsible for managing the herd, and might act as de facto holders in the absence of males (husbands, sons) who sought employment off the farm to supplement family income. Fifty-eight percent of households had off-farm income.

Marketing their products was not a problem for the Wadi Ibn-Hammad women. The data show that 57% of these women market some of their products through traders and middlemen. Direct marketing has been part of the woman's responsibility for generations, as customers for their product were usually relatives and neighbors. Farm income was found to be the main family income, even for families with women as head of household. Some women were members in informal saving societies (savers' clubs). This indigenous credit system was based on the contribution of each woman to the group's fund. The total sum of money paid up by all women was used by one of the women in the savings club, each in turn.

The researcher noted the growing self-confidence among these women farmers and the growing number of women farmers who share in decision--making. This case study is an excellent example for the potential for change in the division of labor and power within rural households and for the need for relevant information about methods of production, animal health, and farm management designed for rural women. Based on his findings, Brockhaus stressed the importance of integrating women in rural development despite and within the constraints of existing social norms. Depriving women of the freedom to control their legitimate share of income, coupled with their systematic lack of access to credit, were identified as critical factors in limiting women's economic and social independence. The researcher called for adopting participation advocacy and reaching women farmers through female extension agents, as well as group extension through cooperatives and tribal structure.

Hatter in a preliminary survey of the women's role in agriculture in Jordan used a random sample of 396 women farmers and agricultural laborers. They were interviewed during 1992–1994. Hatter found that women farmers were relatively old and illiterate. Half of the women were over 40 years old; 71 % were married and 19% were widowed or divorced. Fifty-six percent of the women in his sample were illiterate, and 25% had a basic education. Sixty six percent of the husbands worked away from the farm in civil service positions, were self-employed, or part of the military forces.

On the whole, women's contribution to agricultural production was high (75-91%). They contributed their labor in harvesting, weeding, planting, and packing. Only 42–46% of the women took part in hoeing, irrigation, and fertilization. Similar to the rural realities in other regions, documented in the studies mentioned above, the smallest proportion of women (19–26%) was engaged in plowing, transport, and spraying. The highest proportion of women in this region was found to be involved in activities dealing with animal production (sheep, goats, and cows). Within this labor category, the largest contribution of female labor (68–84% of the farm work) was in milking, processing, feeding, and cleaning. A medium contribution (35% of the work) of female labor was in caring for animals. And a low contribution (22–25% of the work) was recorded in the areas of transport, shepherding, and shearing.

The study also examined the main sources of information for agricultural knowledge by gender. TV and radio programs were found to be the most widely used sources of information – these were mentioned by 50% of the respondents. Women noted that their husbands (40%) and male extension agents (30%) were also important sources of agricultural knowledge. Other women, sons and daughters, female agents, as well as leaflets were valuable means of distribution of such knowledge mentioned by about 20% of the women in the study. The least important sources of information for rural women were newspapers, cooperatives, and private extension agents (mentioned by only 11–18% of the women).

According to the 2003 field survey mentioned above, the ownership of agriculture technology in Jordan is not widespread; only 13 households reported owning agricultural machines: 12 by men and 1 by a woman. Eleven of these machines were located in Aghwar. The share of women in the ownership of agriculture machinery does not exceed 8%. The identified agricultural machines are trucks and pick-ups.

The general problems encountered by women farmers were the hardship of work, which was mentioned by 44%, financing (16%), the high costs of production relative to output prices, and the small size of farms (6–12%). The most important technical problem was related to plant and animal diseases.

Thirty-six percent were satisfied in living in the rural areas and a similar percentage (34%) hoped that their daughters would be involved in farm work. However, more than half (56%) wanted their sons to become involved in farming activities.

Income generating projects are seen as main instrument for the economic empowerment of women. The field survey 2003 demonstrates that men benefit more (44%) than women (36.3%) from agricultural projects. Women in Ajloun benefit the least (28.6%), compared with women in Aghwar (32.5%) and in Badia (46.7%). This is so despite the intended goal of most projects to benefit the whole family (73.6% in Aghwar, 57% in Ajloun and 100% in Badia). Only a few project place women and women's particular needs at the center of their project design. The following is a brief review of such women-focused projects.

Women-Oriented Projects

1. Management of Agricultural Resources Project in Tafeelah and Karak Municipalities (1997–2002):

Goals: Soil conservation, rationalization of available water use and improvement of the living conditions for low-income families.

Activities:
1. Provide women with loans to initiate small income-generating projects.
2. Construct necessary infrastructure to further soil conservation and water harvesting.

Results: Soil conservation projects and rural development projects (home gardening, food production, land reclamation) – 3,370 of these projects were women oriented.

2. Participatory Support and Land Development Project (1997–2001):

Project Goals:
1. Increasing income-generating capabilities of rural women.
2. Increasing the farmer's involvement in production activities by applying modern methods for soil, water conservation and planting fruit trees.

Project Activities:
1. Rangeland development.
2. Focus on women-oriented activities and provision of financial support.

Project Results: In 2002, the number of persons benefiting from agricultural development activity reached 9,000, out of which 100 women benefited financially from the Rural Women Financial Unit. The Women's Cooperation Unions established three diary factories.

3. Income Resources Diversity Project (1995–2001):

Goals: Improving the economic and social conditions for rural families that work in agricultural sector by raising income level to alleviate poverty, as well as providing employment.

Activities:
1. Animal production.
2. Food manufacturing.
3. Water harvesting.

Performance: The total number of persons benefiting from the project activities was 4,665. Only 30% of them were women.

4. Agricultural Resources Management Project in Yarmouk Basin River (2000–2006):

Goals:
1. Improve food security and increase income for target groups and rural woman in the project's region.
2. Develop infrastructure and rationalize water and soil resource use.

3. Improve living conditions of targeted women's groups in project region, by supporting the activities that increase income.

Activities:
1. Construct agricultural roads.
2. Water harvesting activities and maintenance of springs and irrigation canals.
3. Provide loans for families to establish rural income-generating projects.

Performance:
1. Rural developing projects (190 persons)
2. Water collection wells (491 persons).
3. Agriculture roads construction (3,432 persons).
4. Soil maintenance and reclamation activities, (1,970 persons)

5. Agricultural Exhibition Project (2001):

Project goals: Help the rural families in marketing their products including the following:
1. Rural women product exhibition for North County (24–25.7.2001 in Ajloun).
2. Rural women product exhibition for Middle County (28–29.10.2001 in Muaqer).
3. Rural women product exhibition for South County (17–18.10.2001 in Karak).

6. Project Designed to Increase of the Income of Rural Woman in the Eastern Region (1999–2001):

Goals: Improvement of social and economic conditions for poor rural families in the project region by establishing women-oriented agricultural projects and encouraging local resource investment.

Project Activities:
1. Food manufacturing.
2. Goat and sheep rearing.
3. Rearing of Laying Poultry.

Performance:
1. 100 women were taught about different methods of food manufacturing and 70 of them established their own production projects.
2. 32 women engaged in, goat and sheep production activities.

3. 48 women engaged in, laying poultry production activities.
4. A dairy factory for women association in the region was established.

7. Laying Poultry Production Project (2002):

Goal: To improve the economic situation of poor rural families by establishing small projects to increase the income by using local resources, targeting rural women and consolidating their participation in the development process.

Activities:
1. Identify the target category and provide them with suitable training.
2. Distribute tools to participating families needed for raising and feeding the poultry.
3. Publication of laying poultry production brochures.

Performance: Twenty-eight families participated; each family was provided 40 chickens, feed for one month, and production tools. In addition, training workshops on laying poultry production were conducted.

8. Permanent Exhibition For Rural Products Project (2001–2002):

Goals: Improvement living standard of rural families, economically, socially, as well as highlighting the role of rural women in the development processes by achieving the following incremental goals:
1. Increase rural women's proficiency in simple techniques for food manufacturing.
2. Establish income-generating projects using available local resources.
3. Educate rural women about the use of modern methods for   marketing agricultural products.
4. Direct attention and support of organizations that fund rural women's development projects.

Activities:
1. Establish a permanent exhibition for rural products.
2. Train women in targeted categories.
3. Publish technical brochures about suitable techniques to prepare and market rural product.

Results:
1. Increased communication and networking among production associations in different municipalities through the agricultural departments.

2. Growing technical support from women associations, gender units, and various agencies.

9. Establishment of Diary Manufacturing Units Project in Jordan's Badia:

Goals: Encourage and support animal owners in Jordan's Badia. Improve their economic, social and health levels by achieving the following phased goals:
  1. Raise and improve rural women's skills in dairy product manufacturing.
  2. Support and develop marketing of the dairy produce of rural women's.
  3. Establish rural production projects for dairy product manufacturing in order to benefit women associations.
  4. Increase the participation of local organizations in rural development.

Activities:
  1. Form a technical supervising committee for the project. Determine the target area and target groups.
  2. Construct buildings; provide diary-manufacturing units; purchase required equipment.
  3. Provide general training for all women in the region and special training for women who will work in manufacturing units in the future.
  4. Work with interested associations.

Results:
  1. Greater communication between farmers and production associations in different municipalities
  2. Building of infrastructure in selected associations that aimed to establish manufacturing units.
  3. Establishment of training programs on dairy products manufacturing for local community members and participant associations.

Concluding Discussion

The growing interest in promoting women's role in development in Jordan is part of a general trend in the development community at least since the UN Declaration of the Decade for Women in 1975. This call for integrating the issue of gender in all aspects of development planning was enhanced by the principles and measures proposed by the World Conference on Agrarian Reform and Rural Development (WCARRD) in 1979. These proposals were reaffirmed in the UN Conference in Nairobi in 1985 (at the end of the women's decade) and in the conferences organized by FAO in the 1980s to review the progress achieved in implementing the WCARRD Program of

Action. The 4th World Conference on Women held in Beijing in September 1995 was the culmination of this increased international attention to gender issues.

This review of the place of Jordanian women in agricultural production suggests that knowledge of the pattern of women's social and productive activities and the constraints imposed on them is a necessary framework for analyzing the relative success and failure of past projects. A solid database that takes into consideration the gender factor in agricultural production and understands the specific needs and problems of women farmers has to be consulted during the design and implementation of all agricultural projects. Failure to make available to women technological knowledge required to implement modern farming methods often results in under-utilization of women's labor. Ignoring or bypassing female farmers in economies where women's labor accounts for a large share of the labor force in agriculture may have the opposite effect of the hoped-for increase in farm productivity.

Paying direct attention to women's needs is not only a more equitable civil policy, but also will have positive effects on agricultural productivity, increase rural income, and improve the quality of life in rural areas. Traditions are not unchangeable and gender hierarchies are not based on Islamic religious norms. Studies carried out in a range of regions in Jordan since the early 1990s have shown that projects designed in ways that integrate women into the improved agricultural production process may contribute not only to increased production and economic output, but also eventually to a transformation in gender relations in society.

Repeated past failures in programs and policies of rural development are due to the underlying assumption that large groups of people are internally homogeneous, rather than made up of men, women, boys and girls, and various disadvantaged groups with different needs and interests. Goals and objectives cannot be achieved without a clear understanding of the target groups. Knowing who does what and when in providing for household food security is essential in planning policies, strategies, programs, and projects.

Gender mainstreaming became an integral part of most projects in Jordan today. This is an institutional strategy aimed at giving equal rights and opportunities to men and women. Furthermore, it involves the integration of women's concerns in aspects of planning and implementation. By the mid-1990s, the Government of Jordan has increasingly recognized the importance of addressing gender issues in agricultural programs and projects. The Agricultural Policy Charter of the MOA (Jordanian Ministry of Agriculture, 1995) has explicitly recognized the need to target groups not adequately reached by private or other extension institutions. It was stated that efforts would be made to target men and women on the basis of their specific roles, and such intervention will be tailored to meet the needs of the specific target groups. Female economic activity has attracted attention because of its important contribution to alleviating poverty levels and improving the distribution of income.

Many of the new development projects in Jordan took gender issues into greater account and had specific activities geared to women. In 1997, Al-Rimawi traced the increased interest in designing projects sensitive to the place of women in development in Jordan since the early 1990s. Her review concludes that Jordanian government policies have shown firm commitment to integrate women in the process of development. This was manifested at all levels of the educational and health services. The review offered here supports Al-Rimawi's conclusions. We have shown that marked development has been achieved in education in Jordan. This has drastically reduced illiteracy and enhanced women's competitiveness in most fields in the labor market, including agriculture. We have also seen that the active campaigns and development activities of the nongovernmental organizations (NGOs) in Jordan, especially the Queen Alia Fund (QAF) and the Noor Al-Hussein Foundation (NHF) had a critical role in the process. Yet, within this general positive trend we must note that Jordanian working women still face serious social obstacles and various forms of pressure, which prevents their career development. More specifically that:

1. Illiteracy is still high among women, particularly in the rural areas.
2. Women do not have an opportunity to participate in institutional occupations, as the bias in favor of men is clear in this area.
3. Women's lack of training and necessary skills and expertise that could have enabled them to enter the labor market in the various fields of production, including industry.
4. There is a clear failure to deal with the legal aspects of women's rights. Legal regulations must be drafted to encourage women and afford them opportunities.

Recommendations

Gender bias and blindness, prevalent worldwide, constitute the principal constraints contributing to food insecurity. Such gender blindness is not only the bias in agricultural policies against women, but also reflects the sector's inability to take women into account and involve them, both at the household and national decision-making levels. For example, household food production, processing and preparation have traditionally been considered women's work, while cash crop production, men's work. However, women do much of the work in cash crop production, such as seed preparation, weeding and harvesting, even though the income may be attributed to men. Therefore, government and NGO sectors inside Jordan should work to improve the status and condition of women according to these recommendations:

1. Raise women's awareness and educate them about their rights and obligations.
2. Develop and improve the quality of the health services for women throughout the Kingdom, as well as raise awareness regarding health issues by providing women with proper health education.
3. Increase the number of mother and child health centers and makes known the services provided in both urban and rural areas. Improve the performance of these centers and the quality of services they provide.
4. Raise the awareness of women in reproduction relating issues by rewriting school curriculum and public campaign in the media.
5. Establish counseling centers with appropriate services for children in the rural areas in order to maximize utilization of training opportunities provided by the centers.
6. Promote progressive leadership development and empowerment of women. Arrange exchange visits among women, as well as opportunities for informal training, so that ideas, techniques, and information can be shared.
7. There is a need for innovative methods and approaches in order to create greater opportunities to engage women in decision-making, such as by encouraging increased networking and lobbying among women so that they become more influential in our society. It may be prudent to assign gender focal points in ministries and NGOs.
8. Utilize the mass media to improve women's conditions and strengthen the role of women, both within the family and in society. Highlight the productive role of women and their ability to make a contribution to the process of development. Enable women to make an effective contribution to the preparation of media programs directed towards the improvement of women's conditions.
9. Support and encourage the convening of conferences, seminars and workshops relating to women's issues and commissioning of studies, data collection and documentation of information on the status of women's.
10. Enhance the participation of women in the preparation and implementation of plans and programs for the preservation of the environment, matters of rational use of energy and water, by drawing attention to the role of women in environment preservation and use of energy. This will raise environmental awareness in all strata of society, in general, and among women, in particular.
11. Increase Jordan's capacity to finance programs and projects targeted for disadvantaged women to ensure the removal of economic and social constraints they face.
12. Develop new programs to integrate or reintegrate women into productive employment. Such programs should include business counseling, training, job placement, and support services.

13. Encourage self-employment among women; make available more facilities for loans and take the necessary measures maximize investment and minimize production risk.
14. Support conventional and community-organized financial institutions through the provision of capital and resources, which will serve women entrepreneurs.
15. Work on development of women's organizations to raise the internal efficiency, as well as the effectiveness and creativity of organizations, as service providers adapted to different target groups.
16. Initiate extension programs first in the most productive areas, where the perceived needs of women farmers are strongest and the chances of success are highest.
17. Expand agricultural extension programs and combine them with population and family planning programs to upgrade women's capabilities in agricultural work and home management. This can be done through training courses for women in modem agricultural techniques, including productive household gardening and food processing to maintain the quality of products and to sell them in local and regional markets.
18. Include training on techniques and new technologies on food processing for women who work in the animal production/products sector in agricultural courses.
19. Initiate micro studies of socio-economic factors of all aspects of the agriculture in all areas within the Kingdom.

Acknowledgments

I wish to express my gratitude to my research assistants Eng. Kristina Bnayyan and Eng. Mohammad Abu As'ad.

Notes

[1]   Population & Housing Census, 1994, Department of Statistics.
[2]   Life expectancy, 2004, available at:
      http://www.cia.gov/cia/publications/factbook/geos/jo.html.
[3]   Department of Statistics, Jordan Annual Fertility Survey 2000.
[4]   Maternal Mortality Study, Family Health Services Project, 1997, Ministry of Health.
[5]   DHS, 2000, Department of Statistics (preliminary findings).
[6]   Department of Statistics, Employment, Unemployment and Poverty Survey (second round 2001).
[7]   Educational Statistical Report, (1995–1996), Ministry of Education.

[8]   Ministry of Higher Education, 1997.
[9]   Employment and Unemployment Survey, 1996, 2nd Round, 1996.
[10] Correspondence from The Civil Service Commission, 2001.
[11] Department of statistics, 2003, unemployment, Amman.
[12] UNIFEM, 2004, report of Jordanian women status, pp. 50–55.
[13] Ministry of Justice, 1997.
[14] Correspondence from various Professional Unions, 2001.
[15] Correspondence from the General Federation of Jordanian Labor Unions, 2001.
[16] Correspondence from the Ministry of Social Development, 2001.

References Cited

Al-kudauri, A.S., *Rural Women Development in Jordan*, Fridrich-Ebert Foundation Center for Women Studies, 1993.

------- *Rural Pluriactivity in Jordan*, Ph.D. Thesis, Wye College, University of London, 1991.

Brockhaus, M., *The Role of Women on Sheep and Goat Farms in Jordan*, 1996.

Central Intelligence Agency (CIA), Jordan Statistics, 2004. Available from URL: http://www.cia.gov/cia/publications/factbook/geos/jo.html. (Arabic)

Central Intelligence Agency (CIA) and United Nations statistics, 2003. Available from URL: http://www. Nationmaster.com/country/jo.

Civil Service Commission, Jordan, *Correspondence*, 2001.

Department of Statistics Jordanian, "Women: Major Socio-economic Indicators," 2004.

------- "Jordan Annual Fertility Survey," 2000.

------- "Employment, Unemployment and Poverty Survey," 2001.

------- "Unemployment," Amman, Jordan, 2003.

Food and Agriculture Organization (FAO) Technical Cooperation Project, "National Plan of Action for Gender Mainstreaming in Rural and Agriculture Development," *Situation Analysis of Women in Agriculture & Gender Mainstreaming, 2004–2010*, Jordan, 2003.

General Federation of Jordanian Labor Unions, "Correspondence," 2001.

Jordanian Ministry of Agriculture (MOA), *Agricultural Policy Charter*, Amman, Jordan, 1995. (Arabic)

Jordanian Hashemite Fund for Human Development, *Where People Build the Future*, 1999.

Jordanian National Commission for Women. *The Mandate*; Amman, Jordan, 2004.

Jordanian National Committee for Women (JNCW), "National Programme of Action for the Advancement of Jordanian Women, 1998–2002." Within the Framework of the Plan of Action and Recommendations of the IV International Conference on Women, Beijing, 1995.

------- *A Report of Jordanian Women: Major Socio-economic Indicators*, 2002.

Jordanian National Committee for Women (JNCW), *National Strategy for Women in Jordan*, 2000. Available from URL: http://ww.jncw.jo/docs/11.doc.

------- *National Programme of Action for the Advancement of Jordanian Women, 1998– 2002*. Within the Framework of the Plan of Action and Recommendations of the IV International Conference on Women, Beijing, 1995.

Ministry of Education, Jordan, *Educational Statistical Report, 1995–1996*, 1997

Ministry of Health, Jordan, *Maternal Mortality Study, Family Health Services Project*, 1997.

Ministry of Social Development, Jordan, "Correspondence," 2001.

Queen Alia Fund (QAF), *The Role of Women in Economic Development: Equal Opportunities in the Euro-Mediterranean Partnership, A report on Status of Women in Jordan*, Amman, Jordan, 2001.

------- *A Research Study on the Social and Economic Position of Rural Women in the Alkara Region*, Amman, Jordan, 1981. (Arabic)

United Nations Development Fund for Women (UNIFEM), "Progress of Arab Women, Report Launching Ceremony," Amman, Jordan, 2004.

------- "Women's Status Report," National Press, Amman, Jordan, 2004.

References Consulted

Abid-Alhamid, A., *Women and Rural Development*, Center for Agricultural Studies, Institute for Agricultural Studies and Rural Development, Jordan, 1997. (Arabic)

Abu-kaff F., and Matsuy Y., *Income-Generating Projects and the Empowerment of Women: Experience of Family Planning and Gender in Development Project in Jordan*, 2003. (Arabic)

Al-qussous, R.N., *Training Needs and the Development of Skills for Rural Women in the Zarka District*, Faculty for Higher Education, Jordanian University, Jordan, 1998. (unpublished document, Arabic)

------- *Women in Agricultural Development in Jordan Report*, GOPA Consulting Gmbh/German Technical Cooperation, 1997.

Al-Saraf, R.H., *The Role of Women in Rural Development*, Paper presented at the National Conference on Women's Role in Rural Development. Arab Institute for Rural Development, Jordan, 1996. (Arabic)

Choucair, J., *Women in Parliament in the Arab World*, Carnegie Endowment for International Peace, 2003. Available from URL: http://ww.jncw.jo/docs/11.doc.

Dajani, D. and Nafa, R., "Initiative and Change, Promoting Gender Issues through Awareness and Advocacy," in Economic and Social Commission for Western Asia (ESCWA), *Where Do Arab Women Stand in the Development Process*, 2004. Available from URL: http//www.escwa.org.lb.

Himour, K., *Women's Role in Agricultural and Rural Development in the Al' azrak Region*, M.A. Thesis, Department of Agriculture, Jordanian University, 1994. (unpublished, Arabic)

Hagieara, A. and Malkawi, A., "Empowerment of Women through the Participatory Enter-Educat (Pee) Workshops: Report of Case Studies of Female Participant Pee Workshops. Karak Governorate, Jordan." Japan International Cooperation Agency (JICA) 2003, *Family Planning and Gender in Development Project*, 2003.

International Labor Organization (ILO), *Fact on Women at Work International Labor Office*, Geneva, Switzerland, 2002.

Jordanian National Commission for Women, German Technical Cooperation, "Gender for Change as a Winning Option: Door Openers to Equality in Jordan" (Experience, Tools and Success Stories).

Miles, R., "Employment and Unemployment in Jordan: The Importance of the Gender System," *World Development*, Vol. 30, No. 3, 2002: 413–427.

Malhas, H., "The Jordanian Rural Woman: Reality and Observations," Paper presented to the National Committee for Study of the Jordanian Woman, Amman, Jordan, 1985. (Arabic)

Ministry of Agriculture, Jordan, Food Security Program, *Fighting Poverty in Rural Areas, Participation Strategy and Obstacles Analysis*, 2003.

Naeemat, A., *Social Type Department, Productive Project According to Social Type in Arab World, Ministry of Agriculture's Role in Small Projects Development for Rural Families*, Ministry of Agriculture, Jordan, 2004. (Arabic)

Shuqair, M., *The Empowerment of Women in Jordan*, 2003. Available from URL: htpp://www.lebanonwire.com/0301/03010421ds.asp.

Seibel, H. and Almeyda, G., *Women and Men in Rural Microfinance: The Case of Jordan*, University of Cologne Development Research Center, 2003.

Chapter 3

Women in Agricultural Production in the Palestinian Authority

Rema Hammami

Introduction

Women play fundamental roles in the development process, but their contribution often remains invisible. While being primary actors in economic life, their economic activities often remain un-remunerated and underestimated in national accounts and statistics. In paid employment they also suffer from wage discrimination and gender biases in labor law. This situation exists throughout the developing world and Palestine is no exception.

Addressing these fundamental forms of gender discrimination in economic life by paying women equitably for both their productive and reproductive work would have a major impact both on family well being and on human development as a whole (UNDP/HDR, 1995: 6). Thus, mainstreaming women in the development process is not simply a justice issue, but also one of efficiency and economic sustainability:

History and experience show that so long as the different role of women and men have remained 'invisible' to development, planner, efforts to achieve development have too often excluded women. The result has been the marginalization and undermining of women's productive roles both in the household and in the broader economic, social and political spheres. Women, have thus, in many cases been disadvantaged by development, and, through this, the development process itself has been slowed down and distorted (NCRFW, 1993).

This report aims to address some of these issues as they pertain to the roles of women in Palestinian agriculture. It will firstly present a descriptive analysis of the *farming system* of the West Bank and Gaza Strip (WBGS) so as to understand the *farming environment* in which Palestinian farmers operate. This will be followed by an overview of women in the Palestinian economy. The third section goes on to look more specifically at the roles of women in the Palestinian agricultural sector. Finally, the report assesses data needs and gaps in an effort to develop guidelines for the development of a database on women in agriculture. An addendum to the report is a suggested strategy for the development of training packages for women extension agents.

The Palestinian Agriculture Sector

Overview

The West Bank and Gaza Strip (WBGS) encompass five, well diversified, agro-climatic zones allowing for agricultural production throughout the year. Additionally, in comparison with the MENA region, the WBGS have a relatively high level of precipitation; more than 53% of the area receives more than 400mm of rainfall annually and 68% of the area receives more than 300mm, indicating a potential of growing a vast range of agricultural products. These advantages given the right type of support could help mitigate the problem of land shortage.

Most of the total cultivated area in the West Bank (1.7 million dunums) is in only two governorates; Jenin and Hebron, which together make up 40% of the total cultivated area. Looked at from another vantage point, the Northern West Bank governorates (Jenin, Tulkarim, and Nablus) comprise around 60% of the total cultivated area. However, the total areas cultivated in each governorate differ significantly from year to year.

Table 3.1 shows that despite the "formal" decrease in its relative importance in the economy as a percentage contribution to GDP, the added value of the agricultural sector has continued increase in the last years of the 1990s. This increase is mainly due to the growth in the livestock sector, specifically to grazing animals and the high price of meat in the local market. Olive production is the major single agricultural contributor to the GDP, with its contribution ranging from 2% of the total value of agricultural production in bad years to 25% in good years.

Table 3.1 Major agro-economic indicators, 1994–1996

Item	1994		1995		1996	
	Mil. $	%	Mil. $	%	Mil. $	%
Fruit tree production	138	35	125	27	246	40
Olive production	81	20	38	8	154	25
Vegetable production	57	14	95	20	97	16
Cereal production	25	6	47	10	38	6
Livestock production	178	45	182	39	213	35
1. Agricultural output	400	100	467	100	616	100
2. Intermediate consumption	120		193		233	
3. Gross added value of agriculture (1–2)	280		274		384	
4. Gross Domestic product GDP (b)	1715		2022		2227	
Agricultural contribution to GDP (3 of 4)	16		14		17	

Source: (a) PCBS, Agriculture Statistics, Ramallah, several years
            (b) PCBS, National Accounts, Ramallah, several years

However, the agricultural sector plays perhaps a greater social than economic role in Palestinian life than is reflected in the statistical indicators. More than 60% of Palestinians live in the rural areas and benefit directly or indirectly, fully or partially from agriculture. Furthermore, the agricultural sector provides jobs to between 13%-19% of the labor force. In terms of income, agriculture remains a major contributing force with almost 36% of local communities relying on it as primary source of income. This makes agriculture a source of income, at the local community level, only second to wage labor in Israel and Israeli settlements which is the major source of income for 56% of local communities (PCBS, 1994; 1995: 44).

Agriculture Under Adversity

In addition to the regular natural and market risks that farmers worldwide must face, Palestinian farmers have an added and constant risk created by the volatile political environment in which they operate. Land confiscation, lack of access to internal markets caused by closures and blockades, and ongoing lack of access to external markets have been continuing challenges and constraints faced by farmers in the WBGS due to the Israeli occupation and the ongoing expansion of Israeli settlement and their infrastructure in "Area C", which comprises the vast majority of Palestinian agricultural land. A long period of statelessness has also left a deep legacy of under-resourced farmers, with minimal access to credit, lack of subsidies, underdeveloped training facilities and minimal planning and support on the national level. The few years of the peace process and the formation of the Palestinian Ministry of Agriculture (MOA) under the auspices of the Palestinian National Authority made strides in addressing these issues but could not in the short term make up for thirty years of neglect. This is especially the case since the MOA had no authority over land and water in Area C, where most farming takes place, while the PNA had no sovereignty and was unable to exercise authority in relation to external markets.

Since the breakdown of the peace process at the end of 2000, the situation has grown dramatically worse for the population as a whole and for farmers in particular. Sieges, invasions, curfews and internal closures have taken a dramatic toll on Palestinian economic life and have caused immense losses to Palestinian agriculturalists – either through direct destruction of agricultural crops, equipment and tools or through the secondary effects caused by closures and curfews which have both made production costs much more expensive, while making markets (including local markets) often completely inaccessible. The humanitarian crisis in the WBGS has reached dramatic proportions. According to the World Bank:

> Since the outbreak of the intifada at the end of September 2000, all Palestinian economic and social indicators have deteriorated dramatically. The Bank estimates that real Gross National Income (GNI) declined by 35 percent between 1999 and 2002. With the Palestinian population growing at over 4 percent each year, per capita real incomes at the end of 2002 were only about half of what they had been three years previously. Unemployment has increased from 10 percent in September 2000 to over 30 percent of

the Palestinian workforce. In September 2000, some 128,000 Palestinians commuted daily to Israel and the Israeli settlements; by the first quarter of 2003, this figure had fallen to 49,000. At the same time, 143,000 domestic jobs (or 29 percent of pre-intifada domestic employment) have been lost.

Daily Palestinian income losses have been estimated at $7.6 million and since the start of the current intifada overall income losses have been estimated at $3.3 billion. The effects at the household level have been dramatic. The Office of the United Nations Special Coordinator estimates that the 60 percent poverty rate has been reached, with levels at approximately 55 percent in the West Bank and 70 percent in the Gaza Strip. Lack of domestic economic activity has led to an almost 20 percent contraction in employment, raising the unemployment rate from 11 per cent in the third quarter of 2000 to 78 percent in the second quarter of 2002.

The Effects of Military Closure and Settler Violence on Agricultural Livelihoods: The Case of Olive Oil in Beit Furik Village (Nablus Governorate) 2001

The village of Beit Furik with 7,719 inhabitants depends on a mixture of wage labor and dry farming for family livelihoods. Loss of work in Israel and the shrinking of local labor markets have increased the importance of agricultural income for household survival. Olive oil is the village's main agricultural product. In 2001 the village was unable to sell all their olive oil production despite lowering the prices. The manager of Beit Furik's cooperative oil press blamed the military closure of the village and cited three cases:

- A trader who bought 20 gallons of oil in Beit Furik was stopped by settlers or soldiers who destroyed all of the containers, opening them with knives, saying he could be hiding explosives in them.
- A man from Nablus working in the village stone factory ordered 100 kg of oil which was then set aside for him in the village press. The man was not able to collect it, unable to drive his car through the military checkpoint that blocks the entrance to the village. When he goes to work he goes on foot.
- An olive oil trader from Beer Sheva wanted to buy two tons of olive oil from the press but could not reach Beit Furik to collect it.

Israeli settler violence predates the outbreak of the current conflict in 2000, but has continued if not worsened:

- On October 17, 2000 a family went to harvest their olives and was shot at by settlers from Itimar settlement. One man was killed and another seriously injured.
- In 1998, 1999 and 2000 and during the olive season, settlers from Itimar harvested the olives from 200 trees around the settlement that belong to a Beit Furik resident. The Palestinian owner was too fearful of settler violence to intervene.
- In March 2001 settlers cut down the 200 trees and an additional 100 trees in the next plot belonging to the man's brother.

Source: Pederson *et al.*, 2001

The Ministry of Agriculture estimated total losses in the agricultural sector due to direct destruction by military forces and indirectly due to the variety of obstacles and sanctions on economic life at around $1,009,028, 286 between September 2000 and August 2003. In terms of the direct losses incurred by direct military destruction of crops, fields, infrastructure and equipment they estimate that these reached $237,289,756 for the same period. Table 3.2 gives just an example of what the MOA was able to cover in terms of loss of trees, field crops and greenhouses during this period.

Table 3.2 Military destruction of trees, greenhouses and vegetable farms, September 2000 through August 1, 2003

Losses	Unit	Total
Uprooted Olive trees	Tree	251,338
Uprooted Date trees	Tree	22,390
Uprooted Citrus trees	Tree	328,988
Uprooted Almond trees	Tree	64,833
Uprooted Grapevines	Tree	51,462
Uprooted Banana trees	Tree	18,400
Uprooted other Fruit trees	Tree	89,439
Uprooted Forest trees and fences	Tree	113,463
Total Number of Uprooted trees	**Tree**	**940,313**
Total of Uprooted Trees Area	**Dunum**	**29,220**
Uprooted Vegetable Fields	Dunum	20,773
Demolished Greenhouses	Dunum	1062
Destroyed field crops	Dunum	9412
Subtotal Vegetable, greenhouse and Field Crops area destroyed	**Dunum**	**31,247**
Total Uprooted Area	**Dunum**	**60,467**

Source: Palestinian Ministry of Agriculture

In addition to destruction by the military has been the growth in settler violence directed towards Palestinian farmers and the sustainability of their communities and agricultural livelihoods. In a study of only the Ramallah area, it was found that 17 out of 29 villages had experienced threat or violence from local settlers which had included the destruction of crops, water supplies, blocked access to agricultural lands and markets (Oxfam, 2002: 19).

Finally, the extent of curfews, sieges and military incursions into communities throughout the occupied territories has had dramatic effects on the ability of the

Palestinian Ministry of Agriculture to fulfill many of its basic responsibilities to the farming population, female as well as male. Ministry extension workers have often been unable to access communities, often for months at a time. Nor can agriculturalists in many cases reach the Ministry branches for the same reason. MOA staff themselves, are often unable to reach their places of work due to their own communities being paralyzed by curfews or closures. The MOA directorate building in Ramallah sustained destruction to its equipment and physical and informational infrastructure as part of the Israel Defense Forces' (IDF) invasion of all Palestinian Ministries during Operation Defensive Shield in April/ May 2002. The devastation of farms and agricultural livelihoods over the past four years has meant that the Ministry, along with the donor community has had to refocus resources, energy and their priorities towards basic relief and emergency services. Under such conditions the ability to plan for and implement larger goals of sustainable and gender equitable Palestinian agricultural development has continuously been out of reach.

A New Phase of Agricultural Land Loss: The Separation Wall

In June 2002, Israel began to build a highly controversial security wall within the Northern West Bank, which will ultimately extend the entire length of the West Bank.[1] In its first phase of completion (snaking 147 kilometers in length) the construction path of the wall involved the confiscation and destruction of 14,680 dunums. It involved the uprooting of 103,320 trees (predominantly olive trees) and destroyed 30 kilometers of water networks. Besides the loss of agricultural land and crops from the wall's path of construction, is the fact that in this first phase, the wall reached 6 kilometers deep into West Bank territory. Between the green line nearly 122,000 dunums of land totaling approximately 2% of the entire areas of the West Bank was isolated, as well as 51 rural communities from the majority of their agricultural land. Despite the creation of a system of doors, 25 communities have reported no access to land, 4 communities reported that there is limited access and 13 still have access to land. As mentioned, the districts most affected by the wall so far, are also known to be the most agriculturally productive areas of the West Bank. The World Bank says that the three districts (which happen to be most affected by phase 1 of the walls construction) of Jenin, Tulkarim and Qalqilya account for 45% of the West Bank agricultural production. More than 80,000 dunums or over half of the 122,000 dunums caught between the wall and the green line are cultivated with vegetable crops, greenhouses, citrus and olive trees or used for field grazing. In addition, 16 communities are actually located within this zone, and continue to face major access problems to markets and inputs. Based on Israeli government projection maps of the final route of the wall, it is estimated that if these are implemented according to stated plans, ultimately the area left to Palestinians behind the fence will be a total of 54% of the West Bank land area.

The separation wall and its affects are not simply a political issue, but have dramatic effects on rural populations, both in terms of their social and economic well-being, and in terms of their long-term sustainability as communities. In addition, the effects of war, economic destruction and loss of livelihoods are also fundamentally a gender issue. Women are both victims of land and economic loss and community crisis, while having to carry particular burdens of coping and trying to meet the range of household needs associated with crisis and loss. An analysis of women in Palestinian agriculture cannot overlook some of the main processes affecting rural communities and livelihoods which women are a fundamental part of. Empirical studies are still needed to assess the specific impacts of these processes on gender at the household level. However, the fact that women are not excluded from these processes is shown by the very actions of rural women themselves in confronting the ongoing loss of land and destruction to their communities posed by the construction of the separation fence/barrier; in the villages of Salfit, Budrus and Kharbatha Beni Hareth, village women have been at the forefront of non-violent protests against military bulldozers attempting to uproot their patrimony.

Agricultural holdings: Household surveys have shown that almost 31% of households own agricultural land, but these holdings tend to be extremely fragmented.[2] The data indicate that more than 50% of agricultural holdings are less than 10 dunums each (1 dunum=0.1 hectare), less than a quarter are about 20 dunum. Only 10% of households own more than 50 dunums (PIALES, 1996: 7).

Agricultural holdings seem to be larger in the northern agriculturally fertile governorates of Jenin, Nablus, and Tulkarm where the average size of a household's agricultural holding amounts to 12 dunums per household. In comparison the average sized holding of an agricultural household is only 7 dunums in the central governorates of Jerusalem, Ramallah, and Jericho and 4 dunums in the Hebron and Bethlehem regions.

Land tenure system: Land tenure data shows that the family and inheritance remain main determinants of access to agricultural lands and livelihoods. Seventy percent of agricultural holdings are owner operated of which 55% are individually operated. Another 21% are family (collective) owned and the rest or 4% are operated utilizing hired labor, sharecropped or rented (ARCATF, 1995). The implications of an inheritance based land tenure system for women's access to agricultural land is discussed below.

Farm structure: Table 3.3 shows that 50% of households in the southern governorates of Hebron and Bethlehem show patterns of a local integrated farming system (animal husbandry and cropping). Such farming systems are much less dominant in other governorates. Agricultural production of this type tends to be traditional and family-based, suggesting greater involvement of women in agricultural production in these regions.

Table 3.3 Percentage of household with access to land and/or rearing animals (1997)

	Plant production only	Animal husbandry only	Integrated (plant and animals)	Total
North West Bank	15.7	10.9	18.7	45.3
Middle West Bank	13.2	5.1	8.0	26.3
South West Bank	23.2	6.5	20.2	49.9

Women in Palestinian Economic Life

Palestinian women's status is marked by a paradox. On the one hand educational indicators show that women's enrollment and educational achievement is high both relative to men and for the region. In addition, a strong and vocal women's movement and infrastructure of women's rights organizations continues to give voice to and lobby for gender equality in various spheres of life. However, women's representation in formal political structures remains low; 5% of the candidates for the 1996 legislative council elections were women who won 18% of the Council seats (5 out of 82). While women's representation in labor and agricultural unions, local councils and chambers of commerce remain even lower (Hammami, 1997: 47–48). However, women's status indicators are most negative in terms of the persistent high fertility rates and low formal labor force participation.

Women in the Labor Force

Participation of women in the formal labor force has been found to be the most fundamental means for women to achieve equality, even more important than the attainment of voting rights (Portland in UNDP, 1995: 110).

Women's participation in the formal labor force of the WBGS is very low; ranging from 7% in the Gaza Strip and 13% in the West Bank. Women's share in the formal labor force in the Arab countries was estimated at 17% (UNDP, 1995: 24), compared to a MENA regional average of 25% and an average for developing countries of 39% (UNDP, 1995: 38; Hammami 1997).

The context created by the Israeli occupation, of economic and political conflict and instability may have been a negative determining factor since women's Labour Force Participation (LFP) actually dropped throughout the years of Israeli direct occupation of the WBGS, and rose during the period of the Oslo interim agreements. In 1968 women's participation in the formal labor force in Gaza was

6.8% and continued to drop thereafter, reaching a low of 1.8% in 1993. Subsequently in 1995, following the Israeli pullout from the Gaza Strip it rose to 7.6%. In the West Bank, women were able to maintain a relatively higher share in the formal labor force averaging 10% during the occupation, and increased to 12.8% in 1995 (Hammami, 1997).

While women's representation in the formal labor force is low, their employment status levels are positive in contrast to men; with 72% to 84% of females versus only 59% to 68% of males being fully employed (Table 3.4). The reasons for this are because the majority of women are working in pink-collar occupations, with 40% employed as teachers (HDP, 1997: 71). Under-employment is clearly higher for men at 22.9%, versus for women at 10.4%. These figures are for the active job seekers and not for the total population of working age. Male and female unemployment rates are almost equal at 17.8% for women compared to 18.3% for men in 1995 but are worse for men in 2001 at 27%.

Table 3.4 Palestinian labor force participation and their percentage distribution by sex and type of employment 1995; 2001

	Not in Labor Force		Full Employed		Under Employed		Unemployed		Total in Labor Force	
	M	F	M	F	M	F	M	F	M	F
1995	33.1	88.8	58.8	71.7	22.9	10.4	18.3	17.8	66.9	11.2
2001	33.2	89.6	68.4	84.0	4.3	1.9	27.3	14.1	66.8	10.4

Source: PCBS, April 1996; PCBS May 2001

As is apparent in the table above, almost 90% of working age women are outside the formal labor force compared to only 33% for men. The main reason given by women for lack of Labor Force (LF) participation is due to their status as housewives (53%); in other words their involvement in domestic and child raising activities. However, 54% of women outside the LF have high levels of educational achievement (13 years+) attesting to the fact that lack of job opportunity, persistent high fertility and lack of accessible childcare facilities may be causes for their non-involvement rather than lack of educational skills. In contrast only 20% of men outside the LF have such high educational achievement, further re-enforcing the specific gender-based biases that explain women's low LF participation. (HDP, 1997: 71).

As is well known and well accepted in the development as well as economic literature, women's lack of involvement in the formal labor force does not necessarily mean that they make no economic contribution, nor does it mean that they are not working. It simply means that the standard Labor Force Participation (LFP) survey framework cannot account for the entire range of women's work. Hammami (1997) presents this problem for the Palestinian context by dividing the

WBGS labor market into five gendered markets, including non-agricultural economy, agricultural economy, wage labor in Israel, informal economy, and domestic economy. Data concerning labor force in the formal sectors (first two labor markets) are covered in standard labor force survey conducted by Palestinian Central Bureau of Statistics (PCBS) and are of good quality. The wage market in Israel is covered by the Israeli Central Bureau of Statistics (CBS), however their data is never disaggregated by sex. For the informal and domestic economy, data is collected only occasionally in micro-studies (cf. FAFO, 1994) and have good focus on women (Hammami, 1997).

Women comprise more than 50% of the labor force employed in the informal sector, see table 3.5.

Table 3.5 Female percentage of total employment in the five labor markets

	National Agricultural[a]		National non-agricultural[a]		Wage labor in Israel[a]		Informal Economy[b]		Domestic Economy[b]	
	WB	GS	WB	GS	WB	GS	WB	GS	WB	GS
1994/6	39.4	20	18	12	3.6	0.6	55.6	60.6	83.6	85.7

Source: Hammami, 1997 (Data Sources: (a) PCBS, Labor Force Survey, April, 1996; (b) Ovensen, 1994.)

The examples above are only to provide a rough picture of a hidden reality. For instance, data covering informal and domestic labor markets should be interpreted cautiously since the data for West Bank relies on a survey only conducted among the camp refugee population. Secondly, the survey classifies food processing, growing of vegetables and herbs, raising of poultry and other animal as domestic economy, while other household activities as informal economic activities (Hammami, 1997).

The low participation of women in the formal labor force is a crucial issue. At the same time, a focus on formal LFP data tends to hide and underestimate women's actual economic activity which is centered in the informal and domestic sectors. In the formal labor force surveys, unpaid family members constitute 10.8% of the labor force in 1995-1996 (11% in the West Bank and 10% in the Gaza Strip), supporting the fact that women's economic activity is unpaid, underestimated and hidden with the family economy context.

Women and Poverty

In 1997 women headed 9.5% of households in the West Bank and 8% in the Gaza Strip. Despite social support to these families from various sources, 30% of these families suffer poverty, compared to 22% of families headed by men (MOPIC, 1998: 36). Families headed by women comprise 11% of poor families. Hilal *et al.*

(1997) noted that 71% of the single headed households are headed by females, of which 41% receive support from relatives and neighbors. Female-headed households are poorer than those headed by men because they tend to have fewer resident workers and more dependents.

In addition, 73% of these households suffer from acute poverty compared to 63% of those headed by men (MOPIC, 1998: 43). The poverty gap is also greater among the families headed by women reaching 9% or 1.6 times greater than families headed by men, implying that poor families headed by women suffer more impoverishment. Poor households headed by women increased by 4% from 1996 to 1997 while the opposite was true for male headed households – where a slight drop was documented in the same period.

Thirteen per cent of poor families were registered as skilled labors in agriculture, comprising 29.2% of agriculturally skilled laborers, with relatively less acute poverty, 12/8% (MOPIC, 1998: 67).

With the current state of impoverishment brought on following the events of September 2000, and almost 60% of the population having fallen under the poverty line, women face immense burdens in trying to meet the basic needs of their families. Various studies have shown that women are at the forefront of household coping strategies including managing declining household incomes, the reduction of consumption, borrowing through informal social networks, an increased load in food processing and preserving, bartering and recycling in order to cover clothing and school supply needs of children. In addition, in times of economic collapse, women's small personal savings, traditionally held in gold jewelry are most likely to be sold to cover basic consumption needs of families.

The Policy Environment

On the national level, there have been numerous initiatives to strengthen women's roles in all aspects of life so as to enable them to play their full role in social and economic development. In 1996 an inter-ministerial committee on gender with its secretariat in the Palestinian Ministry of Planning, was created in order to facilitate the coordination of gender policy and programming across various branches of the Palestinian Authority. In 2003, an independent Ministry for Women's Affairs was created in order to emphasize the government's commitment to gender mainstreaming. Importantly, gender activists within government have a large and vocal community of Palestinian non-governmental organizations and activists lobbying for women's equality to pull together, and work effectively together around a variety of legislative issues.

Three principles are emphasized in the literature necessary for long lasting, stable and sustainable gender-balanced human development are:

1. Women's equality should be considered as a moral and ethical principal. Institutional, social, economic and legal barriers should be eliminated.

2. The recognition that women are important key-actors and that the involvement, investment, and capacity building of women is a must for sustainable development.
3. That development strategies should not be dictated or imposed but both, women and men should have equal opportunities to select appropriate alternatives.

However, one should be aware of the problem of "policy evaporation." Regardless of stated commitments, in practice commitments to gender equality in development projects and policies are often ignored. Evaluations of several sectoral and public policies and assistance programmes have shown that even at the level of policy studies there has been a failure to emphasize women's role and thus failure to design gender balanced policies and programmes (BZU, 1996). Thus "policy evaporation" is also a phenomenon in the Palestinian Authority.

Table 3.6 below shows the gradual diminution of gender-balanced-policy as the development programme moves from policy statement to policy implementation. This process of policy evaporation is a common phenomenon, especially in the developing countries (Longwe, 1997).

Table 3.6 Gender assessment of XX country development programme

Aspect of Programme	Assessment
Programme Policy	Policy rational is mainly concerned with supporting government policy and endeavors. There is a brief mention of "XX-development agency's" interest in supporting the process of women's empowerment, which is defined as women's increased participation in the development process and increased control over resources.
Situational analysis	There is some identification of gender gaps, mainly in access to resources and skills training. There is no mention of gender discrimination, or lack of women's representation in decision-making positions.
Programme Goals	Here there are several goals, which are concerned with women's increased access to resources, and increased participation in the development process.
Project Goals	There are no specific gender-oriented objectives. When a target group is mentioned, this is sometimes followed by the phrase "especially women".
Project activities	There are no activities which are gender-specific, nor which are concerned with closing gender gaps, overcoming discrimination, or increasing women's participation in the process of project planning and implementation.
Project Implementation	Despite the claims that the projects are implemented in a "gender sensitive" way, project evaluation and visits to various project sites reveal that there is no attempt to identify and address gender issues during the implementation process.

Source: Longwe, 1997

Despite the obstacles posed by the socio-economic and political environment in the WBGS, positive social attitudes can provide opportunities for women to gain greater access to resources and rights. Public opinion polls regularly show a high level of support for enlarging certain areas of women's rights, and tend to show a strong belief in women's abilities. For instance a poll showed that 70% of those believed women are competent to hold leading positions in the society while another 66% of the interviewees believed that women should *not* stay at home and be primarily a housewife only (Qasis 1997: 115). Importantly, these attitudes do not greatly differ between urban and rural areas.

Women in Agriculture

The Feminization of Agriculture

Worldwide there is a trend of the feminization of agricultural production, i.e. women carrying an ever increasing role and burden of agricultural production while accruing few of the rights related to it. This is especially true in the developing countries.

In the West Bank there has been a clear tendency since the 1970s of women replacing men in agricultural work as more lucrative employment sources have become available to men outside agriculture (Arnon and Raviv, 1980: 57). Large numbers of farmers abandoned partially or completely the means of production they owned, their land, and moved into wage work in Israel or joined other money earning sectors. Small-scale farming declined. By the mid 1980's, women were performing an estimated 75% of agricultural work in the occupied territories (Augustine, 1993: 105), taking a larger share as men left the land for jobs in Israel and in other economic sectors.

As agriculture has become the work of women, it seems to have declined in status, acquiring the stigma of "women's work". There are several reasons for this. First, agricultural production has declined as a proportion of the national economy. Second, there has been little investment in research in and modernization of West Bank highland farming, the backbone of Palestinian agricultural economy. Highland farming has remained technologically underdeveloped, while it is the sector in which women play the most prominent role.

Emigration or migration of men may have different consequences on farming households, not always towards the feminization of agricultural production. If new labor markets have relatively high earnings, the family may abandon agricultural production altogether or leave it to wage-workers, tenants or sharecroppers (BZU, 1996: 45). In such cases, women's role in agriculture diminishes. If earnings and remittances are comparatively low, women may have a primary role to play in leading the family's agricultural business. However, both trends show a similar underlying principle – that if family income acquired off-farm is strong, women are expected to withdraw from agriculture and become housewives, culturally considered a higher status. However, a growth in farm-based income tends to correlate positively with women's involvement in agricultural work. Analysts have found that higher incidence of female agricultural labor is positively correlated with agricultural growth, as a response to improved opportunities rather than the pressure of poverty (WB, 1992: 8). Due to the lack of data on this issue for the WBGS, we are unable to assess the nature of these trends regionally.

Women, Extension and Research

The feminization of agricultural production or at least the increased role of women in the system and the shift in the division of labor dictates restructuring the agricultural services supporting systems in order to make them more appropriate and approachable to women.

In the original stage of formation of the MOA in 1995, the system of extension services system was not geared to either the larger shift in the economy nor to engendering a shift in the gender division of labor in agriculture. There were only a few female agricultural extension workers, with the majority of agents remaining men. Male extension agents remained unaware of the need to communicate differently with women farmers, and tended to view them simply as farmers' wives rather than agriculturalists in their own right. In addition, there was little capacity to raise awareness about the roles of women in agriculture, as a whole, as well as increase the numbers of women in agricultural training colleges.

In 1996, the MOA reviewed this gap in its own structure and services and developed a new policy approach and a prerequisite for re-structuring in order to implement it. The new policies emphasized the importance of gender balanced agricultural research and extension services and aimed to mainstream gender in future research and extension activities, based on a commitment to supporting women's roles and developing appropriate extension services to meet their needs (MOA, 1998: 12). The change in policy was especially crucial since by some estimates the MOA performs up to 65% of the extension and services in the Palestinian agricultural sector. In order to implement the new approach in 1998 the MOA set up The Women's Extension Division within the existing Directorate of Agricultural Extension and Rural Development geared to creating a specific focus on delivering gender-sensitive extension services to women agriculturalists (FAO/World Bank, 1997).

At the time, there remained the question of whether creating a women's unit would simply ghettoize women's extension services. Having a special unit for women with women extension agents may increase the efficiency of reaching rural women in general and women farmers in specific, but it may not. In 2000, the Ministry moved the Division from under the auspices of the Extension Services Department and re-located it more directly in the Department of Rural Development. In addition it was now renamed simply, "The Women's Division", in light of the fact that it would no longer be solely focused on extension services.

This move was based both on the experience of trying to address women's needs solely through extension services, as well as the development of a wider vision of providing support to women in the agricultural sector. By situating the Division within the framework of rural development as a whole, the aim has been to promote a more holistic approach to mainstreaming women within the MOA's programs and projects. Indeed, simply the cognitive move has shifted services to women from simply being technical add-ons to being carefully thought out empowerment and income generating strategies in their own right that see rural women as crucial to a host of social and economic transformations such as ameliorating poverty, guaranteeing family nutrition and playing leading roles in family development. The MOA's post 2000 approach is certainly a step up from the preceding one. However, the Women's Division and its role within the MOA is still an experiment in progress, one that needs full assessment in order to ascertain the scope of its impact, as well as uncover existing restraints on its effectiveness. A crucial need in this light is the development of appropriate data tools on rural women, an issue that will be dealt with in the coming sections.

Women in the Agricultural Labor Force

The structure of women's farming today can be divided into three main types. In the first type, some male household members work off the farm while the women continue to work some of the family's land. The second type is women farming full-time with no other major source of income. These are few in numbers and they are mostly cases where the responsibility of a farm has devolved to women when husbands are deceased or have abandoned them. It is worthwhile to know more about the spread of such phenomenon and their particular needs. The third type is women working as agricultural wage laborers for others. This includes women working both for Palestinian farmers but also in Israel or settlements.

According to official statistics (Table 3.7b) around 29.1% of women in the labor force were engaged in agriculture compared to 9.9% of men in 1996. This indicates both the importance of agriculture to women and women's importance to agriculture. This does not mean that there are more women than men engaged in agriculture, but that within the employment opportunities available to women – agriculture is twice as important a labor market for them in comparison to men.

The percentage of women engaged in agriculture in the Gaza Strip is much lower, due to the dominance of intensive and irrigated farming in the Gaza Strip, as well as the critical land shortage there that affects the extent of agricultural production as a whole. In addition, it is clear that women's engagement in agriculture has decreased significantly over the past few decades, from 51%–57% in the 1970s to around 45% in the late 1980s and reached the 30% level during the 1990s. However, as Table 3.7b shows there was a slight retrenchment in the decline of women in agriculture during the late 1990s – reaching a high of 35% in 2000, immediately prior to the outbreak of the second intifada – whether this reflects an actual growth in this period in women working in agriculture, or whether it is a statistical artifact – that for a period and for various technical reasons the PCBS was better able to capture women's agricultural activity needs further inquiry. In comparison, the trend for men shows the regular and constant decline of agricultural activity in comparison to other sectors.

The decline for women does not necessarily mean a decline in pure numbers. Instead since the decline is as a percent of women in the labor-force it means that agriculture is absorbing less of the female workforce as a whole. The reason is that over the past twenty years new areas of work have opened up to women, especially in the service sector. At the same time, the figures for all periods need to be treated carefully, since documenting women's participation in agricultural work is always difficult.

Table 3.7a   Percentage of male versus female labor force engaged in agriculture, 1970–1989

	1970	1975	1980	1985	1989
Female	57.4	51.7	55.1	45.9	45.3
Male	32.4	21.4	18	18.5	17.7

Source: Hammami, 1997 (Based on PCBS 1995 and PCBS Labor Force Survey, several annual reports)

Table 3.7b   Percentage of male versus female labor force engaged in agriculture, 1995–2001

	1995	1996	1997	1998	1999	2000	2001
Female	26.9	29.2	29.8	29.1	31.8	34.6	26.9
Male	10.3	11.6	10.3	9.5	9.3	9.8	9.4

Source: PCBS Labor Force Survey, 2001

Even women resident in urban areas, women in the West Bank and Gaza Strip show some engagement in agriculture. The PCBS Demographic Survey of 1996 revealed that 2.4% of the women labor force living in urban areas (towns and cities) were skilled agricultural laborers (4.3% for men). In the rural areas 20.7% of women in the labor force were engaged in agriculture compared to 10% of men and in the refugee camps 3.6% of the women labor force were engaged in agriculture (compared to 2.8% of men), (PCBS, 1997). This data suggests that one does not have to be part of a rural household to be engaged in agriculture; many women agricultural laborers live in urban and camp areas. In addition, it suggests that households that have migrated to urban areas may still keep active in agricultural work on rural landholdings.

Due to the difficulty of accurately capturing women's involvement in non-formal work, including agricultural activities through the standard labor force survey instruments, various alternative research methods have been developed to better document women's work. One such method is time-use surveys. Between 1999 and 2000 the PCBS undertook a long-term time use survey in WBGS, using daily logs as the means to record daily activities. The findings from the survey are however somewhat disappointing. One category that was supposed to cover informal agricultural work is "Primary production activities" which includes agricultural activities to meet basic needs; animal husbandry; hunting; fishing; collecting wild plants etc. (PCBS, 2000: 15). The survey found that 8% of individuals spend time in primary production activities; 9% of men and 6% of women. The average time spent daily on these activities (specifically crop-farming and market and poultry breeding) was 2.36 hours per/day for women and 3.21 hours per/day for men in the West Bank and 1.31 hours for women versus 4.4 hours for men in the Gaza Strip (PCBS, 2000: 66, 70). The work-time on these activities was greater for married women (4.2 hours) than unmarried (1.9 hours). Surprisingly, the time spent on these activities was almost equal among those living in camp, urban and rural contexts (around 3 hours on average) although it is not possible to disaggregate these last figures by sex (PCBS, 2000).

Demographic Profile

Although agriculture takes a higher percent of the female labor force, in pure numbers there are many more men than women working in the sector. Men constitute 80–90% of the total work force in this sector (women's constitute the rest or 10–20%).

Women employed in agriculture tend to be of older age categories in comparison to males employed in agriculture. Males tend to work in agriculture in the age categories between 15 and 30 years old, while women tend to predominate in the ages between 35 and 50. For both males and females however, the largest single age category of those engaged in agriculture is in the 55 years and older group. This age category is probably dominated by proprietors (employers and self-employed) i.e. it probably represents senior family members of agricultural households. For males and females the life-cycle differences are very clear – women tend to work in family agriculture in their post child-bearing and child-rearing years. It is harder to explain why men begin to drop-out from agricultural work in their 30s – potentially, by this age men in agricultural households are able to find other forms of employment (wage labor in Israel) while leaving female family members in charge of agricultural production.

Table 3.8 Employed in agriculture by age and sex

Age Group	Sex		
	Male	Female	Total
15-20	15.7	8.8	13.7
21-25	16.1	11.0	14.6
26-30	13.8	9.6	12.6
31-35	10.1	9.5	9.9
36-40	6.8	11.8	8.3
41-45	5.5	11.2	7.2
46-50	6.2	10.6	7.5
51-55	4.9	9.4	6.3
55 and above	20.8	18.0	20.0
Total	100.0	100.0	100.0

Source: PCBS 1996 (Due to lack of available data, it is not clear whether this age pattern is
     also true for agricultural production units as well.)

Education

Women engaged in agriculture have the lowest educational profile than any other
of sector of women in the labor force. In 2001, they made up 77% of women in the
labor-force with zero years of schooling, 58% of those with only 1 to 6 years of
schooling, and less than 1% of those with 13% years of education (PCBS, 2002:
79). Due to the organization of PCBS data it is not possible to show the educational
distribution across women in the agricultural labor force. This low educational
profile is congruent with the age profile of women in agriculture, with women of
the highest age groups in the society having the lowest educational attainment.

   Table 3.9 shows that this relationship is continuous. In 1997 and 1998 in the
West Bank 75% of illiterate women within the formal labor force were engaged in
agriculture compared to only 44% of men (in Gaza this was 44% and 16%). The
table shows that the higher the level of education of women, the lower their
participation in agriculture.

   Less educated women are engaged in agriculture perhaps for lack of
alternatives, while educated women are less interested in agricultural production.
The same relationship prevails among men, although it is not as clear.

**Table 3.9   Percentage distribution of skilled agricultural laborers by sex
and Region and schooling years, average for 1997 and 1998**

	0 (illiterate)	1–6	7–9	10–12	13 and over
West Bank					
Women	75.0	56.5	38.9	22.9	0.5
Men	44.0	13.8	6.3	5.2	2.8
Gaza Strip					
Women	43.9	28.5	21.2	9.9	0.2
Men	15.7	6.1	4.5	4.8	1.9

Source: PCBS, Labor Force Survey, several annual reports.

Employment Profile

Out of the female agricultural labor force in the West Bank in 1996, less than 1%
are entrepreneurs (compared to 1.9% for men), 17.3% were owner operators
(50.5% for men), 6.4% were wage earners (20.7% for men) and 76.1% work as
unpaid family members (27% for men), (PCBS, 1996). The pattern is similar in
Gaza with the slight difference that there are more women there working as paid
laborers in agriculture than in the West Bank; see Table 3.10 below. The data
overall suggests that the vast majority of women engaged in agriculture (76%) do
so within the farming household as unremunerated laborers.

**Table 3.10   Percentage distribution of skilled agricultural laborers by tenure
and sex in Gaza and West Bank**

Tenure System	West Bank		Gaza Strip	
	Women	Men	Women	Men
Entrepreneur	0.2	1.9	1.9	2.54
Owner operators	17.3	50.5	1.9	33.0
Paid labor	6.4	20.7	14.2	36.8
Unpaid family labor	76.1	27.0	82.0	27.5

Source: PCBS, Labor Force Survey, 1996

The reason for the low numbers of women entrepreneurs is due to women's
general lack of capital. In addition, the category of 17% of women as owner/
operators in the West Bank probably reflects situations where women and their
spouses operate the farm together, but does not necessarily mean that women are
legal owners of the land. The issue of land inheritance and access to resources will
be discussed later in the report.

Regional Distribution

In terms of region, there are large disparities between women's participation in agriculture both between the West Bank and Gaza, and within the West Bank itself. In a 1993 survey, the highest participation of women in the agricultural labor force was in the Nablus region (25.8% of total female agricultural workers) followed by Ramallah (21.7%) and Bethlehem (21.4%). It was the lowest in the Gaza Strip (1.9%) and in Jericho (5.3%) (AgBase 1994: 34). More recent figures show a quite different trend. As shown in Table 3.11 below, the highest participation is in the Jenin region with 55.3–61.3% of females employed in the region are employed in the agricultural sector, followed by the Hebron and Tulkarim regions.

Table 3.11 Regional distribution of the agricultural labor force by year and sex

West Bank					Gaza Strip				
Province	1997		1998		Province	1997		1998	
	Women	Men	**Women**	Men		**Women**	Men	**Women**	Men
Jenin	**61.3**	24.1	**55.3**	20.1	North Gaza	**17.1**	7.7	**13.2**	6.7
Tulkarim	**35.2**	16.4	**34.1**	15.7	Gaza City	**0**	1.7	**1.3**	1.8
Nablus	**34.7**	7.4	**33.2**	6.3	Gaza Middle	**0**	11.5	**5.1**	10.4
Ramallah	**7.5**	5.1	**13.8**	4.9	Gaza South	**10.3**	10.6	**14.3**	16.2
Jerusalem	**0**	1.1	**0.4**	0.7					
Bethlehem	**31.4**	13.2	**28.6**	10.5					
Hebron	**39.4**	11.9	**40.1**	10.8					

Source: PCBS, Labor Force Survey, annual reports 1997, 1998.

The regional figures also indicate a declining trend between 1997 and 1998 of women's participation in agriculture, as a percentage of the female labor force. Another important phenomenon evident in the table above is the low participation of Gazan women in agriculture, especially in Gaza City. When compared with men's contribution, women have a lower share in Middle Gaza (Khan Younis), where intensive agriculture is dominant compared to Gaza North (Beit Hanoun) and Gaza South (Rafah).

Ultimately, the data suggests that women have a high participation in two very different forms of agriculture; modern irrigated farming (including greenhouses) that predominates in the Jenin sub-district and the more traditional integrated dry farming system of the Hebron region. The specific impact of women's engagement in these fundamentally different types of agricultural relations needs further study.

Livestock

The latest Establishments Census (PCBS, 1997) showed that women constitute 17.9% of the labor supply in agricultural establishments (20.6% in the West Bank and only 2.4% in Gaza Strip). Women's contribution to poultry production establishments (poultry battery farms) is clearly higher for both areas but especially in the West Bank where it is 23.8% while in Gaza it is 3.3%. In the other animal production units or "establishments", women's contribution was 18% in the West Bank and 2.2% for the Gaza Strip. The figures do not necessarily reflect the extent of women's engagement in domestic livestock production – historically and culturally part of women's productive roles at the household level.

While women are only 7.4% of the workers in agricultural industries, they constitute 70% of the administrative employees within agricultural industries in the West Bank in 1994. In Gaza these figures were 0% and 1.6% respectively (AgBase 1995: 10). As such, women are much more likely to work as secretarial staff in an agricultural processing factory than as workers.

New Technologies

There is a growing body of evidence that recently introduced agricultural technologies have not reduced women's workload, and in some instances may have actually increased women's burden. Elmusa (1994: 98) has argued that "gender-related change" in the division of labor should not be viewed as intrinsic to the technology, but rather as stemming from socio-cultural norms and unequal gender relationships. For example, the fact that men perform the essentially mechanized tasks of fertilizer application and irrigation is rooted in the perception that women are not suited or do not posses competence for mechanical work.

Tamari and Giacaman (1997: 57), in a study on the introduction of new technologies in agriculture (especially drip irrigation and plastic covers) in villages in the Jordan Valley, found that these actually increased the workload of women engaged in agriculture without a corresponding redistribution of wealth and power. Technologies increased overall productivity per unit area and thus increased the pressure on women in tasks of planting and transplanting, weeding, harvesting, packaging and other activities considered "women's work". In general women are engaged in time consuming, labor intensive, and low technology agricultural activities. Through households women may have reaped benefits of increased household income, yet the distribution of labor and income within the household has become, with the new technologies, even more skewed in favor of men. While this may be true for irrigated systems, it may not necessarily be true for other farming systems. For instance, in animal production units, automatic feeding, milking and even manure and litter removal have been historically women's work that now may have been eased due to the introduction of new technologies.

Wage Inequality

Women's inequality in agricultural work is most obvious in terms of wage discrimination. In the agricultural sector a woman worker earns on average of only 37 New Israel Shekels (NIS) per working day compared to 43 NIS for male workers. Thus women make only 86% of a male wage for an equal day of work (Ramsis, 1997: 9; cited in Hammami, 1997). In terms of work hours and days of work per/month there is not a large gap between men and women employed in agriculture according to the PCBS Labor Force Survey (LFS) (see table 3.12 below). However, this data should be treated carefully as it most likely covers males and females employed by others in agriculture, rather than men and women working on the family farm.

Table 3.12   Average weekly hours, monthly days and daily wages for agricultural skilled laborers 1997–1998 by sex

	Weekly hours	Monthly days	Daily wages (NIS)
West Bank			
Women	39.5	16.5	27.2
Men	43.5	19.5	45.55
Gaza Strip			
Women	43.0	23.0	26.1
Men	44.0	19.0	29.0

Source: PCBS, Labor Force Survey, several annual reports.

Women, Agriculture and Education

Women constituted less than 15% of the students in agricultural training colleges in the early 1990s (Ramsis, 1997: 3; cited in Hammami, 1997; MOA, 1996). Female university students in the faculties of agriculture dropped from 1% in the 1994/1995 academic year to 0.6% in 1995/1996. More serious is the 0% of female students in the agricultural vocational schools and in intermediate community schools in the academic years – 1994/1995 and 1995/1996 (MOL, 1997: 11).

In addition, females enrolled in agricultural training courses dropped from 0.5% to 0.02% between 1994 and 1995. Only 0.2% of female teachers have agricultural training backgrounds compared to 2.2% of male teachers (MOL, 1997: 28). This highlights the weakness of agricultural education among females in all levels of the educational system.

Clearly, there is a problem but its specific causes are unclear. Is it that the courses and colleges tend to project an image that modern agriculture is not a female domain? Is it that modern agricultural training with its technical focus tends to be viewed as inappropriate for women by women themselves? Further study is absolutely necessary to find out why such a low and decreasing number of young women are pursuing careers in agricultural sciences.

Another feature of gender inequality in the agricultural sector is the poor representation of women farmers in agricultural cooperatives and agricultural training colleges. It was found that only two women were members of agricultural cooperatives and in both cases they were not in the upper levels but lower positions. Although women-only cooperatives are not the (most) efficient alternative, they are still lacking.

Women's Access to Resources

Numerous studies have shown that women's access to capital resources, including land is extremely limited in the WBGS. Access to land is primarily through inheritance, as evinced by the fact that most farmers are either owner/operators or family workers. As in most peasant societies throughout the Middle East, despite women's legal rights to inherit land (sanctioned in religious law), there has been a long historical tradition of women waiving their rights to inherit agricultural land in favor of their brothers. Their brothers in return are expected to support and protect their sisters throughout their lives. This popular tradition is longstanding, and in the past probably played a function in limiting the continuing problem of land fragmentation in a system that had no primogenitor, but in which all sons inherited equally, while daughters were by law supposed to inherit a share equal to half of their brother's share. In the modern period, the situation continues, such that in the 1994 FAFO survey only 8% of women surveyed had inherited immovable property (both in buildings or land), (Heiberg and Ovenson, 1994).

PCBS in the 1999 Survey of Property and Access to Resources found a slightly higher total of 13% of women owning a house/share in real estate or land. Five percent of women in the WBGS (5% in the West Bank and 4% in Gaza) owned land or a share in land. Interestingly, the majority of women owning land resided in urban areas, attesting to the fact that land ownership and agricultural activity do not necessarily go hand in hand. Age-wise, the greatest percent of landowning women were in the 65+ age group, and were divorced or widowed.[3] In line with the historical tradition of women waiving their inheritance rights, it is clear that majority of women still do not receive their partial or full inheritance rights in any form (land, investments, other immovable property). Sixty seven percent of women, claimed in the 1999 survey, that they had the right to inherit but did not get their share; 12% said they received part of their share, while only 20% said they received their full share (PCBS, 1999: 75). The possible inheritance came from parents (41%) or from deceased spouses (36%). The reasons women cite for not getting their share are listed below in Table 3.13.

Table 3.13   Reasons cited by women for not receiving their inheritance share (1999)

Family did not give me my share	I did not ask for my share	I'm not in need of my share	There were too many problems in dividing the inheritance	The share was too small as to make it not worth it	Other
18%	35%	13%	7%	16%	11%

Source: PCBS, 1999

Interestingly for women living in rural areas, the majority (46%) stated that they did not ask for their share – attesting to the strong ongoing social norms that women should not ask for their inheritance rights in land.

Women's access to other property is also very limited either in the form of productive tools or savings and the majority depend on husbands for financial support (BZU/DSP, 1998: 22). At the community level, however one often finds a more complex picture. For instance in a survey of 4 villages in the rain-fed areas it was found that 14% of women rented land, on which they cultivate primarily vegetable and field crops (ARIJ, 1994: 27). At the same time, the survey showed that about 40% of women claimed no assets of their own that could be sold, although 47% reported they could sell their personal jewelry in emergencies (ARIJ, 1994).

Women's access to banking and formal credit systems is no better. Women's experience with formal credit institutions is limited, despite that the higher creditability of women in repayment and the higher loan recovery rate among women borrowers in micro-finance and micro-credit schemes.

Women are even much less informed about credit policies. In general, they lack the knowledge of procedures for getting credit and in terms of traditional forms of lending (such as moneylenders) are constrained by social norms, in which women do not have access to male dominated mercantile networks. Ultimately, the problem is that in order to get access to credit, one needs knowledge and skills but also assets – the latter being the greatest obstacle for women.

In general women have less access to external resources. The Applied Research Institute, Jerusalem (ARIJ) (1994: 28) noted that cooperation among village women is rare in rain-fed farming and where the division of labor based on gender is strict and women are often isolated from each other and they have little access to outside resources independent of the males in their families.

Women's lack of experience, poor access to resources, risk averse attitudes, and lower agricultural productivity levels comprise a typical vicious circle which means they lack the capabilities to enter into and manage technologically intensive agricultural production systems but remain ghettoized in less capital intensive, and more labor intensive agricultural activities.

Importance of Women in Agriculture

Women have always played a major role in agriculture. Their role is even more significant in developing countries given the low level of technology and relatively lower input use efficiencies. This is clear in Palestine were women's roles have a special importance in the rain-fed areas (dry-land farming), and where women bear the main workload especially in the traditional agricultural systems.

Meanwhile women's role in optimal use of available resources is demonstrated in urban farming. Crops produced in domestic gardens mainly managed by women contribute significantly to the household economy but also have a high share in supplying food to consumers (see FAO, 1998). House gardening and agricultural production in the vicinity of the house is not covered in the formal survey's (agricultural or expenditure survey's), in spite of their contribution to the food security and income generation.

The production of secondary food crops (mainly vegetables and fruits) in home gardens, and small livestock and poultry rearing, are often important contributions to improving household food security by improving food consumption, particularly during times of seasonal scarcity of food. In addition, these activities often provide additional income to families from the sale of surplus produce utilizing available family resources, human and natural (FAO, 1995: 336). In a FAO report, house gardens comprised only 2% of Nigerian cultivated family farms but contributes to 50% of food production. In Indonesia, house gardens generate 20% of household income and contribute to about 40% of household food consumption (FAO, 1998).

Palestinians are not only economically attached to farming. There is a strong nostalgia for an idealized vision of the self-sufficiency of the past and its independence from the money economy of the cities. The nostalgia is part of the longing for the lost land and lost way of life. Palestinians in general and women in particular cling to an idyllic view of their past as a defense against dislocation, alienation and powerlessness of their lives today (see Augustine, 1993: 104).

Box 3a   Impressions of a Foreign Agricultural Volunteer in Palestine

I was struck by the hard work carried out by Palestinian women and also the importance of her role. Her role is not confined to housekeeping, baby sitting, cleaning, preparing food etc, she works hard in the fields too, in weeding, harvesting and taking care of animals. Two weeks ago, I was in Gaza, visiting a family, with a small loan they had bought a milking cow. Their cow had a calf when I was there and I witnessed how happy the whole family was because of the new comer and the success of this income generating project. *Janet Saims*

Task Division within Agriculture

While women play varied and active roles in agricultural production, their roles off-farm are more limited; seldom do women contribute to selling of products or buying of inputs (fertilizer, seeds, chemicals, etc.), implying their limited participation in decision making (see UNDP, 1994).

In terms of the gender division of labor, women are engaged more in cultivation, while men are more involved in sales (see box 3b below). Seldom do women participate in the mercantile relationships involved in marketing and producing cash crops. However, in terms of marketing the products from rain-fed agriculture, women often play an important role in marketing, albeit in more local arenas and in reduced quantities, and usually in a more informal marketing setting (such as peddling at the fringes of local wholesale markets). In a survey (ARIJ, 1994: 29), it was found that out of the 58% cases, where agricultural produce that was primarily cultivated for home consumption was sold, around 23.5% were sold by women (wife, mother or mother in law).

In the livestock sector, women have more responsibilities especially in feeding and milking the animals. They are responsible for milking (97.1%) and for processing the milk into products such as yogurt and cheese (94.6%) (ARIJ, 1994: 32). Women's home production of milk products is still a main contributor to these commodities in the local market.

In Palestine, women are seen as key contributors to self-reliance, especially during the first Palestinian uprising or *intifada*. They were encouraged to increase their agricultural production. Women were mobilized through neighborhood committees and clubs into small production group and cooperatives to process local produce into fruit juices, jams, pickles, and baked goods.

Box 3b   Gender-Analysis of Agricultural Activities

Mostly by Women	**by Both**	**Mostly by Men**
Planting	Spraying pesticides	Plowing (tractor or animals)
Weeding		Pruning (trees)
Harvesting		Marketing
Packaging		
Processing		
Feeding animals		
Milking		
Cleaning pen		

Agriculture comprises the working sphere of women, both formal agricultural work or informal. Women's informal work in agriculture includes home-based manufacture of prepared foods or street peddling and selling of agricultural products. Standard labor force surveys do not measure these types of economic activities and there is an absence of data (Hammami, 1997: 13).

On the other hand, farm income generated by women is less than that for men; women tend to grow crops that have less return on investment and more subsistence food crops which are less profitable due to lower market prices due to government subsidization. Due to low access to capital, technology and know-how women are less efficient in making good production decisions but very efficient in allocating and utilizing the limited resources they have.

Even if proven economically not comparatively viable, women's work in agriculture, especially in the past, has two important elements that might be of lasting benefit and can be built on. First, is the experience gained in myriad small, cooperatively run women's "enterprises", and secondly, is the ongoing social value put on women's roles in rural production in the Palestinian community.

Principles and Policies for Women in Agriculture

Constraints to Mainstreaming Women in Agriculture

Previous sections show that the road towards equity is dependent on redressing the gaps hindering the development of gender-responsive plan, policies and projects. These include:

1. Inadequate understanding and appreciation of gender responsive planning among policy makers, planners, and project implementers and managers resulting in the inadequate integration of gender concerns into development programs. The lack of gender policies among planners tends to strengthen existing biases in the legislative arena – such as land inheritance.
2. Inconsistent compliance of implementing agencies to integrate gender responsive policies and rules and the gap in integrating women at the level of implementation.
3. The under-representation of women in community and village councils adds to their marginalization from development projects, including being unable to set local priorities for development. Women constitute less than 4% of those working in local councils in the WBGS. In addition, women are totally excluded from 75% of developmental projects executed by local councils.
4. Inadequate guidelines and tools for the integration of gender concerns in development programs and projects.
5. The lack of sex-disaggregated data and statistics as bases for planning and programming.
6. Weak supporting services for working women and limited participation of women in capacity building and vocational training programs.

In addition, good intentions and development programs alone will not guarantee an improvement in women's situation in agriculture and hence increase in farm productivity. In general women have fewer economic options, access to public space, and less access to information and resources than men. They are less able to improve their farming process and raise agricultural productivity, unless the following constraints/gaps/problems are properly tackled:

1. Limited social and economic opportunities in the rural areas due to limited resources and lack of infrastructures conducive to development.
2. Lack of development programs designed to strengthen the role of rural people and their participation in the development process.
3. Lack of adequate gender balanced data on agriculture.
4. Inadequate adaptive research on technologies and lack of an appropriate technology transfer to agriculturally active women.
5. Lack of qualified and professional female extension agents.
6. Women's lack of access to land and land titles.
7. Lack of access to credit and other agricultural inputs because of lack of collateral, social factors, membership in cooperatives, and lack of time to take care of these matters and transport inputs.
8. Women farmers low level of education and higher rates of illiteracy and, hence, their ability to understand technical information.
9. Women farmers are more risk averse and often lack incentives to increase productivity, especially if they do not control farm income or directly benefit from it.

Why Strengthen the Role of Women in Agriculture

World wide experience has shown that many programs remain socially under-designed and register a high rate of economic, technical and sociopolitical failure (see FAO/WB, 1997: 17).

It is also of extreme importance to keep in mind that social aspects are not the only reasons behind the endeavor of mainstreaming women in the economic activities, especially in agriculture. The overall economic performance of the system will be enhanced through the efficient utilization of factor inputs, especially labor. Several reasons were given to show the crucial importance of strengthening and mainstreaming women in agriculture:

1. It was found that incremental (marginal) productivity of training and capacity building is higher for women farmers.
2. Knowledge acquired and experience accumulated by working women is useful in achieving further progress in agriculture. Women's participation in identifying research themes and directions is crucial since they are the ones who are going to adopt and apply them. Palestinian experience in the

development of local seeds indicated that the involvement of women extension agents and farmers had a significant influence.

3. Strengthening the role of women in agriculture also promoted better agricultural management. This was clearly expressed by (Mook, 1973; cited in World Bank, 1992), "investing in women farmers is worth it since women farmers were found to be more efficient in farm management than men. Given the same inputs, women can produce more."

4. Rural women spend much time in agricultural activities in the vicinity of the house, despite the housekeeping work. Micro projects and income generating projects are needed to support women and increase their productivity.

5. Trends worldwide towards sustainable agriculture have asserted the important role of women in implementing such anticipated changes (DSP/MOPIC, 1998: 18). Utilization and expansion of women's productive potential is a must to the achievement of sustainable development.

Strengthening is a key element in the different levels of actions needed. These levels and action tracks deal with (UNICEF, 1994):

1. Meeting *basic needs* of women cannot be achieved without structural analysis or tackling reasons behind the wider causes of gender inequality in the society.

2. *Access* including access to resources such as education, land and credit. This will contribute significantly to the development of women's roles when addressing with causes of inequality.

3. Supporting women's *awareness* of their needs and potential role.

4. *Participation* of women in identifying these needs and implementing the results and recommendations.

5. Providing women with more *control* over their role in the development process.

Research Findings and Recommendations

Available Data and Data Gaps

The following Box 3c shows the very limited number of indicators on women in the relatively large number of studies, reports dealing with gender. The limited number of gender indicators is obvious in the agricultural fields.

Empirical and quantitative studies may establish that: (a.) women make a major contribution to the wealth of the country and (b.) the use and expansion of women's productive capacities is a necessary condition for social and economic progress. One of the general recommendations made by reviewed/literature is the need for a more in-depth study of women's contribution to agriculture (BZU/DSP,

1998: 16). Since gender-responsive development planning requires a re-examination of the role traditionally ascribed to women and men in society and subsequently a redirection of efforts to ensure a more relevant formulation of a plan, program or project.

Box 3c   Gender Indicators Available in the Reviewed Studies and Reports

- Women's share in Agricultural Labor Force by district (Province/ Governorate)
- Economically active women by sector, schooling year and age group
- Women's share in skilled Agricultural Labor by district, age group, and schooling
- Female students in the Faculty of agriculture and agricultural colleges
- Entrepreneurship of economically active females
- Daily wages by sex and district
- Illiteracy in urban areas, rural areas and refugee camps
- Weekly work-hours by sex and district
- Women headed households
- Women engaged in agricultural establishments by education level and district

---

The first step towards creating gender-equitable policies is to achieve a better understanding of women's status and needs while dismantling constraints confronting their development in each economic sector and its sub-sectors. This requires a gender-analysis, which can best be backed by a specially designed, gender-disaggregated, household survey to furnish researchers and decision makers with needed information. Annex A presents an initial attempt to list data gaps identified after reviewing available literature on women in agriculture in Palestine. The next section explains why, what for, and how to conduct such research and data collection surveys.

Establishing a Gender Database (Suggested Research)

The Database on Women In Agriculture will facilitate empowering decision-makers with relevant data and allow them to reach more balanced decisions specific to women in agriculture. It will be useful in strengthening the role of the recently launched women's program by assisting women extension agents in setting up focus groups in the villages.

Women farmers possess a vital source of local (indigenous) knowledge which is not recorded. Extension agents, and even male farmers, are often unaware of the value of women's information. There is an abundance of aggregate data and information on global and national agricultural issues and problems but often a shortage of information on specific conditions and technological adaptations in the unique individual locations or farms.

On the local and community levels, the better and more accurate the base of information on local needs and resources, the easier it will be to select optimal recommendations and technologies. It is also crucial for working out and implementing approaches to sustainable natural resource management.

The specific objectives of the database are (see Project Document (PD), 1998):

1. To explore the role of women in the different agricultural sub-sectors, especially those identified as program components.
2. To identify problems confronting women's access to services, such as extension and market, and other services that undermine reaching their full potential.
3. To develop a comprehensive and complementary database on women in agriculture to support pm and dt in their dm/t process.
4. To better explain the ties between women and agriculture in order to strengthen and upgrade performance (productivity, quality, profitability, and sustainability).
5. To increase cooperation among all partners in agricultural activities
6. To establish professional networks in agricultural fields and encourage a common approach to the technical problems of the region and promote solutions based on joint research, training and extension efforts.

Suggested Methodology

A two stage methodology is recommended to achieve these goals. The attached TOR (Annex B) sheds more light on this approach.

On the sampling level, it was found that location and farming system are the most distinctive criteria for the classification and selection of representative villages (Arnon and Raviv, 1980:69). Location is the most important single criteria, since it dictates to a high extent the farming system. Examples include; rain-fed farming in the highlands, irrigated vegetables and fruits in the semi-coastal areas, off-season vegetable production in the Jordan Valley.

On the data collection tools, there are several data collection techniques effective in planning services for female farmers. They include farming systems research, combined agricultural calendars and seasonal labor profiles, unstructured survey's, rapid rural appraisal (informal surveys and two-to-three-day field visits to project area), or a combination of these methodologies.

Training and Suggested Training Courses

Development and extension programs are designed and disseminated on the assumption that farmers are males. Considering female farmers on equal footing as male farmers, proportional to their contribution in the production process, is fundamental to designing development and extension programs that meet gender equity goals.

In Palestine, several NGOs have programs for rural women, which extend beyond farming to cover nutrition, agro-processing and domestic technology, usually with a micro-credit component. Their experiences should be reviewed and lessons drawn. This would help in defining what should be done to support rural women and by whom.

Suggested training courses are attached to this paper (Annex C). They cover four issues/tracks:

1. Work environment and conditions conducive to full participation of women in extension services.
2. Constituents of programs necessary to strengthen women's role including; optimal use of local resources, building their capacities and skills in relevant fields, the importance of research to informed decision making, sustainable agricultural and home economics
3. Training in relevant fields. It was found that, the main interest areas indicated by women focus groups include milk and dairy products, small animals (rabbits, chicken, and bees), and micro-credit.
4. Women's access to resources and management/establishment of income generating projects and improve women's access to technology and know-how through positive and active participation in demonstrations, exhibitions, training courses, capacity building sessions, conferences, etc.

Strengthen Extension/Training Services

There is a clear failure of the research and extension systems to respond to the needs of women farmers and rural women's participation in these courses and their continuity. It is crucially important to find ways to get more village women in contact with agricultural services and to improve the way extension agents and women farmers communicate and create direct contact with extension services on a one-to-one basis either as contact farmers or in contact groups. It was found that group meetings offer special advantages to women farmers and are considered an excellent vehicle for technology transfer. In addition supporting and activating existing groups is generally more preferable than creating new ones.

Success factors for conducting an effective training and extension program and increasing the number of female beneficiaries may require:

1. Adequate logistical support and efficient employment
2. Recruitment of female extension agents and build their capacities in extension services, dissemination of information, and communication skills.
3. Locating agricultural rural and training centers in rural areas

4. Easing of admission, entry qualifications and age limits for rural women in these centers.
5. Assuring good geographical coverage of important areas
6. Re-training other rural female agents such as home economists and community workers and integrate their work.
7. Increasing involvement of local women or use of female para-extension agents
8. A prerequisite to a successful gender responsive training/extension programme lies in developing a "demand-driven" and "women-farmer-focused" training materials and approaches.
9. Efficient training courses for rural women that require a continual revision of curriculum in order to identify skill gaps, integrating training into unified extension systems, providing close supervision, support and involvement from agricultural subject matter specialists.

Recommendations

The previous literature review and analysis showed the importance of creating a gender database on agriculture to facilitate implementation and monitoring of development projects targeting or impacting women. Another important track, is evaluation of projects designed to strengthen women's role (income generation projects), provision of work environment conducive to the mainstreaming of women, and developing a gender responsive agricultural extension services. These are cornerstones for efficient and socially balanced agricultural production systems.

Evaluate and Incubate Income Generating (Diversification) Projects

"Diversification is the key to sustainability and variation is the key to adaptation," both are not fully appreciated in the developing countries and need certain intervention programs in order to strengthen existent trends.

Evaluation of women's income generating projects in Gaza, Nablus and Tulkarim were not encouraging (see BZU, 1995). The following needs were highlighted in connection with income generating projects:

1. Better coordination of objectives.
2. Further capacity building and training for women.
3. More efficient planning and management.
4. Proper production and quality control.
5. Better supervision and monitoring (see BZU, 1995: 38).

Mainstreaming women economy-wide which requires:

1. Adoption and implementation of comprehensive development policies based on human development principles that require an active participation of all stakeholders in the development process.
2. Include women's perspectives and needs into the development process, include strengthening of women's role as an objective of development plans, and ensure participation of women in the planning and decision making process.
3. Establish economic systems capable of fairly reflecting the real contribution and participation of women in the informal labor market (especially the agricultural sector).

Develop gender responsive and effective extension services. This requires:

1. Encourage women's groups (that exchange labor, mobilize savings and credit, provision for collective collateral, cooperate and help each other, provide from more cost and time effective extension services, facilitate adoption and transfer of technologies, and more effective response to unpleasant externalities) and promote gender awareness in all extension agents through training.
2. Mainstreaming women's extension program but not overlooking the need for interventions targeting women farmers, which must be tailor-made to fit local situations and needs.
3. Gender responsive (equity) when selecting contact farmers or demonstration sites, any sort of discrimination and bias against women farmers should be avoided.
4. Timing and locations are important for the effective and participation of women farmers.
5. Address the immediate technological needs of women farmers.
6. Increase ability of women farmers to use information and extension services effectively through improving the legal environment, improve women's access to production factors (capital, land, labor) and markets.
7. Training women extension agents in communication skills and in participatory development approaches.
8. Ensure full participation of women farmers in the discussion meetings and their commitment to the development program.
9. Help women in general and women farmers specifically, to discover their own potential and competence. This includes building their own working groups and enabling them to lead the group as a working team.

Ensure the Appropriate Gender Equitable Policy and Legal Environment for Women in the Agricultural and Rural Community Sector

A gender aware policy and legal environment is a must to promote gender equity in agriculture. One ministry with a small group of committed staff can certainly build towards a common goal, but cannot bring about the more comprehensive set of changes necessary for its achievement. On the one hand, legal frameworks both express general social commitments as well as provide mechanisms to promote and ensure their implementation and achievement. Social and economic policies both extend from and are buttressed by legal frameworks. Simultaneously for the law and social policy to be developed and have their effects, the proper institutional mechanisms must be in place. Therefore, three inter-locked spheres of law, policy formulation across government and the proper institutional framework within the implementing institution must be in place and work in coordination, particularly when it comes to the cross-cutting and sometimes thorny issue of gender. In this light, existing legislation that pertains to all aspects of the agricultural sector, across the various legal sectors must be systematically reviewed to ensure that they are in line with the larger policy vision towards mainstreaming women in agricultural development. Necessary as well is the need for exchange and coordination across governmental and non-governmental sectors to ensure a consistent set of policy arrangements regarding the promotion of women's access to resources for equality. Finally, the proper institutional arrangements need to be in place within the MOA so as to both carry out its role within the nexus of policymaking and implementing institutions and to ensure that its own role in carrying out its policy vision will have the necessary impacts. Assessment and further analytical study is necessary in order to understand how the entire range of appropriate legal, policy and institutional arrangements can be promoted.

Notes

[1]   The data in this section comes from, "The Wall in Palestine; Facts Testimonies, Analysis and Call to Action," PENGON, 2003. Their material is based on wide ranging studies undertaken by local and international NGOs, as well as Israeli and International reports. cf. "The Impact of the West Bank Separation Barrier on Affected West Bank Communities," World Bank, 2003. Also see, "The Separation Barrier" B'Teselem, 2002.

[2]   Palestinian Expenditure and Consumption Survey with a sample size of 4500 households.

[3]   Due to the problematic organization of the data, exact percentages cannot be specified. PCBS August 1999, Survey of Ownership and Access to Resources.

References

Agricultural Database (AgBase), "Agricultural Factories in the West Bank and Gaza Strip," Volume 3, No. 2, 1995.

------- "Final Report on Population and Labor, Income and Expenditure in West Bank and Gaza Strip," Volume 2, No. 5, 1994.

------- Agriculture Relief Committees and Arab Thought Forum (ARCATF), "Final Report on Farming Systems in West Bank and Gaza," 1995.

Applied Research Institute – Jerusalem (ARIJ), "Dry land Farming in Palestine," West Bank, 1994.

Arnon, I. and Raviv, M., "From fellah to farmer," Settlement Study Center-Rehovot, Publications on Problems of regional Development No. 31, Rehovot, 1980.

Birzeit University (BZU), "Palestinian Human Development Profile" (HDP), 1996–1997, 1997.

------- Women's Studies Programme, "Gender and public policies," Working Papers No. 2, 1996.

------- Women's Studies Programme, "Gender and Society," Working Papers No. 3, 1995.

------- Development Studies Programme and MOPIC, "Palestinian Women and Development," Planning for Development Series, No. 3, Ramallah, 1998.

Danish International Development Agency (DANIDA), The regional Agriculture Programme in the Middle East: seminar on "Women in Agriculture," Cairo, Egypt, 1st–5th November 1998.

Ebba, Augustine (ed.), "Palestinian Women, Identity and Experience." Zed Books, London and New Jersey, 1993.

Elmusa, Sharif S., "A Harvest of Technology: The Super-Green Revolution in the Jordan Valley." Georgetown University: Georgetown Studies of the Modern Arab World, 1994.

Food and Agriculture Organization (FAO), Nikos Alexandratos (ed.), "World Agriculture: Toward 2010, An FAO Study." John Wiley & Sons, 1995.

------- World Bank cooperative programme, "Agriculture Sector Rehabilitation Project-initial preparation report," draft, 1997.

Hammami, Rema, "Palestinian Women: A Status Report-Labor and Economy," Birzeit University (BZU) Women's studies Program, No. 4, 1997.

Heiberg, Marianne and Ovenson, Geir, "Palestinian Society in Gaza, West Bank and Arab Jerusalem: A Survey of Living Conditions." FAFO: Oslo, 1994: 296.

Longwe, Sara H., "The evaporation of gender policies in the patriarchal cooking pot," Development in Practice, Vol. 7, No. 2, 1997, Oxfam (UK and Ireland) 1997: 148–156.

Ministry of Agriculture (MOA), "Agriculture Research and Extension Policy" (draft), Ramallah, 1998.

Ministry of Labor (MOL), " Labor Force Statistics Guide No. 7 – Women, Work and Education in Palestine," 1997.

MOPIC-national team for combating poverty, "Poverty Report" Palestine, November 1998.

National Commission on the Role of Filipino Women NCRFW, "Guidelines for Developing and Implementing Gender-Responsive Projects and Programs," 1993.

Oxfam International, "Forgotten Palestinian Villages Struggling to Survive Under Israeli Closure in the West Bank." Oxfam Briefing Paper 28: September 2002.

Palestinian Expenditure and Consumption Survey (PCBS), with a sample size of 4500 households.

------- Demographic Survey of West Bank and Gaza Strip, Final Results 1997.

------- Labor Force Survey, 1996.

------- Population, housing and establishment census 1997, Main results 1998.

------- Small Community survey 1994, August, 1995, pp. 44.

------- Time Use in the Palestinian Territory 199-2000, December, 2000.

------- Labor Force Survey Annual report: 2000, May, 2002.

------- Ownership and Access to Resources Survey, August, 1999.

Pederson, Jon, *et al.*, *Paying a Price; Coping with Closure in Two Palestinian Villages.* Oslo: Fafo Institute for Applied Social Science. 2001, pp. 19, 31, 54–55.

Palestinian Institute for Arid Land and Environmental Studies (PIALES), 1996: 7.

Qasis, Mudar, "The individual-society relationship and some Palestinian civil society affairs." in Said, N and R. Hammami (ed.), "Analytical Studies of social and political trends in Palestine," Center for Palestine Research and studies, Nablus, 1997: 115–135.

Said, Nader, "Social, Political and economic women's rights in the Palestinian Consciousness," in Said, N., and Hammami, R. (ed.), "Analytical Studies of social and political trends in Palestine," Center for Palestine Research and studies, Nablus, 1997: 165–200.

Tamari, Salim, and Giacaman, Rita, "Zbaidat: The social impact of agricultural technology on the life of a peasant Community in the Jordan Valley," Birzeit University (BZU), 1997.

The Palestinian Environmental NGOs Network (PENGON), "The Wall in Palestine; Facts, Testimonies, Analysis and Call to Action," 2003.

United Nations Development Program (UNDP), "Human Development Report 1995," Cairo, 1995.

United Nations Children's Fund (UNICEF), "Gender Equality and Strengthening Women and Girls," February, 1994.

Vitullo, Anita, Araj, Hilmi and Said, Nader, Birzeit/Development Studies Programme, "Women and Work in Palestine," Ramallah, 1998.

ANNEXES

Annex A: Data Gaps

For gender analysis, quantitative and qualitative information is needed on (WB, 1992: XIV):

1. Activities: who carry? What tasks? And how is the labor divided?
2. Resources and constraints: Who has access or control? What resources? What are the constraints under which women operate?
3. Benefits: who benefits from or controls income?

From the previous literature review and according to researcher's expressed statements, data is specifically insufficient on the following issues:

*   *Reasons and motives behind the women's engagement in agriculture*: social, political and economic? The need to use all available manpower in the production process, being within the boarders and have no social complications and consequences, women's efficiency in conducting certain agricultural activities such as planting and harvesting.
*   *Alternative work (income generation) opportunities*: within reach of women, in rural and urban areas, including paid work.
*   *Food-deficit (food security) among women and men-headed households?*
*   *Women and sustainable agriculture*: Share of women in adopting environmental friendly agricultural systems, for example IPM, organic farming, integrated farming, low external input agriculture, etc.
*   *To what extent women are innovators and in what direction?* Women started some agricultural activities and was later adopted by men farmers, is this a case in Palestine? And where?
*   *Size and structure of farms managed by women?* Usually it is smaller and capital assets are comparatively less. How diversified is the income source for women in the different economic (agricultural) branches and income level.
*   *Women's access to credit*: Their share in credits and loans from the different sources, by source and type of loan.
*   *Financial aid (loan or credit) by value and number of beneficiaries*
*   *Women's access to information*: Extension services for women farmers (number of visits of or to extension agents) as compared to male farmers.
*   *Access of women farmers to training and capacity building programmes (activities)*
*   *Women's access to and appreciation of technology*: Technology effect on women's work. Hypothesis, technology results in relief of men workers and increases the load for women. Example is the increased productivity.

- *Women's knowledge (awareness)* of optimal agricultural practices adaptable to local production systems, including alternative and low cost technologies, chemical uses, cropping pattern, inputs (manure, seeds, etc.), level of integration of agricultural production units.
- *Performance of women headed agricultural households*: (income, productivity, etc.) and their importance, percentage, distribution, etc.
- *Resource productivity (water, land, labor)*: of men vs. women managed agricultural farms and level of *Generated incomes* by each.
- *Time use*: Women have limited time to spend on activities outside of household management. Are women able to find the time to attend meetings and actively participate at the community level. What other reasons besides time may inhibit women from participating in activities beyond the household?
- *Post harvest techniques* including, processing, storage and reducing significantly the post harvest losses.
- *Women's participation in research*: and direction of research and development to suit women's needs proportional to their contribution to agricultural efficiency.
- *Participation in development and extension activities*: (workshops, capacity building and training courses)
- *Share in the different processes*: (Production, marketing, etc.). What agricultural activities do women carry? And how contributive they are to the overall performance?

Is there a women's crop, i.e. crops selected and grown primarily by women? What are these crops and how they perform in the field and in the market? Why they grow such crops? Do they have different (variety) cultivars? Do the products have different prices? Different marketing channels?

Annex B: TOR for Recommended Survey on "Women in Agriculture"

Background

Helping women to contribute fully to agricultural development requires understanding their role in farming systems and household, making appropriate technical information available; and identifying suitable strategies for reaching women farmers.

Objective

1. Determine agricultural activities of women farmers including crops and livestock, production, processing and marketing tasks.
2. Assess effectiveness of existing research and extension services, and how they meet the specific needs of women farmers, and identify constraints facing the extension system.
3. Assess how the technology generation/research system can respond to the technical needs of women farmers.
4. Identify nature and extent of training needs for both extension agents and beneficiaries to improve performance of training programmes.
5. Participate in planning project interventions to improve extension services for women and plan for monitoring and evaluating the success of the undertakings.

Recommended Methodology

1. Apply same methodology in all countries at least for the basic information needed; modifications on the methodology to accommodate specificity, there should be a discussion within the group first.
2. Select 2–3 villages representing the important agricultural areas, with diversification within the region to ensure complementary information sets is important.
3. Gender Analysis (refer to text)
4. Rapid Rural Appraisal techniques including analysis of project documents and available secondary data, interviews with informant women, farmers and groups :
   a) Discussion with women farmers.
   b) Interviews with extension personnel.
   c) Interviews with agricultural and social workers.
   d) Discussion with relevant people from governmental and non-governmental organizations.
5. Workshops.
6. Reports.

Annex C: Suggested Training Courses for Women Extension Agents and Women Farmers

Capacity Building and Income Generating Courses:

Course (): Low External Input Farming Systems
(Including organic farming, integrated farming and other systems).

Objective
- Introducing low cost farming systems
- Generate more income
- Production of safe food products
- Better utilization of available resources (human and natural)

Course contents
- Meaning, importance, requirements and how to establish Low External Input Farms
- Integrated Farming systems and their application under different farming conditions
- Visits and demonstrations

Course (): Composting Household and Farm Bio-Wastes

Objective
- Beneficial use of household wastes and farm residues
- Production of soil conditioners (compost)
- Higher agricultural production
- Minimize wastes and pressure on environment

Course contents
- Value of household wastes
- Define compost and methods of producing good composts
- Benefits of composts

Course (): Income Generating Projects
(such as bee keeping, growing mushrooms, medicinal herbs, etc.)

Objective
- Generating more income for rural families
- Better utilization of available resources

Course contents
- Technical information on the subjects

- Economically productive activities
- How to start such micro agribusiness

Course (): Food Conservation and Processing

Objective
- Conservation of food products on the household levels
- Improve availability of food products

Course contents
- Importance of proper conservation of food items and agricultural products
- Alternative methods of conserving agricultural products (fumigation, freezing, drying, etc.)
- Affordable food processing methods (juices, marmalade, pickling, etc.)
- Food Quality control methods
- Demonstrations

Course (): managing small business

Objective
- Improve women's administrative skills
- Improve productivity of small businesses

Course contents
- Management skills for women

Women Empowerment Courses:

Course (): Leadership Skills

Objective
- Improve women's leadership skills
- Awareness of women's role in the success of projects

Course contents
- Definition and patterns of leadership
- Role of leaders in the community and factors determining their role
- Factors influencing women's leading role and their participation in decision-making
- Skills needed for leading women,
- Responsibilities and success criteria of leading women

Course (): Communication Skills

Objective
- Improve women's capacity to communicate
- Better chances for cooperation and team work among rural women
- Improve women's chances of benefiting from services (extension)

Course contents
- What is communication, techniques and elements?
- Success criteria and elements of good communication
- Obstacles to effective communication
- Communication networks and networking
- Team work

Course (): Women Empowerment

Objective
- Building and improving women's leading capacities in the rural and national levels
- Improve performance of development programmes

Course contents
- Women's needs
- Bargaining and negotiation skills
- Social and community work
- Active communication and networking on the community level
- Case studies

Annex D: Annotated Bibliography of Women in Palestinian Agriculture

1. Heiberg, Marianne and Geir Ovensen, *Palestinian Society in Gaza, West Bank and Jerusalem: A Survey of Living Conditions.* FAFO, Report 151, Oslo 1993.

   It was the first attempt to produce Palestinian labor statistics based on household surveys. The report is composed of several chapters, among which is one chapter focusing on employment and under utilization of labor with a special section on female labor activity. The study tackles property and access to economic resources including women's access to resources. The report includes sex-disaggregated statistics in appendix A.7 with a comparison between FAFO's and Israeli (CBS) labor statistics.

2. Hammami, Rema, *Labor and Economy: Gender Segmentation in Palestinian Economic Life.* Women's Studies Program, Birzeit University, 1997.

   The report is a separately published chapter of a "Status Report" series. It thoroughly analyzes women's participation on the different labor markets, agricultural, non-agricultural, domestic, informal and wage labor market in Israel. Attempts were made to explain the low participation of women in the wage markets. She argues that women's participation in the available statistics is undermined because of shortage in the available statistical system to reflect the real role of women in the economy. The study includes several tables covering women's participation in the labor force in the different economy sectors disaggregated by sex and region. Some of the tables have also time series data on women's participation in the labor force. Recent data are those collected by PCBS.

3. Hindiyeh-Mani, Suha and Afaf Ghazawneh, Subhiyyeh Idris, "Women Street Peddlers: The Phenomenon of Bastat in the Palestinian Economy," in Tamar Mayer (ed.), *Women and the Israeli Occupation*, Routledge, London 1995, pp. 147–163.

   A micro-study based on interviews with 32 women peddlers in Jabalya (Gaza Strip) and near Jerusalem. The study investigates the peddler's backgrounds, motives, traded materials, division of labor among family members, and involvement in agricultural production.

4. Semyonov, Moshe, "Trends in Labor Market Participation and Gender Linked Occupational Differentiation," in Tamar Mayer (ed.), *Women and the Israeli Occupation*, Routledge, London 1995, pp. 138–146.

   The study is based on the analysis of labor statistical data published by Israeli CBS on trends of women employment in the West Bank and Gaza Strip. The study noted the feminization of agriculture in the territories after the engagement of men in wage labor markets in Israel. The study includes time series (1970–1989) gender-disaggregated data on women participation in the labor force.

5. Farah, Nadia Ramsis, *Situation Analysis and Plan of Action of Gender in Agriculture in Palestine.* 1997.
    Based on the PCBS statistics describing the rural population and division of labor in the agricultural sector and using "Participatory Rural Appraisal" sessions in a number of regions, the study suggested four strategies for narrowing the gender gap in agriculture. These are, mainstreaming gender in the Ministry of Agricultural plans, increasing women's access to credit and technology, empowering women and improving their control over resources, and improving the women's productivity in agricultural production.

6. Tamari, Salim and Rita Giacaman, *Zbaidat: The social impact of agricultural technology on the life of a peasant Community in the Jordan Valley*, Birzeit University 1997.
    The study is an updated view of the agrarian system and health condition in Zbaidat, Jordan Valley, with focus on gender division of labor in rural community and women's outside work as influenced by introduction of new technologies, especially drip irrigation.

7. Vitulla, Anita, Araj, Hilmi and Said, Nader, Birzeit/Development Studies Programme, "Women and Work in Palestine," Ramallah 1998.
    This paper is written in an attempt to identify the existing institutions and mechanisms for advancing women's employment status and to assist the ILO mission to formulate a national plan of action in Palestine for "more and better jobs for women" . The study reviews the Government, NGOs and other civil community organizations active in women strengthening issues. The study includes also a useful annotated bibliography of "Women and Work in Palestine." (To be completed.)

8. Arnov, Isaac and Michael Raviv, *From Fellah to Farmer*, Settlement Study Center 1980.
    The study describes the changes in the agricultural sector of some Arab villages in Israel after the introduction of new technologies and know-how. The major changes, according to the authors, were the elimination of underemployment and the increase in factor productivity.

9. Gad, Islah, *Mainstreaming Gender in the Policy and Programmes of the Ministry of Agriculture*, Jerusalem 1997.
    The author introduced the study as a guide hand book , which came as a result of a series of workshops targeting the top and medium staff of the Ministry. In addition to the theoretical background dealing with gender and development, the study includes a variety of case studies based on the Palestinian experience and gender analysis of some projects proposed by the Ministry.

10. Palestinian Central Bureau of Statistics (PCBS), "Men and Women in Palestine: Trends and Statistics," Ramallah 1998.
    The study accumulates and analyzes data on Gender in the different fields, based mainly on surveys conducted by the PCBS. The study consists of five

chapters, one on demographic gender-indicators, a second chapter on education, another chapter on health, a fourth on labor force and the fifth chapter on political life and participation.

Chapter 4

A Critical Assessment of Research on Gender in the Israeli Rural Sector[1]

Pnina Motzafi-Haller

Introduction

The purpose of this essay is to provide a critical review of research that has documented the place of women in the rural sector in Israel. The analysis progresses from the more general, national level to the more specific rural sector, and finally to micro-level studies carried out in rural communities. The essay distinguishes between the Jewish rural sector and the non-Jewish rural sector in Israel. In the Jewish rural sector, the discussion will focus on research carried out on the two forms of rural cooperative communities, the kibbutz and the moshav. These have been the main rural settings where most Jewish agricultural production was carried out. However, the rapidly decreasing weight of agriculture in the Israeli economy, especially after the mid-1980s' financial and ideological crisis in the cooperative settlement movement has dramatically changed the cooperative nature of these rural settings in Israel. The non-Jewish rural sector includes established Arab villages and newly built semi-rural Bedouin communities. What is the position of women within these diverse rural settings and how has it been recorded in official and academic research?

An Overview of Research on Women in Israel

Only quite recently, during the last two decades, have Israeli social scientists begun to direct their attention in a serious fashion to the issue of the place of women in society. Although there have been studies that investigated the question of gender in Israeli society in the 1950s and 1960s, the penetration of feminist perspectives into Israeli academic work in the early 1970s has refocused attention and opened new, unexplored questions about gender relations, in general, and the position of women in society, in particular (Swirski and Safir, 1993; Izraeli et al., 1999). Most of the recent research on gender has been carried out by women academicians who, themselves, constitute a small and marginalized group within Israeli academe. Research on women in Israel has further been limited in scope when we consider that these women academics were largely concerned with Jewish women like themselves. Moreover, within the Jewish women category, they have focused their research mainly on middle-class, Jewish Ashkenazi women (who originated from Europe) and hardly at all on Jewish Oriental women (who originated from Arab countries).[2]

The main topics of such research have, accordingly, centered on issues such as the struggle of Jewish middle class women for equality in the job market, on the "glass ceiling" encountered by women managers and women entrepreneurs, and on the place of these women in decision-making processes. Examples include work on the unequal structure of the Israeli job market by. Efroni (1997), Zamir's work on the Kibbutz "glass ceiling" (1999), and Izraeli's extensive work on women managers (cf. Izraeli, 1996, 1997a, 1997b, 1999). Herzog (1994, 1999) has written about the place of women in the Israeli local political arena, and the contributors to Ma'or's edited volume (1997) wrote about the rising power of women in business and politics. Most of this research on women in Israel appears in collections edited by a small number of women academics (cf. Swirski and Safir, 1993; Bernstein, 1992; Azmon and Izraeli, 1993; Izraeli et. al., 1999).

Within this limited range of academic research on women in Israel, research on "Other" women in Israel –Jewish-Oriental women, Ethiopian women, lower-class Russian immigrant women, and non-Jewish women – has been further marginalized and it is even more limited both in number and in scope. Elsewhere (Motzafi-Haller, 2000) I reviewed the nature of the few studies that have looked more fully at Jewish Oriental women in Israel since the 1950s. It will suffice to note at this point that Oriental women in Israel are often constituted as a "problem" and that the research about them is often directed at proposing policy solutions for the "social problem" such women pose. A similar perspective frames the research on women immigrants from the former Soviet Union (e.g. Fishman, 1997; and Appelbaum and Zinger, 1995).

Placement of women and their worlds at the center of research has been largely the concern of women anthropologists. Two anthropological studies are worthy of special note here: El-Or's work on women in the ultra-orthodox community and the religious Zionist movement (1992, 1998) and Sered's work on the world of religious Oriental women in Jerusalem (1995). The work on non-Jewish women in Israel has its own limitations which I will discuss at greater length below.

The following observations are offered to sum up this brief general review of research on gender in Israeli academe:

- Social research on women and gender relations has been a relatively recent development in Israel. On the whole, it has been pushed to the margins of mainstream academic research. Most social research in Israel still ignores gender as a central category for analysis.
- The nature of the limited body of research that has begun to explore the place of women in society has been further narrowed down due to the strong influence of liberal feminist concerns. Most scholarly work on

women in Israel reflects liberal feminist concerns that are relevant in the lives of urban, middle-class Jewish Ashkenazi women.

- Very few works have explored the lives of "ethnic" non-Ashkenazi women, and even less attention has been focused on non-Jewish women and their worlds.

- The three observations presented above also suggest that very little sustained work has been carried out on *rural* women in Israel. The rest of this essay sets out to outline the nature of this limited work.

Women in Israel: The National Level

Women's Representation in the Israeli Legislature

Although women had won the right to vote in Israel since the 1920s, the representation of Israeli women in the political system at the local and national institutions is extremely limited today. In 2003, only 15% of the seats in the 16th Knesset (the Israeli parliament) were held by women and even a smaller ratio (13%) of women exists in the Israeli cabinet. For comparative purposes, consider the fact that in 2002 Swedish women held 42.7% of the parliament seats and 55% of seats in the Swedish cabinet were held by women. In Denmark the rates were 38% in the parliament and 45% in the cabinet, in Germany 31.7% and 35.7%, in Britain 17.9% and 33.3% respectively. The Israeli rates were not much higher than those cited for its neighbor Syria with 10.4% of the parliament seats and 11.1% in the cabinet seat held by women (Adva center, Women's representation in the legislature and in the cabinet, www.adva.org/politics 2003). The history of women's participation in the Israeli official political institutions is even less encouraging. In Golda Meir's large cabinet of 24 ministers, there was not even one woman. In most Israeli cabinets there was only one woman-minister; in four other Israeli governments there were only two women-ministers. In the Knesset, the rate of women stood for the first three elections at around 9%, by 1996 it dropped to 8.3% (Herzog, 1999: 314; Yishai, 1997). In the local political arena the representation of Israeli women is even lower. In 1948, with the establishment of the state there were only 4.2% women in local councils. Their rate dropped to 3.1% in 1965. There was a steady rise in women representation in the local political arena since 1969 and by 1998 their rate rose to 15%. For the first time, in 1998 two women were elected city mayors. These low rates are particularly puzzling in light of the fact that Jewish Israeli women, who constitute half of the Jewish electorate, serve in the Israeli army and are known to be equal to Jewish men in their voting participation. Moreover, Arab Israeli women who vote as often as Jewish men and women, tend to be almost absent from the political scene. Since 1948, only six women were elected to local council (Herzog, 1999: 315).

Women in the Israeli Job Market

On the whole, the rate of participation in the labor market by Israeli women is lower than that of most women in western "developed" countries. Table 4.1 records these comparative 2001 rates.

Table 4.1   Labor force participation of 25-54 year olds, by gender in descending order of females participation rates in the labor force

Country	% of men aged 25–54 in labor force	% of women aged 25–54 in labor force
Sweden	85.6	90.6
Finland	85.0	91.0
Norway	83.3	91.4
Switzerland	79.3	96.3
Canada	79.1	91.1
France	78.7	94.1
Portugal	78.1	92.8
United Kingdom	76.4	91.3
United States	76.4	91.3
Hungary	70.0	84.3
Israel	**68.5**	**83.5**
Japan	67.3	96.9
Spain	61.2	91.6
Italy	55.4	86.6
Mexico	45.3	96.2

Source: Adjusted from data provided by the Adva Center for 2001. See: www.adva.org.

Still, as the most recent national data shows, the participation of Israeli women in the labor market has been on the increase in the past two decades. According to the Central Bureau of Statistics calculations, the rate of women participation in the Israeli labor force had doubled over the past two decades. In 1996 women constituted some 46% of the national labor force in Israel. Twenty years earlier, their rate of participation was calculated as 32%. Yet, despite the obvious dramatic growth in the entry of women into the labor force, numerous studies point to the stubborn persistence of gender gaps in the level of income, in the prestige and power of the position held (Izraeli, 1999; Herzog, 1996). Numerous studies and aggregate statistics document the inequality in the earning power of men and women in Israel. These show that the average monthly salary earned by women is about 60% that of Israeli men, and the hourly wages are 80% that of men. A more limited report that compares income levels of men and women in the civil service concludes that women earn 75% of the income of men with the same qualifications and work experience. A 1998 report by the Women's Lobby in Israel shows that about a third of Israeli working women earn minimum wage or less. This compares with 14% of men at that income level. Only 20% of women earn what is defined as the average income as compared to 40% of the men. Finally, since 1993, more than 50% of the unemployed have been women (Adva Center, 1998; Izraeli, 1999: 167).

However, these general figures conceal significant variations *among* Israeli women. In the 25–54 age group, 73% of the *Jewish women* compared to only 18% of *Arab Israeli women* participate in the labor force. Despite the fact that Arab Israeli women constitute 20% of the Israeli women population, the make only 5% of the female labor force (Espanioly, 1994). There are also great variations in the kind of work performed by women in these varied ethnic and religious categories. At the top of the labor market, holding academic and professional positions, one finds Ashkenazi Jewish women. Oriental women cluster at the secretarial and clerical positions. Arab women, although represented in the labor market in small numbers, fall at both ends: either in academic and teaching positions or in low paying jobs on assembly lines (Central Bureau of Statistics, 1996).

In the past two decades the Israeli Parliament, the Knesset, had passed an impressive number of laws that work to prevent gender discrimination in the labor market. These new laws created a public feeling of equality and the legitimated, in the public discourse new norms. Yet in the absence of appropriate budgets that would enforce these new laws, the impact of such laws remains marginal. Employers continue to discriminate women in explicit and more implicit practices (Izraeli, 1999: 209).

Women's Education in Israel

There is a general rise in the achievement of women in formal education, in particular in the rate of high school and university enrollment. In 1995/6, 53% of the seventeen-year old Jewish girls had passed their matriculation exams at the end of high school, in comparison to 41% of the Jewish males of that age group. In the Arab education system, 23% of the females, as compared to 16% of the males, passed these critical exams that are necessary for entry into higher education. Within their respective ethnic categories, women composed 59% of the Oriental university students, 52% of the total Ashkenazi students, 54% of the Christian students, 40% of the Muslim students, and 33% of the Druze students in the country. In general, 55% of the university graduates (at B.A. level), 50% of M.A. graduates, and 39% of Ph.D. graduates were women (Adva Center 1998).

What subjects do women study when they reach university? Their presence has increased in most subjects, including those known as "male" subjects: business administration (43%), law (48%) medicine (48%), and physics (35%). Their presence in engineering and architecture has increased, but remains relatively minor (21%). The number of women in subjects known as "feminine" – which lead to low-paying positions – are the greatest. Humanities (60%), social sciences (63%), languages (82%), and education and teaching (86%). Where do these academic degrees place women? More than one-third of the college-level educated women are employed in education, health and the social services, the very areas that have been cut in recent years by government central planning (Swirski, 1999; Izraeli 1999: 198). All in all, level of education is a critical factor in securing a position in the labor market and women with tertiary education seem to enter the labor market in greater numbers compared with women with secondary or less than secondary education. In 2000, Israeli women with less than secondary education consisted of only 24.7% of the labor force, compare to 61.9% of women with upper secondary level education and 79.9% of women with tertiary education (Adva Center, International comparisons of labor force participation rate of women by educational attainment).

Women in the Agricultural Sector

It is critical to begin our review of the place of women in agriculture in contemporary Israel with the following two facts:

1. Only 2.4% of the Israeli population is engaged in agricultural production.
2. Women who are employed in the agricultural sector constitute only 1% of the total number of women of the Israeli labor power (Central Bureau of Statistics, 1996).

Over the years, agricultural production has shrunk as part of a decline in the rural sector in Israel. Schwartz (1998) reports that the share of agriculture in the country's net domestic product dropped from 12% in 1952 to 2.3% in 1995. Interestingly, the sharpest decline occurred after the 1986 financial crisis that hit Israel's collective settlements. A review of this crisis and the far-reaching changes it brought to the rural segment of Israeli agriculture is detailed in Schwartz, 1995. For our purposes here, it will suffice to state that following the mid-1980s crisis, agriculture lost much of its importance in the national economy. It is also instructive to note that the excellent review of this recent crisis in agricultural production pays very little attention to the impact such a process has had on women and their well-being.

The 1997 National Statistics Bureau data compares males and females according to the economic branch of their employment. It is important to note here that these and other national statistics document only those women who are defined as "employed." The particular nature of women's involvement in agricultural production, as the following discussion will make clear, has often meant that women's work is not defined as "employment." Women contribute many hours of their labor within small family farms, but are seldom reported as "employees" of these farm units (cf. Nevo, 1986). Note also that only 0.6% of women employees are considered "skilled agricultural workers."

Keeping in mind this built-in bias in the aggregate statistical records (the tendency to ignore/not record women's labor in agriculture); we must read the following data skeptically. The national statistics data indicates that those women who are employed in agriculture work less hours per week than men. Specifically, that men work on the average 43 hours; women work an average of 34.9 hours. This gender gap in work performance in agriculture runs across both Jewish and non-Jewish gender divisions, as Table 4.2 records.

Table 4.2 Average work hours per week by economic branch, population group and sex

Economic branch	Arab men	Total Arab[3]	Jewish women	Jewish men	Total Jews	Total men	Total women	Total
Agriculture	45.9	45.1	34.4	42.5	40.8	43	34.9	41.5
"Banking, insurance and other financial institutions"	43.9	42	35	41.4	37.6	41.6	35	37.8
Education	25.1	24.1	25	33.6	27	32.3	24.9	26.7
Health, welfare and social work services	43.3	39.7	30.7	39.5	32.8	40	31.1	33.4

Source: Central Bureau of Statistics, 1996: 189, abstracted from table 41.

The distinction between men and women within the Jewish population on the one hand, and internal gender differences within the Arab population of Israel on the other, leads us to the meso-level. Here one is struck by the paucity of research that concerns non-Ashkenazi Jewish women. Due to particular historical and political circumstances, this ethnic and religious division – between Jewish and non-Jewish women and between Ashkenazi (women of European origin) and Oriental (women of Middle-eastern and North African origin) women – corresponds with types of settlement. A small fraction of the non-Jewish population has clustered in a few urban settings, while the majority continues to reside in rural villages, known in the statistical records as "minority villages" (*kafrie miu'tim* in Hebrew).

The Jewish rural population is divided among the cooperative settlements of the "moshav ovdim" type (here there is an internal division between veteran, established moshavim and moshavim established by immigrants from Arab lands, originally known as "moshve olim" and the collective settlement form of the "kibbutz." The first three settlement types, the moshav (plural moshavim), the moshav shitufi (literally collective moshav) and the kibbutz (plural, kibbutzim) are the main forms of planned settlements among the Jewish population in Israel. The Moshav and the similar Moshav shitufi are forms of cooperative rural settlements distinguished from the collective arrangement of the kibbutz. The distinction among these three settlement forms has been eroding over the years as the kibbutzim have gradually given up many aspects of collective life.

Women in Cooperative and Non-Cooperative Settings in Israel

Table 4.2 records the changing rural population in Israel over the years, distinguishing between Jewish and non-Jewish rural populations. The data shows that the total rural population in Israel has dramatically decreased over the past five decades, from a total of 27.8% of the population in 1948 to less than 9% in 1996. This decline in rural population is much more dramatic among the non-Jewish population than among the Jews. Thus in 1948, the Jewish rural sector was 17% of the population, and this rate has declined in 1996 to about 9%. Among the non-Jewish population, more than 76% lived in rural settlements in 1948, and this rate declined to a low of 7% in 1996.

Table 4.3 The decline in rural population in Israel: Jewish and non-Jewish segments

	Total rural population			Jewish			Non-Jewish		
Year	Total	Rural	%	Total	Rural	%	Total	Rural	%
1948	873	243	27.8%	717	123	17.2%	156	119	76.3%
1951	1578	439	27.8%	1404	311	22.1%	173	128	73.8%
1955	1789	516	28.8%	1591	371	23.3%	199	145	72.8%
1960	2150	501	23.3%	1911	322	16.9%	239	179	74.8%
1965	2598	472	18.2%	2299	267	11.6%	299	204	68.3%
1970	3001	524	17.4%	2561	272	10.6%	440	252	57.2%
1975	3493	491	14.1%	2959	274	9.2%	534	218	40.8%
1980	3922	520	13.3%	3283	315	9.6%	639	205	32.1%
1985	4266	451	10.6%	3517	356	10.1%	749	95	12.7%
1990	4822	458	9.5%	3947	377	9.6%	875	81	9.3%
1996	5759	513	8.9%	4637	433	9.3%	1122	79	7.0%

Source: Israeli Ministry of Agriculture, 1998: 11. Numbers are in thousands.

Table 4.4 shows more detailed data, distinguishing among four types of rural settlements in Israel – "moshavim," "moshavim shitufiyim, "kibbutzim," and "kafre miu'tim." The fourth category lumps together all non-Jewish rural settlements. It indicates changes in the numbers of each settlement type over more than three decades, between 1961 and 1996. Table 4.4 also records a residual category of "Other," which includes rural settings that are not cooperatively run.

Table 4.4 The number of rural settlements in Israel by type of settlement

	Year	Total #	Moshav	M. Shitufi	Kibbutzim	Mi'utim (minorities)	Other
Number of settlements	1961	765	346	20	228	75	96
	1972	780	353	33	233	58	103
	1983	941	405	43	267	61	165
	1990	988	409	45	270	44	220
	1996	757	411	44	268	34	233
Percentages	1961	100	45.2	2.6	29.8	9.8	12.5
	1972	100	45.3	4.2	29.9	7.4	13.2
	1983	100	43.0	4.6	28.4	6.5	17.5
	1990	100	41.4	4.6	27.3	4.5	22.3
	1996	100	54.3	5.8	35.4	4.5	30.8

Source: Israeli Ministry of Agriculture, 1998: 11.

To conclude:

1. Agricultural production has declined dramatically in Israel and constitutes, according to the most recent official data, only about 2% of the country's net domestic product.
2. Most agricultural production is carried out in three main types of rural settlements: the kibbutzim, moshavim, and minority villages.
3. Due to historical, political, and social factors, the population of these three main sites of agricultural production in Israel is diverse and the place of women within this diverse universe of agricultural production varies greatly.

Thus, when we turn to a review of the micro-level, we must devote a separate discussion to each of these varied settlement types. We begin with the most studied, the kibbutzim.

Research on Women in the Kibbutz

There are a relatively high number of studies that have explored the position of women in kibbutz society.[4] A most productive researcher on the topic is sociologist

Talmon-Garber (c.f. 1956, 1970, 1980). Talmon-Garber's work exposed the gender inequality in the kibbutz society and thus dispelled one of the most common myths that gender equality between the sexes did exist in the kibbutz. More recent works on gender inequality in the kibbutz includes that of Adar et al. (1986, 1988, 1993) Adar (1996), Bar-Yosef (1986, 1992), Neuman (1991), and Palgi (1996). Together, these studies document the fact that despite the myth of the equal kibbutz society, women in the kibbutz tended to hold service roles, mostly associated with the caring for children and cooking, while agricultural roles were reserved for men. For example, Neuman's study (1991) records that only 3% of the women in the kibbutz were involved in agricultural production. While 85% of managerial positions were held by men, women fulfilled 85% of the service positions.[5] These data suggest that role segregation along gender lines is higher in the Israeli kibbutz than in urban settings in Israel.[6]

Research carried out after 1985 – the year of the economic crisis of the cooperative movement in general, and the kibbutzim, in particular – reveals that gender inequality in the kibbutzim had, in fact, expanded.[7] This more recent research employs different research methodology and theoretical frames when it explores this post-crisis era in kibbutz society. It tends to use qualitative research methods and asks more open-ended questions such as: have the recent transformations in the kibbutz society and structure created a better environment for gender equality in the kibbutz? For example, Blank (1995) used an interpretive analysis of open interviews conducted with women who had been members of various kibbutzim for at least ten years. Unlike the kind of research that prevailed up to the 1970s, Blank's research did not focus on documenting the statistical gaps between men and women's status in the kibbutz, but chose instead to explore the ways in which these women have *experienced* the recent dramatic shifts in the socio-economic fabric of kibbutz life. Zamir (1999) selected a more focused research sample, choosing to focus on life stories of those 5% of kibbutz women who had reached management and decision-making positions in their respective kibbutzim. Lieblich, who wrote the forward to Zamir's book, makes explicit the shift in focus of both research methodology and questions that this study signal when she wrote (1999: 9):

> The goals of this research have been to explore the lives of those women who had succeeded in reaching the economic elite of the kibbutz and to examine, from their perspective, why they make up such a tiny minority among women. The research is structured thus in a way of learning about the general failure from the understanding of the few success cases.

This recent work has not only finally dispelled the entrenched myth of gender equality in the kibbutz setting; it also documented the ways in which the more recent crisis in the kibbutz movement has exacerbated that tendency. The importance of this research on kibbutz women also lies in its sustained effort to record the voices of women and their particular experiences of the transforming nature of cooperative life in their communities.

Research on Women in the Moshav

One of the most striking facts about the position of women in Israeli moshavim is that until very recently, women did not have the legal right to vote or be elected to the central committee that runs the moshav – the "Agudat Hamoshav." The right to vote was limited to male owners of the family farm units of the moshav. In 1999, the law was changed after a legal battle initiated by a woman from Moshav Zavdiel. Women, according to the new law, could become members of the moshav council (and thus obtain the right to vote), if they were married to the male owner of the family farm or to his son, but only after they had completed a set of bureaucratic procedures of registration (Mualem, 1999; Tal, 1999). The chairperson of one Moshav council was quotes as saying in 2000: "We are used that women do not interfere with business matters. Until now it was fine and created no problems. So why should we change the regulations?" (Frielich, 2000). Despite this blatant contradiction of such statement with the Israeli myth of gender equality, the reality in Israeli Moshavim is such that most women do not bother to come forward and apply for their membership right, enabled by the new law. While all men are automatic members of the Moshav council, the application is necessary for women only. So despite of the enactment of the new law, Moshav women still do not partake in any of the decision-making regarding the distribution of resources made in their respective communal-based councils. While the reality of gender inequality in the Moshav society became a topic of public discussion and the subject of several journalistic essays only after the legal battle for including women as members was won in 1999. Curiously, academic research has not dealt with the phenomenon.

Research on women in cooperative moshav settlements can be divided into three main types: a. economic research, b. social anthropology research, and c. surveys of attitudes held by moshav residents.

a. Economic Research

Two sub-categories of economic research can be identified:

1. Research that considers the family in the rural areas to be the key economic unit. Such research begins with the assumption that the family and the family-centered household units are the basic analytical unit. The early work by Sadan, Nachmias, and Bar-Lev (1976) is a good example of such research. The researchers examined the correlation between the socio-economic background of members of the family unit and the success of its economic management. The researchers compared families of Jewish Oriental and Ashkenazi background and found a direct correlation between the level of formal education of the women, the size of the family, and the level of efficient economic management of the farm. In a recent work, Ayal Kimhi (1996) also considers the family unit to be a factor in his financial analysis. He links the nature of the division of labor within the family with its decision to seek paid employment outside the family farm. Semyonov and Lewin-Epstein (1991) also look at gender-related gaps within the labor market. They propose that because most Moshav women tend to work near their homes, women in rural settings tend to be paid less.

*2. Research that focuses on employment of women in peripheral regions*The key researcher in this category is Fleischer, who, together with several colleagues, have edited several collections of research work published by the Development Studies Center of Rehovot (see Fleischer, Applebaum and Banin, 1990; and Fleischer and Appelbaum, 1992; Fleischer, Rotem and Banin, 1993). This research is based mainly on data culled from questionnaires and examines the characteristics of women's employment in small peripheral towns and moshavim in the south and north of Israel. Among the key research findings are the following:

- Women in peripheral settlements in both the north and the south of the country have a higher rate of unemployment than the national average. (note the grouping together of moshavim with semi-urban peripheral settlements).
- These women are mostly of Oriental (non-European) origin. They are less educated and have less marketable skills and when employed. When employed, they are often found in low-paid, low-status positions.
- The socio-economic profile of this population is the key factor that defines a woman's ability to secure employment.

Rotem and Banin's 1993 research examines a new avenue of income generation for women in the Israeli rural settings – internal rural tourism. The study proposes that women's skills, such as cooking and housekeeping, could be used to build a profitable small business. Several more recent publications by women's advocacy groups (Women's Lobby in Israel 1998), the Ministry of Housing (1994, 1996) and the Association for Small Businesses (1996) have also advocated the engagement of women in this growing non-agricultural, income-generating activity. Yet a 1996 study on rural tourism (Quixchan-Keidar, 1996) reveals that although there is a tremendous growth in rural tourism (from five businesses in the early 1970s to over 200 by the mid-1990s and to more than 7500 by 2004), and despite the fact that about half of these small businesses are owned by women, women of low-income and modest socio-economic background do not take advantage of this economic potential. The person most likely to initiate a rural tourism business (especially renting out rooms, known as "*tzimerim*" from the German word for 'room') is middle-aged and relatively more educated woman, with some relevant professional background and experience (Ibid, 1996: 7). Despite of the importance of this research, little else was reported about the unique potential of engaging Moshav women in this burgeoning economic activity.[8] In fact, most published work on 'non-agricultural businesses' in moshavim have a larger research agenda and mentions women in passing. They do not explore gender distribution in this emerging economic activity (cf. Ilberg, 1984; and Sherman, Kedar and Cohen, 1993).

b. Social Anthropology/Qualitative Research

Anthropological research is characterized by its holistic and qualitative nature. It explores the wider fabric of social life and it employs mostly qualitative and interpretive analytical methods to explain its results. The anthropological body of research on the moshav can be also divided into two subcategories: research that places moshav families and their transformation at the center of the study, and research that is focused on the world of moshav women.

1. Research on families and household units in the moshav settings Women do not constitute the focus of this research, but are considered a part of a larger family/household unit. Shoked's pioneering work (1980) on the changing division of labor in an immigrant moshav in the Negev is a good example. Solomonica (1981) has also recorded changes in family structure in the moshav and explored the implications of such changes on women's status. Solomonica concludes that there have been significant differences in the way economic changes in the moshav structure during the late 1970s to the early 1980s have affected women in veteran moshavim, as against the effects on women in moshavim inhabited mostly by immigrants ("moshavie olim"). He finds that women's roles have changed more dramatically in moshavim in which most of the residents are Jews who immigrated to Israel from Arab lands (Orientals/Mizrahim) than in moshavim in which Jews of European origin (Ashkenazim) reside. Jewish women of Oriental/Mizrahi origin became the main bread winners in their families. Many of them sought cash employment outside the moshav settlement.

Important anthropological work that looks directly at the position of women within Israeli moshavim up to the early 1980s was carried out by Nevo (1986, 1991). Nevo documents the extent to which agricultural work in the family farm is carried out by women. Such work is not recorded, nor paid. Exploring shifts in the ideology of cooperative work in moshavim since 1921, Nevo finds that despite the emphasis on equality between genders in this ideology, the structure of the family within the moshav has remained unchanged over the years. This structure has reproduced inequality between the genders and kept women at a disadvantage.

Very little intensive, anthropological research work has been carried out on moshav women in the 1990s. In her 1991 article, Nevo examines five moshavim that have adopted new technologies for growing greenhouse flowers. She reports that women have found a new focus in managing these greenhouses. However, despite this relative success, Nevo argues that this new economic opportunity for women did not change the lower status of women in the moshav. The engagement of women in public and decision-making positions in the moshav remains minimal, and their marginality in local political life has become more pronounced.

2. Anthropological work that places the experience of women in the moshav society at the center of research.   Included in this category are the work of Wasserfall (1995) on women of Moroccan origin who live in a moshav in the Negev, Katzir's work (1983) on Yemenite women in a moshav near Jerusalem, and Schelly-Newman's (1993, 1997) work on women's narratives among Tunisian moshav women. These micro studies are rich in insights not only regarding gender inequality in the moshav setting, but more critically in the particular ways these women have dealt with the changing conditions of their lives.

c. Sociological Research on Women's Attitudes of their Positions in Society

This kind of sociological research uses questionnaires that record views women hold about their place in society and how they rate their satisfaction with their membership in the cooperative, public, and family life. The following are some results from one early study (Padan-Eisenshtarck and Meir-Heker, 1975):

- Women tend to report a low level of satisfaction with their limited and non-professional engagement in economic activity in the moshav.
- Women have a low level of professional aspiration and thus limit their involvement in the economic life of the moshav.
- Most women in the sample see their role as housewives and mothers as their central social role and draw most of their self-value from these gender-specific roles.
- Although they articulate limited professional aspirations for themselves, most women hope for a professional career for their own daughters.

Research on Women in Non-Jewish Rural Sectors

In a process that parallels the decline of the importance of agricultural production in the Jewish population of Israel, agriculture has been declining in importance in Israeli Arab villages, although due to more specific historical and political conditions (cf. Rabinowitz, 1998). In the late 1960s, only 17% of the residents in Arab villages made their living by cultivating their land (Rabinowitz, 1998: 146). This rate decreased in the 1970s, when more Arab laborers sought jobs in towns, especially in construction (Abu-Rakba, 1993: 187). There is very little recent concrete data that documents the scope and extent of the Israeli Arab women engagement in agricultural production. There is some data on the overall rate of labor participation by Arab women in Israel. On the whole, the rate of the Arab women's labor participation is lower than that of Jewish Israeli women. In 1985, the participation of Arab women in the work force stood at 11%. In comparison, the rate of Jewish women's participation in the labor force in the same year was 39%. Based on an analysis of data provided by the population census of 1983, Lewin-Epstein and Semyonov found (1991) that Arab women's rates of employment was directly influenced by local, community-based economic and social factors. The rate of Arab women's participation in the labor force rose in communities where agricultural production was dominant; it declined in communities with little agricultural work, few job opportunities, and high birth rates.

The labor force of Arab women tends to be sharply divided into low service and industry work and white-collar jobs (Abu-Rakba, 1993: 189). Arab women who work in service jobs, such as cleaning, earn the lowest wages. Many young, unmarried Arab women find employment in textile plants, often located within their home villages or in a neighboring town (Drori, 1996). The low wages earned by these young women are often translated into a social and economic advantage that empowers these women (Goldberg, 1993).

Education among Arab women has also increased over the past two decades. Women constitute about 21% of all Arabs who earned a first degree (Abu-Rakba, 1993). Almost half of the Israeli Arab women in the work force are engaged in white-collar, public service jobs. Shaloufeh Khazen Fatina (1993) argues that the improved economic status of Arab women in the 1980s and early 1990s has resulted in shifts in the patterns of mate selection among Palestinian women in Israel. Women tend to use "modern" criteria (such as emotional compatibility) for selecting their mate, rather than comply with "traditional" criteria (economic or social compatibility). Mar'i and Mar'i (1993) argue that these changes in the position of Arab women have made women important change agents in Israeli Arab society.

Most of the recent research has focused on Arab communities within the "Green Line." Semyonov's 1994 study is unique among Israeli researchers in exploring changing patterns of gender-linked participation in the labor market in the areas occupied by Israel since the 1967 war. Analysis of official national statistics relevant to the population of the West Bank and Gaza since 1970s led Semyonov (1994) to conclude that contrary to general trends documented in other societies of a rise in the rate of women's participation in the labor force, and despite the rapid increase in the male labor force in the occupied territories since the early 1970s, the percentage of women's engagement in the labor force has in fact decreased in these regions.

Yet, as important as these limited data on rate of women's participation in the labor force are, they tell us little about the larger social structures that shape these gender-specific patterns. More theoretical, sociological analyses of the place of women in Arab society in Israel are less common. These include the early important work by Rosenfeld (1958, 1968) and by Cohen (1965), and in the 1970s and 1980s by Marx (1974) and Ginat (1982, 1986). Worthy of mention is the work by social anthropologist Ginat who has devoted a separate book to the question of the status of women in Israeli Muslim rural society (1982). Yet, despite its focus on women in rural Arab society, a critical shortcoming of this body of work produced in Israel until the late 1980s is that it adopts a male-centered perspective in explaining the place of women is society. By the 1990s, one can cite several academic studies that were informed by feminist perspectives. These include the works by Jareissi, 1991; Espanioly, 1994; Ibrahim, 1997; and Hasan, 1995, 1999.

Conclusions

Any review of the existing knowledge on gender in the Israeli agricultural sector must distinguish among the various ethnic/national segments of what is generally defined as the "rural sector". The positions of women within the Jewish cooperative settlement of the Moshav and the Kibbutz on the one hand, and that of Arab women in Palestinian villages within the Green-Line and in recently-settled Bedouin villages on the other hand are two very different realities. Moreover, within each of these "rural" settings, relations of production and relations between the genders vary greatly. Not only do we find variations in gender relations according to distinct ethnic, class, national and religious communities, but as the overview presented in this essay suggests, the particular gender relationships within each "rural segment" have dramatically shifted over the past decade or more. The decline in agricultural production in Israel had reached a crisis situation in the mid 1980s, transforming in the process the shape of Jewish rural communities and the position of Arab village society within and beyond the 1967 boundaries of the Israeli state.

   This essay offered a critical overview of the existing knowledge on women in these various rural segments of the changing society and economy of Israel. It suggests that, on the whole, and maybe despite more naïve expectations, research on gender relations in Israel in general, and on the rural sector in particular is rather limited and relatively recent. Gender began to be considered a relevant category for analysis and research mainly since the early to mid 1970s when feminist research made its way into Israeli academe. Still, because gender-focused research tended to focus, until quite recently on urban, middle-class Jewish women, we know relatively little about rural women and about their diverse role in agricultural production. While research on kibbutz women is relatively an exception in this general gap of our knowledge on women in the Israeli rural sector, we have extremely limited knowledge on Jewish women from non-Ashkenazi origin and on the shifting gender relations in non-Jewish rural settings. What, for example, have recent shifts in the demands for labor by the expanding Israeli economy meant for women in Arab villages within Israel? And what does the continuing trend over the past decade to import foreign agricultural workers from the Far East (mainly Thailand) mean for Jewish moshav women? For example, when Jewish men left their farms to work outside their homes, women became managers of foreign agricultural laborers. No serious research has documented the meaning of such a new situation for the Jewish women who were left to manage these workers. We also know little about the changing lives of Bedouin women and girls who seem to do the major part of goat and sheep herding in their Negev communities when Bedouin men seek paid jobs in Jewish urban centers. There is similarly little or no systematic new research that documents the lot of poor Oriental women in failed family farms in many Negev moshavim.

The Israeli Ministry of Agriculture does not have a special gender officer, nor is it set to develop projects and program that will consider gender as part of their planning. To understand this obvious omission one must consider the political settings within which rural women from marginal ethnic and national groups are defined by Israeli policy makers. Put bluntly: in the Israeli setting ethnic and national affiliations are more critical than gender in shaping access to resources. Because we are not dealing with a uniform population of rural women in the Israeli case, no clear, comprehensive gender-focused policies or directive has been developed by the Israeli Ministry of Agriculture or by other concerned policy makers. "Gender mainstreaming" or any other catch-all gender-conscious recommendations presented in the other essays of this book, and in the development literature in general, are thus exposed as meaningless in social realities that are sharply divided by other lines of inequality based on national, religious or ethnic affiliation. This is perhaps the most critical conclusion that emerges from the review of the Israeli case of gender, knowledge and rural relations of production.

Notes

1 This is an expanded and updated version of an article published in 2001 in the *Journal of Rural Cooperation*, vol. 29, no. 1, pp. 3-25, under the title "Research on Women and Rural Israel: The Gender Gap". I wish to thank the Journal for granting me the permission to publish this essay in its expanded form.

2 Oriental Jews are Jews who originated from Arab lands. They are known in Hebrew as "Mizrahim."

3 Official data for Arab females is not available. Note that the average total work hours are lower than the average for males only, evidently due to the lower average of Arab women working hours.

4 There is no space in this brief section to review all the work published on women in the kibbutz. The limited selection I have cited intends to support the argument I am developing here about the changing nature of academic scholarship on women in the kibbutz due to the growing influence of feminist theories and perspectives.

5 Adar (1996: 27) supports this data when she argues that "there are more men than women in jobs of managerial nature." She adds another interesting twist to this statistics when she argues that despite the fact that women have gained higher education in larger numbers than men, they have fewer opportunities to make use of their educational skills in their work. (op. cit). For a detailed discussion about the meaning of the categories "service" and "managerial," see Palgi 1996 page 14ff.

6 Feminism in the Kibbutz, Adar writes (1996: 24) "exposed the nakedness of the double message that was prominent in kibbutz society. On the one hand it was argued that every woman can work in any branch of kibbutz economy she wishes to work in...on the other hand, there were clear signals that the primary duty of each woman is to care for her family, especially her children" (my translation from the Hebrew original text). Adar reviews a range of research work documenting women inequality in kibbutz society of

the late 1980s and 1990s and provides several tables based on data culled from the kibbutz research center files. Against the 3% of women who participate in agriculture in the late 1980s, she notes 22% of men in that field (i.e., more than seven times more men than women participate in agricultural production). By the early 1990s, the relative numbers of men and women engaged in agricultural production rose to 23 and 5 percent, respectively. (Adar, 1996: 27, table 3).

[7] The list for such research is long. Interested readers might consult the excellent review essays and many references cited in Palgi, 1996; Adar, 1996; and Neuman 1991.

[8] In a recent comprehensive survey carried out by Fleischer with others it was found that the *tzimer*-renting business is growing at a rate of 10% per year, producing, by December 2004, 1650 full-time jobs and 2600 part-time positions.

References

Official Documents

1. Association for Small Businesses in Israel, "Committee for Women Entrepreneurship," 1996. (Hebrew)
2. Israel Ministry of Agriculture. "An Economic Account of Agriculture and the Rural Sector," 1998. (Hebrew)
3. Central Bureau of Statistics, Israel, *Statistical Abstracts*, 1996 (Jerusalem, Israel)
4. Central Bureau of Statistics, Israel, "Labor Force Survey," Publication No. 1100, 1997. (Jerusalem, Israel)
5. Ministry of Housing, Israel, Department of Housing Restoration, "Little Secrets on the Way to Big Success: Guide for Business Entrepreneurship for Women." 1994 (Hebrew)
6. Ministry of Housing, Israel, Department of Neighborhood Social Restoration. "'Tnufa' [momentum] Plan in the Realm of Occupations: Program for the Advancement of Women Business Entrepreneurship, Israel," 1996. (Hebrew)
7. Women's Lobby in Israel, "Equality for Women in the Welfare State of Israel." Workshop Report, Tel Aviv, Israel, 1998. (Hebrew)

Published and Unpublished Articles and Books

Abu-Rakba, S., "Arab Women in the Israeli Labor Market," in Swirski, B., and Safir, M., (eds.) *Calling the Equality Bluff: Women in Israel.* New York and London: Teachers College Press, 1993: 187–192.
Adar, G., "Women in the Kibbutz: Change and Continuity (1980–1995)" in Adar, G. and Palgi, M. (eds.), *Women in the Changing Kibbutz.* Haifa, Israel: Haifa University, Institute for Kibbutz Research, 1996: 21–38. (Hebrew)
Adar, G. and Louis, H., "Kibbutz Female Members: A Survey of Women Holding Public Positions." Haifa: Yad Tabenkin and the Institute for Kibbutz Research, 1988. (Hebrew)
Adar, G., Torniansky, B. and Rozner, M., "Ways to Infiltrate Reform." Haifa, Israel: Haifa University, The Institute for Kibbutz Research. No. 131, 1993 (Hebrew)

Adar, G., *et al.*, *Women in the Kibbutz of Tomorrow.* Ramat Efal: Yad Tabenkin, 1986. (Hebrew)

Adva Center, "The Center for Alternative Information," Tel Aviv, Israel, 1998.

------- "Women's representation in the legislature and in the cabinet," 2003. URL: www.adva.org/politics.

Al-Haj, M., "Problems of Employment for Arab Academics in Israel." Haifa, Israel: Haifa University, The Jewish-Arab Center, 1988.

Azmon, Y. and Izraeli, D. (eds.), *Women in Israel.* New Brunswick and London: Transaction Publishers, 1993.

Appelbaum, L. and Zinger N., "Integration Patterns of Women Immigrants from the F.S.U. in the Labor Market of Israel." Rehovot, Israel: Development Studies Center, 1995. (Hebrew)

Bar-Yosef, R., "The Women's Issue is Universal: How Disappointing this is the Case Even in the Kibbutz" in Adar, G., et. al., *Women in the Kibbutz of Tomorrow.* Ramat Efal, Israel: Yad Tabenkin, 1986: 20–30. (Hebrew)

------- *The Kibbutz at the Turning Point of the Century.* Discussion Paper. Ramat Efal, Israel: Yad Tabankin, 1992: 53–95. (Hebrew)

Bernstein, D. (ed.), *Pioneers and Homemakers: Jewish Women in Pre-State Israel,* New York: State University of New York Press, 1992.

Blank, D., "Women in the Process of the 90s Transformation in the Kibbutz Society." *Ayin Bohenet Research Report Series,* Pamphlet B, Ramat Efal, Israel: Yad Tabankin, 1995. (Hebrew)

Cohen, A., *Arab Border Villages in Israel.* Manchester: Manchester University Press, 1965.

Drori, I., "The Work Culture of Arab Women in the Galilee Sewing Workshops." Discussion Paper No. 86, Golda Meir Institute of Work and Social Research, 1996. (Hebrew)

Efroni, L., "Compensations in the Wage System in Israel," in Ma'or, A. (ed.), *Women, The Rising Power.* Tel Aviv, Israel: Sifri'at Po'alim, 1997: 44–45. (Hebrew)

El-Or, T., *Educated and Illiterate.* Tel Aviv, Israel: Am Oved Publishers, 1992. (Hebrew)

------- *In the Next Passover.* Tel Aviv, Israel: Am Oved Publishers. 1998. (Hebrew)

Espanioly, N., "Palestinian Women in Israel: Identity in Light of Occupation" in Mayer, T. (ed.), *Women and the Israeli Occupation: The Politics of Change.* New York and London. Routledge, 1994: 106–120.

Fleischer, A. and Applebaum, L., "Spatial Differences in the Labour Force Participation of Married Women: The Case of Israel's Peripheral Areas." *Journal of Rural Studies,* 1992: 293–302.

Fleischer, A., Appelbaum, L. and Banin, T., "Employment and Unemployment of Women in Peripheral Areas." Rehovot, Israel: The Development Studies Center, 1990. (Hebrew)

Fleischer, A., Rotem, A., and Banin T., "New Directions in Recreation and Tourism Activities in the Rural Sector in Israel, Demand and Supply Factors." Rehovot, Israel: The Development Studies Center, 1993. (Hebrew)

Fishman, D., "New Immigrants from the F.S.U. at Work in Israel: A Report," in Ma'or, A. (ed.), *Women, The Rising Power.* Tel Aviv, Israel: Sifri'at Po'alim, 1997: 243–246. (Hebrew)

Frielich, R., "In the Moshavim Mahasiya, Gefen and Lozit Women do not have the Right to Vote." *Maariv*, 4.1.2000.

Ginat, J., *Women in Muslim Rural Society: Status and Role in Family and Community*. New Brunswick, N.J.: Transaction Books, 1982.

------- *Blood Disputes Among Bedouins and Rural Arabs in Israel*. University of Pittsburgh Press and Jerusalem Institute for Israel Studies, 1986.

Goldberg, D., "Is there Really a 'Double Disadvantage? The Social and Economic Status of Arab Women in the Israeli Labor Market." M.A. Thesis, Tel Aviv University, 1993.

Hasan, M., "Murder of Women for 'Family Honour' in Palestinian Society in Israel," M.A. Dissertation. University of Greenwich, 1995.

------- "The Politics of Honour: Patriarchy, the State and the Murder of Women in the Name of Family Honour," in Izraeli et. al., *Sex, Gender, Politics: Women in Israel*, 1999: 267–307. (Hebrew).

Herzog, H., *Realistic Women: Women in the Local Politics of Israel*. Jerusalem, Israel: Jerusalem Institute for Israeli Research, 1994. (Hebrew)

------- "Women in Politics and the Politics of Women," in Izraeli *et al.*, *Sex, Gender, Politics: Women in Israel*. Tel-Aviv, Israel: Hakibbutz Hameuchad Publishers, 1999: 307-357. (Hebrew)

Ibrahim, I., "The Arab Woman at Work," in Ma'or, A. (ed.), *Women, The Rising Power*. Tel Aviv, Israel: Sifri'at Po'alim, 1997: 238–242. (Hebrew)

Ilberg, N., "The Infiltration of Non-Agricultural Occupations into the Moshavim." M.A. Thesis, Dept. of Geography, Bar-Ilan University, 1984. (Hebrew)

Izraeli, D., "Report on Women on Boards of Governors in Government Companies." Ramat Gan, Israel: Sociology Department, Bar-Ilan University, 1996. (Hebrew)

-------- "Culture, Policy and Women of Two-Income Families in Israel," in Waller, R. and Cohen, R. (eds.), *Family and Insight, A Current Look at the Family*. Jerusalem, Israel: Ministry of Education, Culture and Sports, 1997a. (Hebrew)

-------- "Women Directors in Israel," in Ma'or, A. (ed.), *Women, The Rising Power*. Tel Aviv, Israel: Sifri'at Hapo'alim, 1997b: 56–75. (Hebrew)

-------- "Gendering the Labor World," in Izraeli D. *et al.*, *Sex, Gender, Politics: Women in Israel*. Tel-Aviv, Israel: Hakibbutz Hameuchad Publishers, 1999: 167–217.

Jareissi, R., "The Working Arab Mother's Ways of Dealing with Dual Roles." Haifa University, M.A. Thesis, 1991. (Hebrew)

Katzir, Y., "Yemenite Jewish Women in Israeli Rural Development: Female Power versus Male Authority." *Economic Development and Cultural Change*, 1983. 32: 45–61.

Kimhi, A., "Demographic Composition of Farm Households and its Effect on Time Allocation." *Journal of Population Economics*, 1996, 9, 4: 429–439.

Quixchan-Keidar, P., "Census of Home Businesses Owned by Women in Jewish Settlements." The World Zionist Organization. Department of Settlements Development, Rehovot, Israel: The Development Studies Center, 1996. (Hebrew)

Lewin-Epstein, N. and Semyonov, M., "Modernization and Subordination: Arab Women in the Israeli Labour Force". *European Sociological Review*, 1992, 8: 39–51.

Ma'or, A. (ed.), *Women, The Rising Power*. Tel Aviv, Israel: Sifri'at Po'alim, 1997.

Mar'i, M. M., and Mar'i, S. K., "The Role of Women as Change Agents in Arab Society in Israel," in Swirski, B. and Safir, M. (eds.), *Calling the Equality Bluff: Women in Israel.* New York and London: Teachers College Press, 1993: 213–222.

Marx, E., *Bedouin Society of the Negev.* Tel Aviv, Israel: Reshafim, 1974.

Motzafi-Haller, P., "The Double Erasure: Mizrahi Women in Israel," in Epstein, H. (ed.), *Jewish Women 2000.* Waltham, Mass: Research Institute on Jewish Women, 1999: 79–97.

Mualem, M., "Elections to Moshav Peduyim Council were Postponed because Women were not allowed to Vote." *Haaretz.* 3.8.1999. (Hebrew)

Nevo, N., "Unpaid Work in the Rural Family in Cooperative Farming." *Israeli Social Science Research,* 1986, 4, 1: 44–59.

-------- "Technology as a Factor in Gender Differentiation of Work Roles: A Case Study of Israel's smallholder Cooperative Villages." *Journal of Rural Studies,* 1991, 7: 31–36.

Neuman, S., "Occupational Sex Segregation in the Kibbutz: Principles and Practice." *Kiklos,* 1991, 44, 2: 203–219.

Padan-Eisenshtarck, D. and Meir-Hecker, H., "Women on the Collective Moshav in an Ideological Trap." *Megamot,* 1975, 21, 4: 423–428. (Hebrew)

Palgi, M., "Women in the Changing Kibbutz Economy," in Adar, G. and Palgi, M. (eds.), *Women in the Changing Kibbutz.* Haifa University, The Institute for Research in Kibbutz and the Idea of the Collective, 1996: 2–22. (Hebrew)

Rabinowitz, D., *Anthropology and the Palestinians.* Tel Aviv, Israel: The Institute for Israeli Arab Studies, 1998.

Rosenfeld, H., "Processes of structural change within the Arab village family." *American Anthropologist,* 1958, 60: 1127–1139.

-------- "The Contradictions Between Property, Kinship and Power, As Reflected in the Marriage System of an Arab Village," in Peristiany, J.G. (ed.), *Contributions to Mediterranean Sociology,* 1968.

Sadan, E., Nachmias, C. and Bar-Lev, G., "Education and Economic Performance of Occidental and Oriental Family Farm Operators." *World Development,* 1976, 4: 445–455.

Schelly-Newman, E., "The Woman Who Was Shot: A Communal Tale." *Journal of American Folklore,* 1993, 106 (421): 285–303.

-------- "Finding one's place: Locale narratives in an Israeli moshav," *Quarterly Journal of Speech,* 1997, 83: 401–455.

Schwartz, M., "The Transformations of Israel's Moshavim," in Schwartz, M. and Hare, P. Agricultural Cooperative Resettlement: Applying Israeli Experience in Zambia, Nigeria and Nepal. An Unpublished Report to Netherlands-Israel, 1998: 43–63.

------- *Unlimited Guarantees: History, Political Economy, and the Crisis of Cooperative Agriculture in Israel.* Beer Sheva, Israel: Ben Gurion University of the Negev Press. 1995.

Semyonov, M. and Lewin-Epstein, N., "Suburban Labor-markets, Urban Labor-markets, and Gender Inequality in Earnings." *Sociological Quarterly,* 1991, 32: 611–620.

Semyonov, M., "Trends in Labor Market Participation and Gender-Linked Occupational Differentiation," in Mayer, T. (ed.), *Women and the Israeli Occupation*. New York: Routledge, 1994: 138–146.

Sered, S., "Women's Spirituality in Context," in Azmon, Y. (ed.), *Window to the Lives of Women in Jewish Societies*. Jerusalem, Israel: Zalman Shazar Center of Israeli History, 1995: 245–258. (Hebrew)

Shaloufeh Khazan, F., "Change and Mate Selection Among Palestinian Women in Israel," in Swirski, B. and Safir, M. (eds.), *Calling the Equality Bluff: Women in Israel.* New York and London: Teachers College Press, 1993: 82–90.

Sherman N., Kedar P., and Cohen (Kadman), M., *Non-Agricultural Businesses on Moshavim.* Rehovot: The Development Studies Center, 1993. (Hebrew)

Shoked, M., "Transformation in the Division of Labor between Men and Women in Families of Moroccan Immigrants," in Shoked, M., Marx, E. and Deshen, S. (eds.), *Essays in Social Anthropology*. Schoken Publishers, 1980: 141–152. (Hebrew)

Solomonica, D. D., "Recent Drastic Changes in Moshav Farming and Some Implications on the Role and Status of Women." A paper presented at the International Interdisciplinary Congress on Women, Haifa, Israel, 1981.

Swirski, B. and Safir, M. (eds.), *Calling the Equality Bluff: Women in Israel.* New York and London: Teachers College Press, 1993.

Swirski, B., "Money is the Name of the Game – Women in the Israeli Welfare State." *Noga,* 1999, 36: 18–23. (Hebrew)

Tal, R., "The Right of the Voter." *Maariv,* 4.8.1999.

Talmon-Garber, Y., "The Family in Collective Settlements." Amsterdam*: Transactions of The Third World Congress of Sociology,* 1956: 26–116.

-------- *Individual and Community in the Kibbutz.* Jerusalem, Israel: Magnes, 1970. (Hebrew)

-------- "The Family in the Kibbutz," in Shoked, M., Marx, E. and Deshen, S. (eds.), *Essays in Social Anthropology*. Tel Aviv, Israel: Schoken Publishing, 1980: 120–141. (Hebrew)

Wasserfall, R., "Fertility and Community: The White Ribbon Ceremony and the Green Ribbon Ceremony in an Ethnic Moroccan Moshav," in Azmon, Y. (ed.), *Window to the Lives of Women in Jewish Societies*. Jerusalem, Israel: Zalman Shazar Center of Israeli History, 1995: 258–271. (Hebrew)

Zamir, A., *Through the Glass Ceiling – Women in Senior Management Positions in the Kibbutz*. Ramat Efal, Israel: Yad Tabenkin, 1999. (Hebrew)

Chapter 5

Gender and Agriculture in Egypt

Zeinab El-Tobshy

Introduction

About 47% of the total active female population in Egypt is engaged in agricultural work. Agriculture accounts for 40% of Egypt's gross domestic product (GDP) and 22% of Egypt's exports. More than half of Egypt's population, which reached 64.7 million in 1997 and is growing at the rate of 2.3% per year, live and work in the rural areas, drawing a large part of its livelihood from agriculture.

Over the last decade or more, it became increasingly clear that the role of women in agricultural production in Egypt could no longer be ignored. A key factor in this realization is that most available arable land in Egypt is already being used in agriculture and improving food production cannot be directed to increasing agricultural production within existing cultivated plots, nor via expansion of agricultural land. The efforts of the Egyptian government at reclaiming land through the project at Toshki cannot be the main way for increasing food production. An increase in food production could be attained through minimizing post-harvest losses that are estimated at 5-40% for cereals and horticultural crops. These losses are due to inadequate post-harvest handling technologies and shortage of trained and experienced manpower. The critical role women play in the post-harvest process must therefore be considered with greater care by planners.

Yet, there are numerous constraints on any effort to address the question of integrating women into projects designed for increasing food production in Egypt. Critical among these is the general lack of awareness of gender issues at all levels of the society. Such lack of awareness by policymakers and planners is reflected by the fact that most planned projects ignore the requirements and particular interests of rural women. Because most extension service systems are dominated by men, women seldom express their needs and are effectively excluded from access to technological knowledge, which is transmitted by male extension workers. Another critical constraint on integrating women into projects and policies intended to improve agricultural production and better living conditions in the rural areas is the lack of access by rural women (most of whom are illiterate and poor) to credit and potential markets. A final and major barrier for women's participation in plans designed to increase production in the agricultural sector are customs and traditions which inhibit women from accessing services and benefits that might be offered by the state. Indeed, overcoming these traditional barriers requires structural and fundamental changes, which are not accomplished in short-term projects and perspectives. One important step in this direction is the task of making the woman's role in the agricultural sector more visible. That is, in order to increase awareness of gender issues among policymakers, it is necessary to provide them with as complete a picture as possible of the ways in which rural women are crucial to agricultural production activities in Egypt. The purpose of this essay is to begin this task by reviewing existing databases that document the nature and extent of women's participation at all levels of agricultural production in Egypt. We hope that such an integrative database will serve as an important instrument in the long process of enhancing the status of our rural women.

More specifically, the main objectives of this essay are:

1. To highlight the position of Egyptian women in social, economic, and political structures of society in order to place a more focused concern about women's role in agricultural production and the position of rural women in society in a more general frame of reference.
2. To document the position of women in the agricultural sector in order to provide policymakers with a better understanding of existing gender gaps in this segment and to point to areas where policies and programs can benefit women and improve their lot.

Table 5.1 Demographic trends in Egypt

	1975	1997	2015
Total population (millions)	38.3	64.7	85.2
Annual population growth (%)		2.3	1.5
Urban population (% of total)	43.5	45.1	53.5
Dependency ratio (%)		70.1	47.3
Population 65 and above (% of total)		4.0	5.2
Fertility rate	5.3	3.4	
Contraceptive prevalence rate	1990–98: 55%		

Database and Gender Analysis

General Socio-Economic National Indicators

By the year 2015, it is projected that Egypt's population will exceed 85 million. Most of this growing population will cluster in urban areas and will tend to be older. Table 5.1 records several critical demographic trends in Egypt. The rapid growth in Egypt's population and its tendency to cluster in urban areas is accompanied by an alarming rate of human poverty (Table 5.2).

Table 5.2 Poverty indexes in Egypt

Human index (HPI) 1997	Rank: 57; Value: 33.0	
People not expected to survive	10.3% (1997)	
to age 40 (% of total population)		
Adult literacy rate (%)	47.3% (1997)	
Population without access to:	1990–1997	1981–1992
Safe water	13%	
Health services		1%
Sanitation	12%	
Underweight children less than	15%	
5 yrs. (%)		
Real GDP per capita (PPPS)		
Poorest (20%)	1990–1997:	1.653
Richest 20%	1980–1994:	7.809
Richest 20% to poorest 20%	1980–1994:	4.7
Population below income poverty line (%)		
$1/day (PPPS, 1985)	1989–1994:	7.6
National poverty line	1989–1994:	36.0

Table 5.3 documents the gaps between the rural and the urban populations in Egypt with regard to access to sanitation and the people's level of literacy. A closer examination of the data presented in Table 5.3 reveals, however, that the gaps between rural and urban areas change according to location.

Table 5.4 shows additional indexes for the gaps between the genders within the various regions in the country. Some of the conclusions from Table 5.4 are: (1) the life expectancy of women is higher than that of men; (2) in 1995, for example, and with some significant variation among the regions in the country, women entered the labor force at a much lower rate than men. The lowest rate of women's engagement in the labor force was recorded for the region of Alexandria (14.3% of the male rate) and the highest rate (57.1%) was recorded for the Sharkia region in Lower Egypt. On average, and across regions, women constituted about 30% of the male rate in the labor force in 1995.

Women are less literate than men and their enrollment in education decreases as the level of schooling increases. In 1996, the literacy rate of women who completed 10 years or more of school was about 66% of the male literacy rate. Female literacy is higher in urban areas across the country (77%) and lower in rural areas (54%). Yet these 1996 figures are higher than the rates recorded a decade earlier. In 1986, female literacy stood at 60% of the male literacy and the urban/rural rates were recorded at 74% and 44%, respectively. Internal variations among regions are exemplified by an interesting figure recorded in Table 5.4: while women constitute only 34% of the male literacy rate in rural areas in Upper Egypt, their literacy rate in Cairo reaches 80% of the male record. The table also documents the significant rise in primary school enrollment by females over the past four decades. In 1960 this was 63.2% of the male rate, by 1994/5 this rate grew to 81.7% of the male rate.

Table 5.3 Rural-urban gaps in Egypt

Rural population (as % of total)		Population with access to:								
		Piped water %		Sanitation %		Literacy (10+)		Rural-Urban disparity		
		Urban	Rural	Urban	Rural	Urban	Rural	Water	Sanitation	Literacy
	1960	1996	1995	1995	1995	1995	1996	1996	1195	1995	1996
Cairo	0.0	0.0	--	--	--	--	76.7	--	--	--	--
Alex.	0.0	0.0	--	--	--	--	75.5	--	--	--	--
Port Said	0.0	0.0	--	--	--	--	77.3	--	--	--	--
Suez	0.0	0.0	--	--	--	--	76.3	--	--	--	--
Urban Govs.	0.0	0.0	99.0	--	98.6	--	76.4	--	--	--	--
Domietta	75.1	72.5	96.7	94.9	97.3	94.6	73.2	65.2	98	97	89
Dakahlia	81.9	72.2	96.5	77.1	99.6	83.5	73.5	60.3	80	84	82
Sharkia	83.8	77.4	99.3	64.6	100.0	92.0	74.6	53.4	65	92	72
Kalyoubia	74.6	59.2	98.8	83.5	95.3	66.8	71.7	60.3	85	70	84
Kaft El-Sheikh	83.0	77.1	100.0	95.8	99.0	80.8	66.8	49.2	96	82	74
Gharbia	71.8	69.0	99.2	87.9	97.0	87.6	78.5	59.9	89	90	76
Menoufia	86.4	80.1	100.0	88.6	94.1	58.8	73.6	62.0	89	62	84
Behera	81.8	77.1	99.6	76.4	99.4	83.0	70.0	49.4	77	84	71
Ismailia	0.0	52.3	94.2	78.6	97.9	88.6	79.1	59.5	83	91	75
Lower Egypt:	78.3	72.5	98.2	79.8	97.7	81.1	73.4	56.6	81	85	77
Urban	--	--	--	--	--	--	--	--	--	--	--
Rural	--	--	--	--	--	--	--	--	--	--	--
Giza	67.6	45.8	89.1	65.6	99.5	80.6	75.6	54.3	74	81	72
Beni-Suef	78.6	76.5	88.9	45.1	87.8	48.4	65.1	40.8	51	55	63
Fayoum	80.7	77.5	92.7	80.8	88.3	45.5	62.3	37.5	87	52	60
Menia	82.8	80.6	94.5	39.0	91.1	45.8	68.9	38.6	41	50	56
Assyout	78.2	72.8	94.7	63.5	88.7	70.3	69.0	40.6	67	79	59
Suhag	81.9	78.1	89.8	57.6	84.5	62.7	65.3	42.3	64	74	65
Quena	86.3	68.7	89.9	47.2	79.1	43.1	63.7	44.7	53	54	70
Aswan	74.6	57.2	95.4	92.8	90.9	80.3	73.9	62.3	97	88	84
Upper Egypt:	79.4	68.3	90.7	55.8	93.1	57.1	70.2	43.7	62	61	62
Urban	--	--	--	--	--	--	--	--	--	--	--

Rural	--	--	--	--	--	--	--	--	--	--	--
Red Sea	0.0	11.0	--	--	--	--	81.3	54.7	--	--	67
New Valley	0.0	51.7	--	--	--	--	82.9	67.0	--	--	81
Matruh	0.0	46.9	--	--	--	--	65.8	40.7	--	--	62
North Sinai	0.0	41.0	--	--	--	--	77.4	43.6	--	--	56
South Sinai	0.0	46.2	---	--	--	---	88.1	50.3	--	--	57
Frontier Govs.	0.0	39.0	--	--	--	--	77.5	49.6	--	--	64
Urban	--	--	--	--	--	--	--	--	--	--	--
Rural	--	--	--	--	--	--	--	--	--	--	--
Egypt:	62.0	57.0	96.5	69.4	97.2	70.9	74.0	51.1	72	73	69
Urban	--	--	--	--	--	--	--	--	--	--	--
Rural	--	--	--	--	--	--	--	--	--	--	--

Table 5.4 Male-female gaps in Egypt by region (females as % of males)

	Life expectancy	Population	literacy rate 10+		Primary enrollment		Preparatory enrollment	Secondary enrollment	labor force (15–64)
	1993	1994	1986	1996	1960 *	1994/ 95	1994/95	1994/95	1995
Cairo	105.0	95.0	78	80	80.5	94.5	97.6	106.8	23.2
Alexandria	104.0	94.8	78	80	75.7	90.4	96.8	103.1	14.3
Port Said	103.0	93.8	80	83	83.7	94.8	97.6	104.1	51.1
Suez	103.0	92.2	72	76	69.1	92.4	98.5	108.9	38.1
Urban Govs.	104.0	94.8	78	80	78.7	93.1	97.4	105.8	22.5
Domietta	104.0	94.7	81	84	79.6	90.0	108.0	109.2	16.5
Dakahlia	104.0	95.5	61	68	65.8	91.0	95.8	101.0	32.1
Sharkia	104.0	94.4	54	62	55.9	85.3	84.3	85.4	57.1
Kalyoubia	103.0	93.0	58	64	59.8	88.5	88.8	93.4	28.9
Kaft El-Sheikh	106.0	99.0	50	60	56.9	84.8	84.4	83.4	25.9
Gharbia	105.0	97.5	57	64	61.7	91.1	90.5	91.8	46.3
Menoufia	103.0	94.3	55	62	54.4	86.8	84.8	88.4	62.5
Behera	105.0	97.0	49	58	52.8	76.0	76.3	73.1	15.6
Ismailia	103.0	95.3	65	70	60.5	88.6	91.4	94.1	26.3

Lower Egypt	104	95.6	57	64	59.7	86.3	87.4	89.4	26.5
Urban	--	--	72	76	--	--	--	--	45.4
Rural	--	--	49	58	--	--	--	--	33.0
Giza	102.0	93.9	64	69	58.1	83.0	81.2	85.4	17.7
Beni-Suef	105.0	96.5	41	50	69.4	60.5	56.2	57.2	48.6
Fayoum	104.0	92.5	46	56	74.2	62.0	57.4	54.0	20.7
Menia	102.0	95.8	42	52	54.2	59.2	54.0	49.9	38.6
Assyout	101.0	93.5	46	56	54.0	66.9	63.9	58.1	18.1
Suhag	101.0	96.2	42	54	35.8	67.1	61.0	52.1	22.3
Quena	102.0	97.8	41	54	53.1	77.2	67.2	49.1	36.5
Aswan	102.0	99.3	57	79	60.9	88.9	86.6	73.7	28.1
Upper Egypt	102.0	95.3	49	58	55.6	70.8	66.3	60.4	27.7
Urban	--	--	70	74	--	--	--	--	30.2
Rural	--	--	34	48	--	--	--	--	26.4
Red Sea	--	--	70	75	--	94.0	94.1	89.8	20.9
New Valley	--	--	67	72	--	89.4	88.7	83.3	44.5
Matruh	--	--	42	53	--	47.0	52.5	47.6	27.9
North Sinai	--	--	56	64	--	79.4	70.6	66.0	30.2
South Sinai	--	--	34	53	--	71.1	57.7	64.5	--
Frontier Govs.	102.0	90.4	57	64	--	79.7	74.0	71.3	31.2
Urban	--	--	67	72	--	--	--	--	32.5
Rural	--	--	40	52	--	--	--	--	29.1
Egypt	104.0	95.3	60	66	63.2	81.7	81.4	81.7	30.7
Urban	--	--	74	77	--	--	--	--	31.2
Rural	--	--	44	54	--	--	--	--	30.2

Various indicators of female educational status clearly reveal the vulnerability of women as a result of poor educational levels. Although the proportion of girls in primary education has increased over the past four decades, women's educational achievements fall short in comparison to those of men. Several programs have been launched over the last decades to deal with this situation. These include governmental and nongovernmental projects that targeted women and aimed at eradicating their illiteracy, for example, the creation of a single class school where all illiterate people, regardless of their age, can enter, programs such as 'Reading for Everybody', and the establishment of mobile libraries in a large number of villages. These recorded rates of the women's low level of educational achievements are only one indicator of the general situation of female poverty in Egypt. The cycle of poverty is illustrated in the following flowchart:

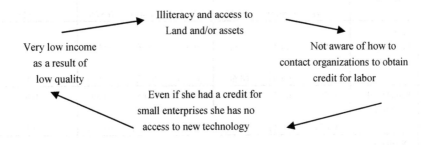

Table 5.5 **Employment and unemployment rates by gender and place of residence, 1997**

Employment Status	Urban		Rural		Total	
	Male	Female	Male	Female	Male	Female
Work for pay	66	73	51	24	58	44
Owner and manager	11	1	20	5	16	4
Work on his own and does not employ workers	13	2	12	12	12	8
Unpaid work with in the family	4	3	12	40	9	24
Unemployed previously employed	1	1	1	1	1	1
Newly unemployed	5	20	4	18	4	19
Total Ratio	100	100	100	100	100	100
Total Number	58,800	15,827	76,343	21,791	135,143	37,618

Source: Institute of National Planning, 1999

Table 5.6 Gender of head of household and level of income

Sex of Household head	The Poor			The Non-Poor			Whole Sample
	Urban Income (Exp.) L.E.	Rural Income (Exp.) L.E.	Total Income (Exp.) L.E.	Urban Income (Exp.) L.E.	Rural Income (Exp.) L.E.	Total Income (Exp.) L.E.	Annual Income (Annual Expenditure) L.E.
Male	4082 (3552)	3410 (3021)	3635 (3199)	11587 (8452)	7137 (4857)	9642 (6867)	7809 (5714)

Female	2761	2077	2241	10402	4715	8438	6186
	(2278)	(2046)	(2102)	(8041)	(3503)	(6474)	(4883)
All households	3945	3201	3440	11446	6936	9502	7632
	(3419)	(2868)	(3045)	(8403)	(4746)	(6826)	(5624)
Ratios							
Female/Male (2:1)	0.68	0.61	0.62	0.90	0.66	0.88	0.79
	(0.64)	(0.68)	(0.66)	(0.95)	(0.72)	(0.94)	(0.85)
Female/All (2:3)	0.70	0.65	0.65	0.91	0.68	0.89	0.81
	(0.67)	(0.71)	(0.69)	(0.96)	(0.74)	(0.95)	(0.87)
Distribution of Income							
~ >200 M	0.21	0.19	0.20				
F	(0.35)	(0.61)	(0.55)				
2000<4000 M	0.34	0.52	0.46				
F	(0.47)	(0.26)	(0.31)				
4000<6000 M	0.29	0.21	0.23				
F	(0.12)	(0.13)	(0.13)				
6000≤ ~ M	0.16	0.08	0.11				
F	(0.06)	(0.00)	(0.01)				

Source: Egypt Human Development Report, 1996

Poverty and Gender

Women are four to five times more prone to be unemployed in both urban and rural settings. In the rural areas, the rate of women's unpaid work carried out within family settings is almost four times that of male unpaid family labor. The situation in the urban areas is not as severe (see Table 5.5).

Although the majority of rural households in Egypt are headed by men (87.4%), the number of women-headed households (WHS) is increasing as a result of male migration and widowhood. The percentage of female-headed households has reached 12.6%, and is lower in rural and Upper Egypt. According to the Egyptian Human Development Report of 1995 (EHDR), the ratio of female-headed households is highest (16.1%) in urban Lower Egypt, followed by urban Upper Egypt (13.4%) and the urban governorates (13.0%). Rural Upper Egypt and rural Lower Egypt have the lowest rate-12.9% and 11.6%, respectively. The same study notes that in most households, men have almost exclusive authority to make decisions in matters related to the use of seeds, source of seeds, buying and selling of livestock and land, use of herbicides, use of agricultural machinery, what to grow, and where to sell produce. The wife makes minor decisions in buying and selling poultry and poultry vaccination. When the head of the household is female, most decisions, agricultural and nonagricultural, are made by the women. Yet these female-headed households tend to be the poorest. Table 5.6 shows that the total expenditure of female-headed households is lower than that of male-headed households, across all economic strata. Female-headed household expenditure amounted, on the average, to about 85% of the expenditure of male-headed households, and 87% of the overall average of the whole sample. The average annual income of female-headed households was 79% of the corresponding average for male-headed households and 81% of the overall average for all households.

In conclusion, three critical observations can be made in describing women's labor status in Egypt.

- A significant proportion of female work is unpaid and is not taken into consideration in the national income accounts.
- Work, especially for poor women, is not regarded as a source of empowerment, but rather as a source of income for their families.
- Women are paid two-thirds of men's wages for the same type of work.

The Status of Women's Health

Indicators of women health conditions illustrate one of the most important aspects of their vulnerability. During the past six years, public expenditure on health has increased (from 1% of the GDP to 1.5%). However, this increase has been only a small step in the right direction. The health needs of women, and especially rural women, are dramatic. For example, maternal mortality is 174 per 100,000 live births. In a recent field study (EHDR, 1996) the recorded percentage of anemia cases among women in Egypt reached 22.1% for pregnant women; 25.3% in breast-feeding women; and 22.4% for the total sample. Anemia is a result of malnutrition, prevalent among women in low-income households and particularly characteristic of pregnant and lactating women. The same publication indicates that women in these lower socio-economic levels (not working for cash, no education) are also under a greater risk because they tend to deliver at home. Table 5.7 records changes in the rates of life expectancy at birth since the 1980s.

Planners must realize that good health and proper education of rural women contribute to the goal of national food security by allowing women to be more productive. The specific health and educational needs of women must be identified and become the focus for policies, programs and projects.

Table 5.7 Life expectancy at birth, by gender and year

Age	1980		1991		1996	
	Male	Female	Male	Female	Male	Female
Less than a year	61	64	63	66	65	69
1–4	61	65	63	66	64	68
15	52	55	53	57	55	59
25	43	46	44	48	45	49
50	21	23	22	24	23	26
60	14	16	15	17	16	17

Source: CAMPAS, 1997

Table 5.8 Female members in the local public councils (all governorates)

Public Local Councils	Female %
Governorates	3.22 %
Districts	1.02 %
Cities	1.70 %
Suburb	4.47 %
Village	0.74 %

Gender in the Political Arena

Egyptian women have full political rights-they can vote and hold political positions. Yet despite the established constitutional rights, it is a well-documented fact that women's impact on political issues in the country is very limited. In 1996, women members of parliament constituted 2.2% of parliament. The numbers of women elected to local, district, and governorate levels are not much higher than their rate in the national parliament. Table 5.8 records the percentages of female representatives elected to these local bodies. On the average, women, constitute less than 2% of the respective total membership of these elected bodies. However, Egyptian women are entering the political arena in growing numbers. Table 5.9 records the increasing percentages of women registered for election between 1985 and 1995. The rate increased from 26.5% in 1985 to 33.16% in 1995.

Having reviewed the general status of women in the educational, health, and political arena, and the labor market systems in Egyptian society, we are now in the position to turn to a closer look at the place of women in the Egyptian agricultural sector.

Table 5.9 Political participation of the Egyptian women (1985-1995)

Year	Percentage of Females to Total Registered
1985	27.51
1986	27.59
1987	28.53
1988	28.44
1989	28.09
1990	30.23
1991	31.04
1992	31.71
1993	33.26
1994	33.16
1995	33.73

Table 5.10   Legal instruments available to women for obtaining land, livestock, credit, employment, and social insurance

Legislation	Year Enacted	Specific provisions to eliminate discrimination against women or enhance their status
Social Insurance Laws 1. No. 79	1975	* Covers all working groups (men and women) in the Government and Public and private sectors.
2. No. 108	1976	* Covers private business-men (commerce, industry, craft-men workers in free jobs; land owners and land holders by rent or crop-sharing (10 feddans and more).
3. No. 50	1978	* Covers all persons working outside Egypt (men and women).
4. No. 112	1980	* A comprehensive social insurance covers anyone 65 years old and over; disable persons; or any person who died before the enforcement of this law and didn't benefit from any other retirement laws and in particular the following groups: A. Temporary agricultural worker who work less than months/year. B. Land holders of less than 10 feddans including owners or tenants (cash or sharing). C. Land owners but not holders of less than 10 feddans. (Article No. 5).
Income Tax. Law No. 157	1981	Cancelled war tax for land holders of 3 feddans or less (Article No. 3).
Law No. 96 (Concern some adjustments of the Agrarian Reform law no. 178, 1952	1992	Article No. 33 (z) stated: the land contract during the enforcement of this law (in cash or share) will discontinue by the end of Agricultural year 96/1997 unless the two parties agree otherwise. - In case the owner or the tenant dies the contract continues valid for the stated period. - In case the tenant dies the rights of contract go to his family for the remaining period.

Source: Mansour, 1994

Gender and Agricultural Production

Women's Legal Rights

The Egyptian constitution gives women equal access to education, employment and work opportunities, equal work, and social security. Egyptian civil law, in accordance with Islamic law, gives women the right to possess and control property and to inherit, although women receive only half as much as men. While no laws restrict women's ownership of land and livestock or access to credit, discrimination may exist due to custom and tradition, women's lack of awareness of their rights, or lack of strict implementation of the laws.

Most of the Egyptian women who inherit land do not have it registered in their names. These women are unaware of their land rights and the importance of having property registered to them. As a result, they give away their rights and do not understand that this will limit their opportunities to access credit for micro enterprises. Egyptian women also have a legal right to possess and control livestock. The most common livestock owned by women are buffaloes, cows, and sheep; men own donkeys, camels, cows, and buffaloes. Table 5.10 provides an overall view of the various legal statements relevant for women's right and the year of their introduction.

The Role of Women in Agricultural Production

The majority of rural women participate in agriculturally-productive activities, particularly in work related to food security and animal husbandry. More than half of the rural women are actively involved in agricultural tasks, such as weeding, harvesting, sacking, marketing, and storage. About 70% of their working time in agriculture is devoted to animal husbandry. Women are involved in almost all aspects of crop production, with the exception of land preparation and mechanized activities. Women sow seeds and spread fertilizers; they do most of the hand weeding, harvesting, and the work necessary to store cereals. Women spend many hours in post-harvest activities, such as threshing, cleaning, sorting, grading, and packing. There is a clear division of labor between men and women in agricultural production, and it varies by crop. Overall, men carry out most of the land preparatory tasks-planting, weeding, irrigation, and pest control. Women participate in seed preparation, fertilization, harvesting, post-harvest processes, and marketing. In recent years, as crops for export increase (e.g., citrus fruit, grapes, strawberries, peanuts, potatoes, and snap beans), there are more girls and young women laborers working in production, a process often known as 'feminization of employment' in agriculture.

The active role women take in livestock production has been extensively documented. They feed and care for small ruminants, rabbits, and chicken; clean stables; collect dung for fertilizer; make dung cake for fuel; care for sick animals; and milk the animals and process milk products. Yet, because most of the work they perform is unpaid, their labor is often not recorded in official statistics. If they do get paid, their wages constitute only half or two-thirds of the wages earned by men for the same task (Mansour, 1994). In the fisheries, fishing, feeding, and marketing are primarily men's tasks, while women contribute about 52% of the labor in fish processing and net making, and carry out 42% of maintenance and repair of the nets. There are significant disparities in the access to agricultural resources and services between men and women. These gender-based disparities in access can be discussed under four sub-headings: disparity in access to land, to credit, to technology, and to extension services.

Access to Land

The distribution of agricultural land is one of the most important determinants of household living standards and income generation and distribution in rural Egypt. Inequality is a major characteristic of the agricultural land distribution, hence of income, in the rural areas. A human development report published in 1996 records that almost 70% of landowners own less than one feddan; 93% of landowners own between 1-4 feddans each; and 15% of the total cultivated land in Egypt is owned by 0.3% of the landlords.

This general uneven distribution of land is one of the major factors in explaining the extent of poverty in rural Egypt. Although, as we noted above, Egyptian women have the legal right to inherit and purchase land under the Inheritance Law based on Islamic Sharia, the fact is that for a range of reasons, most Egyptian women who inherit land do not have it registered in their names. Such women are unaware of their land rights and the importance of registering such property in their own names. As a result, they have limited access to credit, which is given only to registered land owners. In 1989, 76% of the registered land owners were male, while only 24% were female. Moreover, records show that the area of the land held is larger for men than for women.

This gender discrepancy has not been corrected in the recent national project of newly-reclaimed lands. Data shows that the number of females who apply for obtaining land under this new scheme is much smaller than that of males (FAO, 1996; CSPP, 1997). In the Mubarak Project, designed for the resettlement of graduates (started in 1989), only about 8% of land recipients are women (see USAID report No. 50, and unpublished field records based on visits to Adam village). Indeed, direct access to financial resources is dependent on registering land ownership. Most women in Egypt do not own any land, and those who rightly inherited land tend not to register it, and thus curtail their access to other resources, such as credit and agricultural extension services.

Access to Credit

Women's access to credit is limited mainly because many do not own land or other property that could be used as collateral, as required by most formal lending

128   *Women in Agriculture in the Middle East*

agencies. Until recently, loan criteria were heavily biased toward male-headed households. The most common loans to those who can provide collateral are input loans to finance crop production. In 1993, men received 88% of the short-term production loans and 84% of the investment loans from Principal Bank for Development and Agricultural Credit (PBDAC), while women received 12% and 16%, respectively (FAO, 1996). Women have greater access to credit through agricultural credit societies than through PBDAC (FAO, 1996).

Data collected by the USAID and the Ministry of Agriculture and Land Reclamation (MOALR) demonstrate that women receive fewer loans than men. Although data are not available on the loan amounts, we know that the few women who did secure agricultural loans supported very small enterprises with their loans (USAID Report No. 1 and an unpublished report by El-Sanabary, Nagat et al., MOALR, the Agricultural Policy Reform Project).

Access to Extension Services and Agricultural Training

A recent FAO survey records that female farmers receive only 5% of all agricultural extension services worldwide, and that only 15% of the world's extension agents are women. In Egypt, while 53% of agricultural labor is carried out by women, only 1.9% of Egyptian extension agents are women. Data produced by the MOALR shows that between 1987 and 1993, only four women were contacted by the Ministry's extension staff, as compared to 7,367 men. Another set of data produced by the Statistical Department of the MOALR in 1994 notes that in a sample of 50 families, 47 husbands were contacted, as compared to only three wives. In meetings and contacts regarding issues of crop production, the extension staff met with 156 men; there were only three meetings with women.

Agricultural extension services are mainly provided by the MOALR, through the Central Agency for Agricultural Extension. The majority of extension workers are male (95%). Male extension agents largely work with male farmers. Most extension services directed to women are restricted to subjects such as home economics and related subjects. The women extension agents specialize in home economics instruction and do not devote time and expertise to communicating new technical knowledge that might alter the way women carry out their diverse agricultural tasks.

Access to New Knowledge and Technology

Women in Egypt perform their agricultural tasks with little or no access to labor-saving equipment (e.g., tools, threshers, harvesters, cream-milk separator churn) or technology (e.g., improved seed, fertilizers etc.). Women's access to technology is limited (see Table 5.11), since rural women lack cash to purchase necessary tools. Their awareness and interest in such knowledge and technology is low due to lack of contact with extension service workers.

This lack of access to technology preserves traditional patterns of gender based division of labor. It encourages men to have control over mechanized land preparation, sowing, fertilizing, and pesticide application, leaving women the more intensive and time-consuming non-mechanized tasks, such as sowing, hand weeding, harvesting, and picking fruits and vegetables. There have been multiple attempts to address the issue of the limited attention paid to women's agricultural work. Several institutional bodies and short- and longer-term projects were established. A brief review of these efforts to promote the advancement of women is given. I will first trace the national institutional machinery and then the agricultural rural organizations.

Table 5.11 Use of labor-saving technology for carrying out agricultural and household chores

Rural Technology Use	Total			Male			Female		
	1980	1985	1993	1980	1985	1993	1980	1985	1993
Improved animal traction	100	110	120	100	115	130	100	105	110
Electricity or other energy producing devices	100	108	113	100	106	110	100	110	116
Irrigation tools	100	110	129	100	115	150	100	105	108
Improved post-harvest threshing devices	100	113	125	100	120	140	10	106	110
Piped water	100	118	160	100	116	160	100	120	160
Improved stoves	100	115	135	100	100	100	10	130	170
Improved food processing devices	100	115	135	100	105	110	100	125	160
Improved food storage devices	100	120	143	100	110	126	100	130	160
Cold storage devices	100	125	150	100	130	160	100	120	140
Improved transport	100	115	155	100	120	180	100	110	130
Other	100	1360	170	100	140	200	100	120	140

Source: Unpublished data provided by Dr. Ragab A. Rassoul, 1994

National Machinery

Six bodies are included in this category:

1. The Department of Women's Affairs in the Ministry of Social Affairs, created in 1977, is the technical secretariat for the National Commission for Women. Revitalized in 1993, the commission is comprised of four committees: information, legislation, economy, political life, and decision-making. It executes projects recommended by the Commission, and in 1994, it handled 13 donor-sponsored development projects in literacy, income generation, family planning, and health.
2. The Egyptian Central Agency for Public Mobilization and statistics (CAPMAS) established a Women In Development Unit (WID) in 1987. The unit consults the national database for women regarding all aspects of life-social, economic, health, environmental, educational, and agricultural-in its effort to help policymakers formulate gender-sensitive projects and plans.
3. The Policy and Coordination Unit for Women in Agriculture (PCUWA) was established in the MOALR in 1992. It aims to increase women's access to agricultural services and resources, improve their socio-economic status, and increase agricultural productivity and production. It works with the various departments and institutes of the Ministry to integrate issues of concern to women into the mainstream of the MOALR's programs and policies. Funding is still required to fully operationalize the Unit.
4. The Ministry of Social Affairs is designated as the official body responsible for the coordination of a range of Non-Governmental Organizations (NGOs) working in the field of women and development.
5. The Social Fund for Development (SFD) established the Gender and Development Unit in 1996. The goal of this unit within the SFD is to mainstream gender issues in SFDs overall activities by adopting approaches such as greater engagement of women in all Social Fund Programs, and by developing special women's enterprise development programs. About 1,500 women have received loans from the SFD, thus constituting a significant ratio of 26% of the total number of loans provided by the Fund. The average loan amount is Egyptian Pounds (L.E.) 18,000.
6. A Gender Planning and Policies Unit within the National Planning Institute was also recently established. It is intended to bring the gender question to the attention of national planners.

Agricultural Rural Organizations

Agricultural rural organizations include: local cooperatives agricultural societies, cooperatives at district levels (often focused on the concerns of particular crop growers, e.g., potatoes growers, cotton growers), and local women's groups. The local, village-level agricultural societies are multi-purpose. They offer agricultural and social services, as well as small loans to their members. In 1995, the Arab Organization for Agricultural Development reported that between 1987 to 1991, there were 527 such local cooperatives in Egypt-with an exclusively all-male membership of 453,622. By 1994, the number of these agricultural societies grew to 5,193, with more than three million members. These local societies work under the supervision of the General Authority for Agrarian Reform in the Ministry of Agriculture and Land Reclamation.

In addition to these rural agricultural organizations, which tend to be all male, recent organizations are trying to direct their activities to promote rural women's concerns. Since 1990, these organizations have worked for women's illiteracy eradication projects and have provided home economics classes designed for rural women's development. Table 5.12 records the participation of women in several governorates in Egypt in these home economics activities.

Assessing the Impact of Agricultural Policy Reforms on Women

In closing, we would like to present a comprehensive review of the various policies and reforms enacted in Egypt since 1980. The table composed by Nagat El Sanabary (1999) records the dates on which these policies were issued and implemented, the stated purpose of the policy, its target population and, most critically for our concerns here, the constraints placed on women who might wish to be part of the proposed policy or action Table 5.13. A close reading of El-Sanabary's table will show that since the 1980s (and probably earlier), specific needs of women were overlooked or simply unattended to. Women's access to resources offered by the proposed projects and resources has been systematically ignored.

Table 5.12 Rural women's participation in home economics activities run by agricultural cooperatives in the governorates (1995-1996)

Governorates	No. of Districts	No. of Cooperatives	No. of Training rounds	No. of Trained women
El-Behera	1	2	3	100
El-Dakahlia	3	7	7	122
El-Sharkia	1	2	25	496
El-Ismailia	4	6	6	159
El-Sues	1	1	3	45
El-Fayoum	4	4	18	230
Total	14	22	62	1152

Source: MOALR, 1998

Table 5.13 Agricultural policy reforms and their potential impact, 1980 to present

Policy/Action	Purpose	Target Population	Constraints on Women
Land • Improve tenancy law (Issued 1992, implemented, 1997)	Raise land rent crop sharing value; stimulate investment in land; promote cultivation of high value crops; foster a free market for land transactions	Landlords and tenants	Female tenants lack information and negotiation skills; women are unaware of their legal land rights and lack the skills to manage their land
• Adopt land reclamation (1980)	Expand agricultural land areas; increase agricultural products; substitute for government jobs; settle new communities beyond the Nile valley	Private-sector landlords; new graduate; farmers	Inadequate infrastructure and support services; restricted eligibility for unmarried women; inadequate extension farm services for women
Credit and Finance • Shift from credit based on collateral to credit based on need. (1987) • Restructure financial institutions. such as PBDAC and its regional banks (1987)	Convert to a market-driven economy; compete for customers in free markets; improve terms of trade for agriculture and private-sector agricultural investments	All investors in the agricultural sector	Collateral still required for some loans; lack of information; few female credit officers; lack of knowledge about viable micro-enterprises.
• Improve import and export regulations. (1984-1986)	Impose restrictions on imports; liberalize exports	Agricultural input/output traders	Government's low prices for exports are not competitive Decreased crop prices; increased agricultural input prices, especially for small farmers
Cropping Farming • Reform the structure of seed production and marketing (1987)	Promote greater involvement of the private sector; improve the market environment	Agricultural researchers; investors in the agriculture sector	Women may be unable to function in a competitive environment because of a lack of

			cropping-pattern knowledge and extension information
• Remove procurement quotas for all crops except sugar cane (1787-1994) • Eliminate subsidies on all inputs (1787-1994) • Eliminate cropping-area restrictions (1787-1994)	Allow greater choice for farmers; increase productivity and incomes; reduce the burden on the government of controls; release government subsidies for other productive areas	Agricultural producers and traders; input suppliers	Yields may stagnate because of high production costs; small farmers, especially women, cannot afford higher prices on inputs. Uncontrolled cropping diversity (small farms); declines in cotton cropping area.
• Strengthen food security through subsidies for essential food, such as bread and oil (1980)	Ensure a minimum level of food supply	Poor classes (urban/rural)	Subsidies are not well targeted
Water Resource Policies • Improve irrigation-water cost recovery/sharing (1995)	Foster more efficient water usage	Farmers/water users	*Decreases the number of cultivated areas that require heavy water usage*
• Improve the irrigation system. (1994)	Foster more efficient water usage	Farmers/water users	*Fosters cost-effective water usage*
• Create water user associations. (1994) • Reuse drainage (1994)	Foster more efficient water usage	Farmers/water users	*Ensures water supply to end users; ensures principal users are represented in the decision-making process*
Agribusiness • Support food processing/fiber manufacturing and biotechnology; increase the role of the private sector in agribusiness (1980)	Enhance business; reduce food gaps; increase exports	Poor classes (urban/rural); farmers, growers, traders	Increase farm income; stabilizes the economy and promotes economic growth; creates loose alleviated land
Technology Transfer • Use modern technology in farming; expand the use of food technology (ongoing)	Increase the number of products and	Farmers, growers, exporters; extension agents	Women have limited access to new technology;

	improve product quality; increase marketing, exports, and farm income		majority of extension workers are male; women lack information to increase farm output and lack marketing skills
Market and Trade • Promote exports (ongoing)	Promote economic growth through exports		Women are engaged mainly in limited vending activities and lack relevant information and marketing skills
Associations (ongoing)	Promote sector participation through associations; encourage formation of rural associations		Women's access to associations in general is limited.

Source: El-Sanbary *et al.*, 1999

Case Studies: *The stories of individual women and their daily life experiences in rural, agricultural settings in Egypt.*

Case 1: Fatma, The Married Farm Manager: A Married Woman Managing Her Husband's Land

Abd El-Naby, Azza Mohamed *et al.*, 1998. "Gender Analysis of Irrigation Activities and Water Resource Management: The Case of Several Villages in Minoufeya Governorate."

   Fatma is 39-years old and lives together with her three young children in the village of Zueir, located on the right-hand bank of the El Atf Canal. Fatma did not have the chance to go to school during her youth, and thus she is struggling very hard so that her children will attain an education. Ever since she married, her husband worked as a clerk in one of the schools in the city of Shebin El Kom. The family derives its means of living not just from the husband's salary; they also have 20 kirat of reclaimed land, in addition to engaging in animal husbandry.

   Fatma's husband comes home every three days, and thus she is the one primarily responsible for farming the land. She is the one who is responsible for watering her field. When her husband comes home, they both operate the *saqia* (the irrigation); she drives while he irrigates the land. Fatma is the one who keeps an eye on the water flow. She sometimes depends on her in-laws, who help her clean the irrigation ditch. The canals in her surroundings are cleaned by the Land Reclamation Cooperative by tractor, and the fee for this service is then subtracted from the monies they receive after bringing their cotton to the cooperative. When they hire any laborer, her brother-in-law pays the fees, and she is the one who settles the accounts with him later on. Fatma is also the only one responsible for the management of the water supply for her household. She gets the water from the family's pump. The used water is discarded into the pit latrines.

Fatma's network is quite widespread. She collaborates with her in-laws and with many of her neighbors. They support her in her agricultural tasks, and she, in turn, helps them in their fields. Her network extends beyond local people and institutions. For example, she knows the village head and refers to him in times of trouble. She also meets the agricultural extension staff of the cooperative when they go to the fields to teach farmers how to combat the cotton worm. Whenever the water pumping machine in the station fails, she does not hesitate to complain to the irrigation engineer so that he will fix it. Fatma knows that the water station was installed 12 years ago, and is well aware that the machine broke twice during last year.

Fatma primarily deals with two problems related to irrigation. During the season, due to a fall in water pressure during the day, there is a need to irrigate fields in the evening. Fatma reports that in several instances she had gone out with a friend to irrigate the field during the night. Fatma also faces problems caused by the need to collaborate with other farmers in the station. She notes that these problems are better handled when the other farmers are also women, like herself. Fatma says, 'We women are much more tolerant towards each other. We bear each other much better'.

Fatma needs to get her husband's approval for all the decisions she wants to make regarding the managing of her farm. She convinced her husband to join a rotating savings scheme, and despite his initial objection, they joined a group of 22 people. Fatma is proud of her decision. The total amount she received from the savings scheme the first time was L.E. 1,100, which she used to install wooden windows and build a ceiling for their home. Fatma claims that although she knows that her husband will object to every new decision, she trusts her ability to persuade him to change his mind.

Case 2: Om Mukhtar: The Married Woman Managing Her Own Land

Om Mukhtar is a 39-year old woman who lives in the village of Zueir, located on the right-hand side of the El Atf canal. Her household comprises five members: herself, her husband, and three children. She never attended school. The family has three sources of income: agricultural land, animal husbandry (in partnership), and her husband's salary. Her husband is employed as a tractor driver. From her family she inherited a piece of land of 11 kirat in her name; her husband rents an additional 6 kirat in his name.

Om Mukhtar is heavily involved in the farming of their lands. With some help from her son and her brother-in-law, she is often the one to open the water flow to their fields, and even goes out to irrigate her land during the night when her turn comes. Om Mukhtar mounts the irrigation pump on her own and then sits and waits for any man (even her young son) to pass by so she can ask him to operate the machine. She does not dare to do it by herself, because the handle is quite heavy and she is afraid she will be injured. However, she is the one to stop the machine when the land has been watered sufficiently. It usually takes about three hours to oversee the watering of her field. Sometimes her husband supervises the water in one field, and she supervises her own field. However, most often she performs that task for both fields. Both her husband and herself clean the ditch, but due to her husband's absence because of paid employment, she does most of the ditch cleaning, which takes over an hour.

If laborers are needed, she or her husband will hire them and pay their wages. Om Mukhtar and her husband have a water pump at home for household consumption. Om Mukhtar is responsible for disposing the used water. All the agricultural tasks are carried out in tandem by both women and men in the family, including the labor contributed by both her in-laws.

Even though Om Mukhtar is the main decision maker with regard to the daily performance of agricultural activities necessary for their household, her contacts with the outer world are limited and are often confined to other members within the agricultural cooperative and the village head. Because she is a member of their local agricultural cooperative, Om Mukhtar often turns for advice to other members of the agricultural cooperative. In case of trouble, she might address the village head. If a matter is urgent and her husband is away, Om Mukhtar does not wait for her husband's approval. The agricultural extension staff are also helpful when she calls on them.

Om Mukhtar is acquainted with the neighboring farmers and had decided to join them in their rotating savings scheme even prior to getting her husband's consent. She makes her own decisions about the way to use the money she receives from the scheme-most often it is spent to cover her children's expenses.

Om Mukhtar listed the following irrigation problems as central: (1) Low water pressure in the canal; (2) Station pipelines situated higher than the canal; (3) The opening valve of her neighbor blocks the path of water flow to her field; (4) Her own water valve is broken and due to the problems mentioned above, she had to stop using the station. Om Mukhtar wishes that the station would organize a system of rotation for irrigation, for example, by assigning two days of irrigation to each circle of fields.

Case 3: Khadra: A Married Woman Managing Her Husband's Land

El-Din, Soreiya Salah *et al.*, 1998. "Gender Analysis for Irrigation Activities and Water Resource Management: The Case of Several Villages in the Minia Governorate."

Khadra is a 33-year old, illiterate woman who lives in the village of Tahnasha, located on the canal of Beni Obeid. Khadra is the de facto female head of her household because her husband has been working in Saudi Arabia for more than 20 years and returns only for brief holidays. They have four children, and she is entirely responsible for their upbringing. The family's income is derived from agriculture and her husband's salary. The land title is in her Husband's name, and the size of the land is one feddan and one kirat. They had been renting out the land, but two years ago due to the enforcement of the new tenancy law, they took back their land, and her husband announced that she was the official agent for the land. Their piece of land lies in the advanced irrigation scheme zone, but there is still no collective irrigation pump. Khadra has planted fenugreek, cotton, wheat, and beans *(foul)* all by herself. Farming the land provides her with great joy, especially when she harvests all by herself. Khadra is very familiar with the amount of irrigation required by each type of cultivation and is responsible for all farming activities. She is the one who opens the water valve, hires an irrigation pump, cleans the ditch, hires a male laborer to dig a small ditch close to her field, supervises the water in the field, and also pays the laborer's wages.

Even though Khadra manages her field and is the sole decision maker within her household (due to her husband's long absence), her external contacts with the institutions or local people that deal with water management is very limited. She is acquainted only with the agricultural cooperative from which she gets seeds and insecticides, and knows only the head of the cooperative (who has helped her to register their land), the village head (who supported her by signing for the transfer of the land), and the major of the police in the area, to whom she complained about the 'Bahar' (river) and the previous tenants. Khadra does not know about any water group in her area. When the name of the group head was mentioned, she said that she knew him personally, but did not know what he did. She probably would be able to take the initiative to start a group and encourage its members to buy their own shared irrigation pump, because she suffers often from the lack of irrigation machines. Rather than irrigating the feddan for L.E. 7.50, based on the usage of a communally owned pump, she pays L.E. 20 for 1 feddan for use of a machine which is not always available when she needs it. She had been irrigating at night. However, due to safety considerations in Upper Egypt, the security police forbade this practice. Khadra has installed a hand pump for drinking purposes close to her field for common usage and wishes that the members in the water group would soon purchase a water pump together.

Case 4: Hanem: The Female Head Managing Her Own Land

Hanem is an illiterate, 53-year old woman who was abandoned by her husband. She heads a household of six children and lives in the area of 'El Deir Attia, 'Tehnasha', located on the canal of Beni Obeid. Hanem rents a piece of land of 1.25 feddan from the Waqf Ministry. To obtain drinking water, she depends on a common hand pump located in the street. Hanem manages the farm work all by herself. During peak seasons, she may hire a male worker to plough the ditch or does the work herself with the help of her children (both sons and daughters).

Her contacts with different institutions related to irrigation are quite limited. She turns to the agricultural cooperative in order to receive seeds; to the local council, when she needs help to process her papers; and to the agricultural department, where she pays rent for the land. She knows several of the officials with whom she needs to work with: the head of the water group, the head of the cooperative, the village head, and the local police officer. Hanem heard about the head of the water group only after he had been selected. In her water group, there are more women farmers than men. The average size of the land tenures of those farmers is ca. 16 kirat. The turns for irrigation, she says, are usually done by mutual consent of the farmers. Hanem mentioned that there is often mutual exchange of labor among female farmers in her village. She also is very much engaged in that exchange.

Acknowledgments

I would like to thank Dr. Kamla Mansour, Dr. Effat Abdel Hamed, and Mrs. Hala Yousri for their help in preparing the report on which this chapter is based.

References

Annual Book of Statistics, Egypt, "Central Agency for Public Mobilization and Statistics (CAPMAS)," 1997: 428.

Egyptian Ministry of Agriculture and Land Reclamation, "Human Resources in the Agricultural Sector," Agriculture Research Center: Center of Information and Documentation, 1996: 303.

El-Messiri, S., "Baseline Gender Study for Grapes." Agricultural Technology Utilization & Technology Transfer Project (ATUT), Ronco Publication, USAID Project No. 263–0240, 1997.

------- "Feminization of Strawberry Production." Agricultural Technology Utilization and Transfer Project, Ronco, USAID Project No. 263–0240, 1999.

El-Sanabary, N. *et al.*, "The Impact of Liberalization and Privatization on Women in Agriculture in Egypt: Agricultural Policy Reform Project." Ministry of Agriculture and Land Reclamation, 1999: 64.

Food and Agriculture Organization (FAO), "Rural Women and Food Security: Current Situation and Perspectives." 00100, Rome, Italy, 1996: 137.

Faris, A. *et al.*, *Egyptian Women in Agricultural Development.* London: Boulder, 1994: 153.

Fong, S.M. and Bhushan, A., "Toolkit on Gender in Agriculture," in *Toolkit on Gender in Agriculture*, Series No. 1, Washington, DC: The World Bank, 1996: 92.

Institute of National Planning (INP) and ESCWA, "Women and Men in Egypt: Statistical Portrait," 1999: 98.

------- "Nast City Cairo, Egypt, Egyptian Human Development Report (EHDR)," 1996: 103.

Mansour, K., "Egyptian Women in Agriculture." Cairo, Egypt: Ministry of Agriculture and Land Reclamation. (Unpublished report), 1994.

------- "Strategy 2017." Ministry of Agriculture and Land Reclamation. Policy and Coordination Unit for Women in Agriculture, 1998.

------- Cotton Sector Promotion Program (CSPP), 1997.

Chapter 6

An Annotated Bibliography on Women and Development in Egypt

Zeinab El-Tobshy

Abaza, Mona. 1987. "Feminist Debates and 'Traditional Feminism' of the Fellaha in Rural Egypt." Bielefeld, Germany: University of Bielefeld, Sociology of Development Research Centre. Mimeo, 26 pp.
Abaza concentrates on three areas: the transformation of social relations, patterns of sexual division of labor, and cultural representation of sex roles in a small village. The study was carried out in a small village in the region of Mansoura, governorate of Dakhahlia. It attempts to describe women's strengths by depicting their daily activities in a rural setting. This strength is imbedded in peasant culture which, historically, has always been threatened by the state, as well as by recent open-door policies of 'modernization'. Migration to the oil-producing countries, proliferation of the informal sector, monetization of social relations, acquisition of better education and jobs in state administration, and the frequenting of mosques and thus access to formal channels of religion are all new opportunities offered to males, leaving women in the shadows and often undermining their former base of power.

Abaza, Mona. 1987. "The Changing Image of Women in Rural Egypt." *Cairo Papers in Social Science,* 10:1–119, Monograph 3.
This study investigated the changing lives of rural Egyptian women in light of the increasing migration of males to the oil-producing countries. Working within the dependency paradigm, it related changes in gender relations to economic and social processes unfolding in the national and global arenas.

Abd El-Kader, Mohamed A. 1997. "Determinants of Rural Women's Participation in Community Activities." *Minofia Journal of Agricultural Research.*
This study examined the relationships between specific characteristics of rural women (their age, level of formal education, family size) and their tendency to take part in economic, social, and political activities in their communities. Data were collected through personal interviewing and questionnaires from a sample of 100 women from the villages of Al-Helbawy and Al-Nashw in Kafr El-

Dawar, Behera. The findings revealed that, on the whole, there was no direct correlation among age, educational level, and family size with the rate of participation in economic, social, and political activities. However, age was a factor when political participation was examined.

Abd El-Kader, Mohamed A. 1997. "Social Status of Rural Women in Village Community: A Study of Some Villages in Kafr Al Dawar, Behera." *Minofia Journal of Agricultural Research.*
The study aimed to assess the social status of rural women in village communities. A personal interview questionnaire was used to collect data from 100 rural male farmers in the villages of Kom Al-Berka and Al-Baslakon, Kafr Al-Dawar country, Behera. The findings revealed that there is no correlation between the age and education of the men interviewed and their views about the "right place" for rural women in the process of local development. Regardless of their age and level of education, rural men expressed conservative "traditionalist" views that had a dramatic impact on the low social status of rural women in their village community.

Abd Ellatief, Sawsan O. 1993. "A Study of the Role of Small Industries in Women's Development: Between Theory and Practice." Symposium on the Role of Productive Enterprises in Women's Development, Ministry of Social Affairs, in cooperation with UNICEF.
The study aimed to identify obstacles that might inhibit women's participation in, and benefit derived from, projects designed for small industries. The author listed the following obstacles: (1) Small industries often fail to succeed due to the unstable business environment they must operate in; (2) the underdeveloped socio-economic structure of Egyptian villages, with particular regard to certain negative beliefs, values, and patterns of behavior; (3) Insufficient market research; (4) Lack of training in the technologies of small industries; (5) Shortage of credit necessary for on-going operations, replacement of equipment and for expansion; (6) Lack of predetermined or prearranged marketing channels; (7) Inefficient monitoring and evaluation.

The author recommends establishing a local agency responsible for developing small industries; state intervention that will support small industries through proper financial planning and legal protection; and direct attention to the development of women through such projects.

Abo Taleb, Mha S. 1991. "The Impact of Family Income and Food Management Upon Food Consumption Patterns and Nutritional Status of Some Rural, Urban, and Bedouin Families in Alexandria and Matrooh Governorate." Ph.D. Thesis, College of Agriculture, University of Alexandria.
The study attempted to identify the extent of female labor participation in agricultural production in populations of diverse socio-economic background.

The study compared results of a sample of 300 families: 100 urbanites from Haiy-Shark Alexandris, 100 from Abis-Extension, Alexandria, and 100 Bedouin families from the Hammam area, Matrooh. Analysis of the data revealed that in all three areas, women carried out the majority of the labor in processing of grain. Women were also engaged in dairy product processing and vegetable and fruit cultivation and processing. While the urban families in the sample spent over 63% of their income on food, the rural households spent 68% and Bedouin families spent 72%. The higher the income of the family, the better the nutritional status of its members.

Adams, Richard H., Jr. 1991. "The Economic Uses and Impact of International Remittances in Rural Egypt." *Economic Development and Cultural Change*, **39: 695–722.**
This article examines the debate over the use of international remittances by comparing the expenditure behavior of a set of migrant households with those of a control set of non-migrant households. The article is divided into six sections. The first provides an overview of the data set. Section 2 presents the predicted income and expenditure functions used in analyzing migrant and non-migrant behavior. Section 3 discusses the choice of the functional form for the model. Section 4 specifies the model and simulated results are given. Section 5 presents the empirical results, and Section 6 summarizes the main findings.

Al Deeb, Amal A. 1993. "Rural Women's Extension Needs in the Area of Minimizing Postharvest Loss in Horticulture." Master's Thesis, Extension and Rural Sociology Department, Faculty of Agriculture, Cairo University.
The study tried to identify extension needs of rural women in order to minimize post-harvest loss of tomatoes and citrus fruits. The findings revealed that: (a) respondents did not know certain recommended procedures, such as the proper method for collecting tomatoes, the use of shallow containers, picking the tomatoes when they start to turn red, the use of smooth containers, and the need for speed in packing them; (b) the most important sources of information were kin and relatives, followed by personal experience; (c) the most favored extension methods were practical demonstrations, extension meetings and rural television programs; and (d) the most important problems were high wages, scarcity of farmhands, and the scarcity and high price of plastic containers.

Al-Garhy, Aman A. 1997. "Socio-Economic Variables Affecting Women's Agricultural Production in a New Valley Village." Second Conference on the Role of Women in Production and Agricultural Development, Productive Activities Project for Women Beneficiaries in New Lands, Alexandria.
The objectives of this study were: assessment of the relationship between the socio-economic variables of rural women and their participation in some agricultural production activities pertaining to plant, animal, and poultry

production and the food and nonfood industries, and identification of the relationship between the socio-economic activities of rural women and their participation level in some areas of home economics with regard to food and nutrition, maternity and childhood, and public health and hygiene. The results revealed that the age of a woman was directly correlated with participation in food production and with the degree of her application of public health and hygiene practices. Her educational level correlated significantly with the degree of her participation in food production and also with food and nutrition practices. The husband's age correlated with the degree of the woman's participation in agricultural and livestock activities. The husband's education correlated significantly with the degree of a woman's participation in food production.

Al-Hanafy, Mohamed Ghanem and Mohamedy Shalaby. 1997. "Some Variables Affecting the Degree of Rural Wives' Participation in Agricultural Labor." Bulletin No. 173, AERDRI, Agricultural Research Center.
The study aimed to estimate the degree of rural wives' participation in agricultural labor, and its relationship with 13 independent variables. Extension training programs necessary for rural women were also specified. The findings illustrated that 70.4% of rural wives were characterized by an average or a high degree of participation with their families in agricultural labor. There was a significant correlation between degree of participation and the wives' popular (community) participation, wives' leadership status, their level of education, family size, and husbands' age. These independent variables explain 21.54% of the variability of wives' participation in agricultural work. Wives also participated actively in animal production, showing that training programs in this area are also required.

Al-Henaidy, Abdellatef. 1997. "Strategic Importance of Providing a Database and Required Information about Women in Agriculture." Second Conference on the Role of Women in Production and Agricultural Development. Productive Activities Project for Women Beneficiaries in New Lands, Alexandria.
This study illustrates the significance of human resources for socio-economic development. The census of 1996 indicated that women comprise 48.8% of Egypt's population. However, the proportion of women in the labor force is only 28%, as compared to over 40% in some countries. The number of females in rural areas is 16.5 million, compared to 12.4 million in urban areas. Database and other information regarding rural women are vitally important for the maximization of the role of women in agricultural activities through education, training, and dissemination of information. Illiteracy among rural women reached 58.8% in 1995, as compared to 33.7% for urban women. The author assessed three problems of women's employment: job isolation where women

are allowed to fill only certain jobs considered suitable for their nature; discrimination against women, whether job-wise or wage-wise; and the conflict between roles imposed upon women with regard to motherhood, household, and work obligations. The study also presents a plan for building a database on the status of women in agriculture.

Ali, Zeinab A. and Laiyla H. Al-Shennawy. 1994. "The Role of Rural Women in Decisionmaking Related to Tomato Crop in Some Egyptian Villages." Research Bulletin No. 128, AFRDRI, Agricultural Research Center.
The study identified the role of rural women in the productive process and in decision-making with regard to the tomato crop. The findings suggested the following: (1) rural women devoted 20% of their working hours to the tomato crop; (2) no significant relationship was found between a woman's participation in agricultural production and the number of family members participating in agricultural labor, respondents sharing labor with others, or amount or possession of household equipment; (3) participation of women in decision-making about the tomato crop was positively correlated with their degree of participation in agricultural work; (4) it was found that size of the area cultivated with tomatoes was the only significant variable that explained the respondents' variability of participation in agricultural labor-more than 15% of variability could be thus explained. Finally, there were significant variations in the extent of women's participation in making decisions and in their involvement in agricultural production in the four regions where the study was conducted.

Al-Mallah, Galal. 1997. "Financial and Training Needs of Women's Small Enterprises: On the Role of Women in Production and Agricultural Development." Productive Activities Project for Women Beneficiaries in New Lands, Alexandria.
The study called attention to the importance of small industries in the economic development of both developed and developing countries. The small industries not only generated income, but also provided new expertise and technical, organizational, and managerial skills. There was an emphasis on the economic importance of financing women's small enterprises and on the training needs of women-operated small enterprises.

Amer, Moh. El Sayied Abu El Magd. 1999. "Identify the Variables Concerning Rural Environment Pollution and Social Services Role." M.A. Thesis, Institute of Environment Studies and Research, Ain Shams University.
The study looked at the links between socio-economic and cultural practices and the environment. It showed that there was a positive correlation between pollution of the rural environment and the low level of social services in the rural periphery.

Anker, Richard, and Martha Anker. 1989. "Measuring the Female Labour Force in Egypt." *International Labour Review*, **128: 511–520.**
The authors looked into the question of whether Egyptian women are as economically inactive as official statistics suggest. If not, why are the statistics inaccurate, and how they can be improved? In the first section, the authors present the official labor force data for Egypt and indicate how recent changes in data collection procedures and questionnaires used by the Egyptian Central Agency for Public Mobilization and Statistics (CAPMAS) have affected responses and, consequently, official estimates of the female labor force. The next section briefly describes the results of the methodological household survey conducted jointly by the International Labour Office and CAPMAS and discusses several potentially important ways to improve data collection on the female labor force.

Badran, Hoda. 1993. "Women's Human Rights: A Conditionality for Sustainability," in Faris, Mohamed A. and Hasan Khan, Mabmood (eds.), *Sustainable Agriculture in Egypt.* **Boulder, Lynne Rienner Publishers.**
Sustainable agriculture is the focus of this chapter, specifically the status of rural women in Egypt. The author stresses that rural Egyptian women do not have basic human rights. Several indicators are presented, such as maternal mortality, malnutrition, and lack of education. Finally, the author discusses the inadequacy of community delivery systems to meet the basic needs of rural women.

Brink, Judy H. 1987. "Changing Extended Family Relationships in an Egyptian Village." *Urban Anthropology*, **16: 33–149.**
Participation, observation, and interviews in a modernizing Egyptian village revealed that the availability of wage labor and modern education for young people in rural areas has changed the nature of family relationships within the extended family. In early stages of development, older men lose power when their sons leave the family farm and enter the wage labor market. Older women, however, retain their position of power within the family because their daughters- in-law remain in the home under their authority. In later stages of development, when young women become educated and enter modern wage labor, older women lose power within the family as their daughters-in-law gain autonomy and are accorded decision-making ability. It is suggested that if a majority of rural Egyptian women become educated and employed, a reversal of daughter-in-law and mother-in-law roles may occur, and the mother-in-law will lose her position of power and prestige within the extended family.

Brink, Judy H. 1991. "The Effect of Emigration of Husbands on the Status of Their Wives: An Egyptian Case." *International Journal of Middle East Studies*, **23: 201–211.**

This study analyzed labor migration, using a micro approach. Employing Egyptian household data for 1983 and 1984, the author analyzed the impact of emigration of husbands on the lives of women. Of the 79 women interviewed in the village of Sadeeq, eight had husbands working abroad. The status of this subset of women was compared with that of the women whose husbands were at home and was measured by four variables: the ability to allocate food money; the ability to allocate money for routine expenditures, such as clothing, medicine, and educational supplies; the ability to make decisions about purchasing expensive items, such as a television or a washing machine; and the freedom to leave home without permission.

In the extended families, food money is allocated by mothers-in-law. In nuclear families, wives allocate this money. The effect of migration on this variable was that families with migrant husbands were able to build a nuclear family home sooner than most. Emigration provided the money to build a house and enabled the couple to leave the extended family. Thus, wives in these nuclear families were able to control food money at a comparatively younger age. The ability of the wife to allocate money for food and routine expenses and to leave the house without permission was affected by the husband's migration. Six of the families in the sub-sample lived in nuclear households.

The absence of husbands from the nuclear family further increased the status of wives by freeing them from supervision and by increasing their ability to make financial decisions regarding routine expenditures and ongoing projects.

Brocas, Anne-Marie, Anne-Marie Cailloux, and Virgine Oget. 1990. *Women and Social Security. Progress Towards Equality of Treatment.* Geneva: International Labor Office, 116 pp.
The study contains two parts. The first explores whether men and women in equivalent employment enjoy equal rights regarding social security and highlights discriminatory provisions that still exist. The second covers women's special needs as mothers and as workers with family responsibilities. Policies to help women who are in precarious situations or who live in poverty are also discussed.

The authors argue for a move toward personal entitlement to social security for women regardless of their financial and marital status. This, however, is likely to be achieved only when women are fully integrated into the workforce (with compensation for periods of maternity and childrearing) and when tasks and roles in society are genuinely shared between men and women.

Egypt, Arab Republic of, Central Agency for Public Mobilization and Statistics (CAPMAS), and United Nations Children's Fund (UNICEF). n.d. *The Situation of Women in Egypt.* Cairo: Shorouk Press, 51 pp.
This analysis covers the status of Egyptian women in the areas of education, the labor force, legislation, political and community participation, the contemporary Egyptian family, and the media. The final chapter offers

recommendations to ameliorate the status of women and increase their contributions in these areas. A critical overview of women's development projects in Egypt is also presented.

Egypt, Arab Republic of, Ministry of Social Affairs, and International Labor Organization. 1992. "Training Rural Women in Income Generating and Basic Life Skills." Cairo: State Information Service Press, 6 pp.
This project was designed as a demonstration effort to meet the needs of village women through training, with the aim of achieving specific goals. These aims are to expand the resource base of the village women by providing the skills, knowledge, and experience necessary to generate reliable and sustainable income; to increase the earnings of rural women and their access to resources; to promote rural women's participation in community services and activities; to encourage rural women to hold positions in community organizations; to improve the social and economic position of women; to encourage groups of women or individuals to set up workshops or home production units; and to train women leaders so they can implement training programs.

El-Bendary, A.T. and M.A. Saad. 1999. "Women's Response to Environmental Problems in Old Reclaimed Desert Lands in Egypt: The Case of the Mariout Area." Sixth International Conference of the Development of Dry Lands, Desert Development Challenges Beyond the Year 2000, ICARDA, Cairo, Egypt, 9 pp.
This study investigates the impact of environmental problems on rural women's livelihood and women's responses with regard to soil salinity and the rising ground water level in their family land holding. Results show that there are highly significant differences between the affected and non-affected group with regard to the increasing burden of farm activities, the women's feelings of economic hardship, their satisfaction with services and facilities in their community, and their role in the decision-making process. The relationship between the independent variables and family coping strategies were significant. There is a significant relationship between housing condition, family size, family landholding, and the subjective coping strategies the families have used.

El-Gingihi, Hoda M. 1985. "The Role of Mass Media in Nutrition Education Programs for Rural Women." *Bulletin of Faculty of Agriculture,* **University of Cairo, 36: 681–709.**
Rural women play a vital role on the farm and at home. They need continual educational programs, especially those that relate to family health and nutrition, including food selection and consumption. These programs reach rural women through different mass communication means such as radio, television, and publications. This research was conducted in the village of Elkounayesa, Giza governorate, in order to learn what kinds of radio and TV programs people like;

the source of nutrition knowledge and its relation to mass media; and the proportion of people who watch television and listen to the radio. The study included 100 randomly-selected women. The socio-economic data pertaining to the study were collected by personal interviews.

El-Katsha, Samiha, and Anne U. White. 1989. "Women, Water, and Sanitation: Household Behavioral Patterns in Two Egyptian Villages." *Water International*, 14: 103–111.
Understanding the behavioral patterns of women in rural households regarding water and sanitation may be the key to solving the problem of why improvements in facilities are not always accompanied by a reduction in disease prevalence. An interdisciplinary team surveyed 312 households in two Delta villages in Egypt, examining 46 of them in depth, by participant observation. The patterns of storing water and its use for drinking, cooking, washing, animal rearing, and waste disposal are rooted in women's beliefs regarding cleanliness and what enhances the health and well-being of their families. The women suggest practical solutions for their water and sanitation problems, such as carts for collecting wastewater, but they feel powerless to influence local governments or even to pressure their husbands to institute such new practices.

El-Katsha, Samiha, Younis Awatif, Olfat El-Sabie, and Ahmed Hussein. 1989. "Women, Water, and Sanitation: Household Water Use in Two Egyptian Villages." *Cairo Papers in Social Science*, 12: 1–96, Monograph 2.
The objectives of the research were: (1) to determine the patterns of women's behavior related to the handling and utilization of water and associated materials for household purposes and disposal of sewage; (2) to identify some linkages between behavioral patterns and the transmission of water-borne diseases; (3) to seek an understanding of the cultural and household economy contexts within which the behavioral patterns find their rationale; (4) to determine present environmental sanitary conditions, both at the village and the household level; and (5) to investigate the extent to which women understand the mechanisms of disease transmission. The research was conducted in two villages in Menufia governorate, located approximately 70 kilometers north of Cairo.

El-Shennawy, Layla H. 1998. "Farmers' Environmental Behavior in Some Egyptian Villages." Arab Countries Conference, Arab Council for Studies and Scientific Research, Association of Arab Universities, pp. 521–539.
This study aimed to examine farmers' awareness of concepts of environment, problems associated with the environment, their own environmental behavior, and their role in the protection of the environment. The results revealed that:
- Farmers were not aware of the environment as a concept, but were aware of types of environment, such as house environment, social environment, farm

environment, and natural environment. While the mass media play a positive role in their awareness, academic studies have no such role.

- Farmers were aware of pollution problems and their effect upon environmental elements.
- Farmers engaged in a variety of wrong practices which affect the environment.
- In the farmers' view, the Ministry of Agriculture, Public Works and Water Resources, and Health, as well as the local council are responsible for the environment.

El-Shennawy, Layla H. *et al.* 1994. "The Contribution of Rural Women in the Production of the Potato Crop in Some Egyptian Villages." Mimeo.

The study aimed to identify the degree of rural women's participation in the production of the potato crop. The study also sought to discover the impact of some independent variables on the degree of participation, and also to ascertain the production area impact upon women's participation in agricultural processes. The findings revealed that: (a) the proportion of rural women's participation in all agricultural processes of potato production reached 20%; (b) the highest participation ratio of rural women was in seed preparation-it reached 40%, followed by fertilization, 28%, and by cropping, 26%; (c) a significant relationship between women's participation in potato production, on one hand, and the number of family members participating directly in farm labor, family size, and amount of household equipment, on the other, was found; (d) no significant relationship was found between women's participation in potato production and the respondents' participation in work for their amount of agricultural machinery possessed; (e) women's participation n potato production differed significantly according to location of he study, i.e., Behera, Menoufia, Giza, or Gharbia.

El-Shennawy, Layla H. 1998 "Farmers Irrigation Behavior in Some Egyptian Villages." 3rd Conference: Role of Agricultural Extension in Rational Use of Irrigation Water in the Egyptian Old Valley Lands, pp. 221–237.

This study aimed to examine farmers' awareness about limited water resources in Egypt, irrigation problems, water-saving practices, their role in irrigation management, as well as what would be the preferable communication channel. The results of the study revealed that:

- Farmers (especially women) were not aware of national water limits. They do not know the source of the Nile.
- Farmers are aware of local water topics, such as water shortage, pollution, drainage problems, and watering by drainage and underground water.
- Farmers engaged in a variety of practices that resulted in saving water, such as watering at night and leveling the land. Farmers took several factors into consideration in choosing crops that required little water.

- In the farmers view, the Ministry of Public Works and Water Resources (MPWWR) is responsible for the entire irrigation system. They did not speak positively about the irrigation engineer and his assistants. The farmers tried to influence the MPWWR through complaints.
- For both men and women, TV is the most important communication channel, followed by radio and the newspaper. They like some of the dramatic shows, news, and religious programs.

El-Tobshy, Zeinab, M. 1998. "An Approach for Promoting Egyptian Women Farmers in Sustainable Agricultural Development." International seminar on women's leadership, "Help Women Help Themselves," Israel, 18–23 October 1998.
An innovative program to support women in agriculture was initiated by the Egyptian Ministry of Agriculture through the National Agricultural Research Project (NARP). The Technology Transfer Component (TTC) focused on developing the skills required by rural women to carry out agricultural tasks through the training of village extension workers (VEW).

A needs assessment for rural family development was conducted in eight governorates of Egypt to determine the training needs of the VEW with regard to field crops, animal and poultry production, bee-keeping and silkworm rearing, and marketing, as well as home economics and agricultural extension areas. Barriers facing the VEW in their attempt to develop rural women at village level were identified. This was carried out using special questionnaires filled out by the VEW. The study identified the main constraints in the transfer of a new technology to rural women at the village and examined the role of extension workers in that process.

Fathy, Shadia H. 1985. "A Study of Motivations and Needs For Participation in Informal Education Programs Among Young Rural Women in the Mariut Area, Alexandria Governorate." *Alexandria Journal of Agriculture Research*, 30: 1213–1226.
The study focused on 115 village girls in the Mariut area. The girls were classified into groups according to their intention to enroll and their actual participation in formal education. It used a range of statistical analytical tools (The Kendal rank correlation coefficient, the expectancy value of Fishbein, and standard chi-square test) in order to examine the subjects' perceptions of their educational needs and the degree of consensus among these groups about such educational needs. No significant differences were revealed among the various groups in the overall perception of their educational needs. The differences were found mainly in the basic personal values underlying the perception.

Fong, S. Manica and Anjana Bhushan. 1996. "Bedouin Women's Role in Management of Natural Resources in Egypt," in *Tool-Kit on Gender in Agriculture.* **Series No. 1, Washington, DC: The World Bank, 93 pp.**

The main objective of the Matruh Resource Management Project (Cr. 2504) in Egypt was to break the cycle of natural resource degradation and poverty in the fragile ecosystem of Matruh. In view of the critical role Bedouin women play in rural production and environmental management, the project worked closely with community groups through traditional channels to: (1) define the needs of women and men; (2) ensure men's and women's participation in preparing and implementing local resource management plans and; (3) to determine income-generating activities for women.

To fulfill these objectives and to address gender issues effectively, the project staff received specific gender training from the very initial phases of the project. In addition, women extension agents were based in each subproject area so that they could work directly with women. Audiovisual communications were also directed to women.

Gamal Eldine, Nadia, and Mohamed Saied Heikal. 1988. "Educational Needs of Illiterate Rural Women: A Case Study in Barahamh and Qualaa Villages, Qena Governorate." Cairo, Regional Center for Illiteracy. Mimeo, 102 pp.
This study presents the educational needs of rural women, with the aim of improving their knowledge in various domains so that they can exercise their full potential influence in the economic sector and the development of the country.

Hassan, Naima A. 1985. "Studies on the Role of Women in Better Family Living and Community Development with Special Reference to Rural Industries." Master's Thesis, Cairo University.
The aim of this study was to investigate the role of rural women in various agricultural operations, including crop production, animal husbandry, poultry, and small-scale agro-industries. These have a direct impact on family income and the standard of living. The author examined the correlation between the additional income of females and certain key independent variables such as family size, number of educated children, and amount of modern household equipment. The study concludes by identifying the needs of rural women and suggesting various policy options to meet those needs.

Hassanein, Laila M. 1986. "Extension Training Needs for Rural Women in Family Development Areas, Nobar Hamlets, Alexandria Governorate." Ph.D. Thesis, Alexandria University.
The main objective of this research was to study the training needs of rural women in order to enhance their status and the development of the family. Based on responses of randomly-selected rural women, the study found a high correlation between the female's (wife's) education and her participation in the decision-making process at home and on the farm. According to the results of this study, extension programs for women are clearly important in increasing

their understanding of their role in the social and economic development of the family.

Helal, Samia Abdel-Samie. 1988. "Role of Rural Women in Family Decisionmaking in Elwan Village." M.A. Thesis, Assiut University.
The objectives of the study were to determine the role of rural women in family decision-making and the effects of certain characteristics of rural women upon their role in family decision-making. The results show the following: (1) rural women play an important role only in certain aspects of family decision-making; (2) a positive association was found between cosmopolitanism, age and educational level of women and their role in family decision-making; and (3) a negative association was found between the educational level of the husband, family size, and farm size, and the role of rural women in family decision-making

Helali, Ahlam Moustafa. 1989. "Study of Some Dimensions of Organized Women's Activities in Rural Egypt." M.A. Thesis, Ain Shams University.
The improvement of society and of rural communities in particular, depends upon the range and degree of the members' participation in making such improvements. In Egypt, planners of development programs have considered women in the process of development by encouraging them to be members of organizations and to participate in community projects. The object of this study was to analyze the nature of rural female participation and the women's motives for participating in development projects, the fields of such participation, major social factors that affected the degree of participation, the nature of benefits for rural females, major social factors that affected the benefits, and the relationship between rural female participation and how the projects benefited the women.

Helmy, Enayat, and Kamilia Sboukry.1991. "Promotion of Women's Role in Food Production: Draft Terminal Report." Cairo, Cooperation Project Between the Egyptian and Netherlands Governments and the Food and Agriculture Organization. Mimeo, 25 pp.
The project's aims were to develop, test, and evaluate an experimental approach to multiple socio-economic activities. The implementation environment was unfavorable at the beginning, mainly because most of the rural female beneficiaries lacked experience in dealing with various institutions and authorities, such as banks and technical and local governmental staff. Also, a majority of the needy rural women had never previously established or participated in organized private enterprises, but through an appropriate policy and a careful plan, encouraging results were obtained during the execution of the three-year project.

Hendi, Nabila Abde El Megeed M. 1999. "Some Factors Affecting Women's Awareness of Maintaining an Agricultural Environment in Reclaimed Areas." Dept. of Agricultural Science, Institute of Environment Studies and Research, Ph.D. Thesis, Ain Shams University.

The research aims were to: (1) define the sources of pollution in the agricultural environment in newly-reclaimed areas, and assess how these differed from pollution in other areas; (2) delineate the degree of women's awareness and behavior concerning the agricultural environment; (3) define the relationship between a woman's awareness and the behavior of women who attended special classes in the newly-reclaimed areas; and (4) define the factors affecting both environmental awareness and behavior.

The results were: (1) the sources of environmental pollution in the village under study included the unsafe use of agricultural pesticides, crop residues, animal waste, and house wastes; (2) the female graduates of the classes offered on this topic had the highest level of awareness of the impact agricultural practices on the environment. While the wives of male graduates of these classes had a medium level of such awareness, the wives of the men who had not attended classes had the lowest level of awareness and behavior.

Henein, Samia H. and Hamed, Nefisa A. 1998. "Knowledge Needs of Extension Workers Related to Rural Women Development in El-Fayoum Governorate." Arab Countries Conference at the Arab Council for Graduate Studies and Scientific Research. Association of Arab Universities, pp. 655–673.

The goals of this research were to recognize the knowledge needs of female extension workers in the area of rural women's development, and to determine the relationship between these needs and the studied independent variables. Training courses were surveyed to determine what information was transferred to the rural women and by which methods. Also problems facing the extension workers were examined and solutions suggested.

Findings indicated that 60% of the extension workers were in the high needs category. Information on obtaining credit was rated as a high need, as was the need for knowledge in the fields of marketing and nutrition. It was found that extension workers transfer information in the fields of agricultural and environmental manufacturing, as well as livestock raising, more than the other fields. The no availability of transportation was the main obstacle preventing extension workers from achieving their goals.

With regard to the training courses, it was found that those dealing with credit, livestock, and agricultural and environmental manufacturing had the highest degree of attendance. Courses dealing with social and political participation, marketing, and environment had the lowest attendance. The length of courses in the fields of social and political participation and obtaining credit was said to be adequate, but courses dealing with the environment, marketing, and agricultural and environmental manufacturing were too short.

Hopkins, Nicholas S. 1985. "The Political Economy of Two Arab Villages," in Hopkins, Nicholas S., and Eddin, Saad (eds.), *Arab Society: Social Science Perspectives*. Cairo: American University in Cairo Press, pp. 307–321.
This chapter analyzes the political economy of two Arab villages, one in northern Tunisia and the other in Upper Egypt. First, the geographical setting of the villages is put into context; then, the patterns of agriculture, in particular the social organization of agricultural production, are analyzed. These data are followed by an examination of the social organization of the village in general, with emphasis on the problem of the emergence of class and the significance of political action. The discussion stresses common features in the two cases, illustrating the process of agrarian transition within the Arab world. Not only the similarities, but also the contrasts between the two cases help us see the general pattern. The methodology is thus a comparative one, in which the distinctive elements of each case are used to clarify obscure parts of the other and features of both contribute to the development of a general theory.

Hopkins, Nicholas S., Abderrahman El-Haydery, Salah El-Zoghby, Hanaa Singer, Sabea Hanen, Rania Sholkami, Saad Reem, and Ahmed Bahaa El-Din Ziad. 1988. "Participation and Community in the Egyptian New Lands: The Case of South Tahrir." *Cairo Papers in Social Science*, 11: 1–127.
This study describes the results of research carried out by the Desert Development Center of the American University in Cairo in the summer of 1986. It deals with the processes of community formation and local participation in the institutional structure of the New Lands villages. The purpose of the research was to refine existing knowledge of this structure in the New Lands, in order to evaluate the success of different experiments in creating viable human settlements and communities in the desert areas of Egypt. The research was carried out in three villages in South Tahrir: Omar Makram' participation in the institutions of government and the community.

Ibrahim, Mostafa Hamdy A. 1989. "Some Factors Affecting Fertility of Rural Women in the Assiut Governorate." Ph.D. Thesis, Faculty of Agriculture, Assiut University.
This study examines the factors affecting fertility in rural areas, with special reference to the Assiut Governorate. The study concentrates on social and economic factors affecting fertility.

Ibrahim, Mostafa Hamdy A. 1996 "A Study of the Relationship Between Women's Education and Socio-Economic Status and Demographic Development in Selected Villages of the Assiut Governorate." *Journal of Agricultural Sciences*, 27(3), Faculty of Agriculture, Assiut University.
The main objective of this paper was to examine the relationship between women's education and socio-economic status and demographic development

in selected villages of the Assiut Governorate. The study was based on data collected by means of personal interview of 380 women, randomly-selected from four villages in the Assiut Governorate. Results showed that a rural woman's education affects her life in several aspects-demographic, education, health, economic, social, home economics, and agricultural.

Ibrahim, Mostafa Hamdy A. 1996. "Associated Factors with Rural Participation in Local Development Projects in Selected Village Communities." Faculty of Agriculture, Assiut University, Egypt.

The main objective of this paper was to determine the factors associated with rural women's participation in local development projects in selected village communities. The study was based on interviews with 300 women, randomly selected from three villages in the Assiut Governorate. The results of this study show that the participation of rural women is affected by several factors: the woman's education, her age, and her contact with those in a position of leadership and with female extension workers.

Ibrahim, Samya. 1999 "Gender and Institutions: Gender Analysis of Two Institutions of the Ministry of Public Works and Water Resources." Mimeo.

In this study, two sectors from the Ministry of Public Works and Water Resources were chosen as case studies for an examination of gender sensitivity in governmental institutions in Egypt. Results of the study show that gender Ministry through joint work with external donor agencies. It appears that the topic of gender was inserted into official projects because of the donor agencies' agenda and was not an integral concern of the institution in its daily practices. Moreover, males held almost all the managerial posts, while female staff members were predominantly represented in the secretarial and administrative ranks in both institutions studies. Therefore, even the direct experience and insights of female staff members were excluded from project planning since only men carried out all the decision-making. The final results show that sensitivity to gender is carried out in an unsystematic and irregular fashion, depending on the project and the agenda set by the donors.

Ibrahim, Soumaya. 1998. "Discussion and Reflections about Gender Roles and Responsibilities in Irrigation Activities and Water Resources Management." Mimeo.

The study aimed to make visible women's activities related to irrigation in the agricultural production process and to assess the extent to which women have access to and control over irrigation facilities. The study wished to shed light on the constraints women face in the realization of gender needs. It examined the process of social construction and the importance of the integration of gender concerns into irrigation activities. The study revealed the following:

- There is a relatively large percentage of female-headed households or women managing their own farms or those of their husbands. This remains invisible to a very large extent due to the stereotypical assumption that households are always headed by men and that women do not irrigate land.
- A lack of communication exists between men and women with regard to irrigation. For example, women were not informed about the process of the selection of the Water Association's board members.
- All members of the Water Association are men. This male domination reflects the in particular, are a male affair.
- As a result of these gender conceptions, the women themselves explained that they did not participate in the Water Association's meetings since this was a masculine arena better suited to male representatives. Women perceive themselves as farmers who perform agricultural labor.

Ibrahim, Soumaya. 1999. "Gender Concerns in Water Policies: Gender Analysis of Egypt's Water Policy for the 21st Century." Mimeo.
Egyptian water policies are analyzed from a gender perspective and an attempt is made to incorporate gender concerns into them.

Ishak, Yeldez, Zeinab El Tobshy, Naima Hassan, and Collen Brown 1987. "Egyptian Women in Agriculture." Cairo, Egyptian Major Cereals Improvement Project (EMCIP), Ministry of Agriculture and Land Reclamation.
Two studies are included in this publication. The first study used case studies to show the quality of time spent by the family in agricultural production. It describes the amount of time spent on animal care, household work, personal needs, and leisure by women and girls of the family. The second study mainly used questionnaires to document the knowledge of women compared to that of men with respect to new technologies and their effect on the implementation of new practices.

Ishak, Yeldez, Zeinab El-Tobshy, Naima Hassan, and Collen Brown. 1985. "Role of Women in Field Crop Production and Related Information." Cairo, Egyptian Major Cereals Improvement Project (EMCIP), Ministry of Agriculture and Land Reclamation. Mimeo, 45 pp.
This report is based on research conducted in the Gbarbiya and Minya governorates to document the agricultural tasks performed by women. Because women are important in the production and utilization of food in Egypt (and the EMCIP's purpose is to contribute knowledge that will increase food production), studies were undertaken to document specific tasks that women perform in the production of maize, wheat, rice, soybeans, and forage flora; the utilization of maize, wheat, rice, soybeans, and forage; women's participation in animal and poultry care and household tasks; and the extent to which they participate in decisions about household budgets and farm operations.

Jennings, Anne Margaret. 1985. "Power and Influence: Women's Associations in an Egyptian Nubian Village." Ph.D. Thesis, Riverside, University of California.
This dissertation employs the results of field research in a Nubian village to question the validity of the stereotype and widely-accepted model of Muslim society in which men dominate and women are seen as the subservient, passive party. The author finds that the two genders are interdependent and complementary. Sexual segregation, seemingly detrimental to women, does not exclude them from important decision-making, but gives the sexes differential control over separate aspects of village life. The social networks developed by women from childhood on allow them to acquire information through which they exercise significant social and economic control in both male and female spheres.

Kazem, Fatima M. 1995. "The Role of Rural Women in the Promotion of Community Development Prospects in the Assiut Governorate." A paper presented in "The Societal Requirement for Economic Reform: The Neglected Dimension in Rural Development in Egypt." The 1st National Conference for the Egyptian Rural Sociological Society.
The level of voluntary participation of rural women in community-oriented activities was studied with regard to the social, economic, cultural, political, and environmental conditions found in the Assiut Governorate. It also explored the possibility of enhancing rural women's development and their increased participation in rural development programs. Recommendations were made to promote the role of women in community development projects in the Assiut Governorate.

Khafagy, Fatma, Hania Sholkami, and Hanaa Singer. 1987. "Impact of Income-Generating Activities on Rural Women." Cairo: United Nations International Children's Fund. Mimeo, 83 pp.
The objectives of the program were to improve knowledge, attitudes, and practices of rural women in various areas of family life; to provide rural women with income-generating opportunities through skill development; to support activities that enable women to increase family income; and to provide daycare facilities for children of rural women.

Kotby, A. Fawkia, A.R. Hosini, and Zeinab M. El-Tobshy. 1999. "Rural Family and Technology Transfer of Sericulture Development in Egypt." The 2nd International Conference on "Women, Science, and Technology for Sustainable Development." Third World Organization for Women in Science (TWOWS) 8–11 Feb., Cape Town, South Africa.
A previous needs assessment indicated a high need for the training of female extension workers in Egypt in various agricultural activities. One of these was natural silk production development. Therefore, the Technology Transfer

Component of the National Agricultural Research Project and the sericulture department developed a program for sericulture development through the introduction of appropriate new technologies for natural silk production. The basic objectives of this program were: to raise the skill of the extension agents, both male and female, to further cocoon production and cultivation of the mulberry, to increase the number of families rearing silkworms, and to increase the cocoon crop per egg box.

For two successive seasons of TTC involvement, practical demonstrations on silkworm rearing and cocoon production were conducted for 182 trainees (extension agents, male and female) in seven Governorates. This detailed practical training covered all relevant stages of silk production, from egg hatching, up to cocoon harvesting, drying, reeling and re-reeling, to marketing. In addition, methods for using the new mulberry cultivates were taught so that the maximum yield of fresh green leaves could be attained. Steps were illustrated either through video, slides, and dry or living material. A highly selected capable team was formed of seven specialists (28% female), each being responsible for one governorate. They were assisted by 20 TT specialists at the regional sites (20% female) and 70 Village Extension Workers "VEW" (93% female) in the selected villages.

The goals of the program were to build an integrated extension team for sericulture, to train skilled female Village Extension Workers, and to increase the cocoon yield per egg box.

Lanson, Barbara K. 1991. "Women's Work and Status in Rural Egypt." *National Women Studies Association (NWA) Journal,* **3: 38–52.**
This article examines the nature and significance of women's work in rural Egypt and its implications for the status of women. What kinds of work are available to women in rural Egypt, and what is the relationship between women's work and their status? The author does not pretend to answer these questions for all of Egypt. Her attention is directed primarily to rural women in the governorate of Beni Suef, where she carried out anthropological research on rural markets and marketing during the years 1981-1982 and again in 1984-1985. The author believes her findings from Beni Suef were typical for most of Egypt, where the seclusion of women is prevalent and women's participation in marketing activities appears to be restricted.

Lotayef, Karima. 1987. "Report on Socio-Economic Status of Women in Egypt with Considerations for Implementing a WID Project." Cairo, Canadian International Development Agency (CIDA) Egypt Desk for Anglophone Africa Branch. Mimeo, 52 pp.
The consultant was asked to update statistics on the socio-economic status of women in Egypt, including life expectancy, fertility, literacy and education, legal rights, attitude toward family planning, participation in the labor force, access to credit, and the general degree of independence. Available literature at

CIDA was examined, as well as international and Egyptian (Arabic) reports, articles, books, and audiovisual materials, and telephone interviews conducted with personnel at agencies such as UNCEF, the International Women's Tribune Center, the Population Council, and the World Bank. Much of the information regarding attitudes, existing WID activities, and constraints is summarized here.

Mansour, Kamla. 1997. "Some Results of the Analysis of Questionnaires [administered] to Rural Women in the Four Governorates: Sohag, El Fayoum, El Behera and El Kaloubiya." Unpublished report. Ministry of Agriculture.
The study delineated the principal indicators necessary for policymaking and examined the special programs for enhancing participation of women in agricultural development.

The study discussed in detail more than a dozen specific policy recommendations, among which were:

- Rural women need training programs and loans to enable them to use suitable technologies and take advantage of natural resources that protect the rural environment. The training programs should also help rural women handle income-generating unconventional projects.
- The role of women extension workers should be fortified; the concepts of social, cultural, health, and psychological development should be integrated into their work with clients. More female agricultural extension workers should be trained in order that more rural women can be reached.
- There should be coordination among all governmental and nongovernmental organizations dealing with the development of rural women. The senior female staff of women's organizations should be trained in technical and administrative aspects of development.
- Media tools and direct communication systems and education should be enhanced in order to integrate women in development through special programs that address rural women and respond to their immediate needs. In doing this, care must be taken to preserve fundamental rural tradition and customs.
- More studies and research need to be conducted to investigate the gender gap in other governorates so as to cover the geographical and cultural variations and furnish the extensive information and a database on rural women.

McCann, Barbara. 1988. "Women in Development." Canadian International Development Agency (CIDA), Egypt Program. Ottawa, McCann Consulting, Mimeo, 106 pp.
This report is divided into four major sections. The first section deals with the context in which CIDA's development assistance functions. The second section addresses women in Egypt and the influence of such assistance on their lives.

The third section covers donor experiences. The last section reviews current and planned CIDA projects in Egypt and their considerations for and impact on women. The report also gives recommendations for implementation of the WID strategy within CIDA.

Morsy, Soheir A. 1990. "Rural Women, Work, and Gender Ideology: A Study in Egyptian Political Economic Transformation," in Shami, S., Taminian, L., Soheir A., Morsy, S.A., El-Bakri, Z., and El-Wathiy, M. (eds.), *Women in Arab Society: Work Patterns and Gender Relations in Egypt, Jordan, and Sudan.* **Providence: Berg Publishers, pp. 87–217.**
This comparative study of rural women in two Egyptian villages of the Nile Delta focuses on work, social position, and gender ideology in relation to the transformations in the Egyptian national and regional political economy. Informed by a holistic conception of work that transcends remunerative wage labor, it examines women's roles in production and social reproduction. Fieldwork conducted in the villages of Fatiha and Bahiya during the mid-1970s and early 1980s, respectively, provided some of the data on which this study is based. Attention is focused on the social and material conditions and ideology that produce and reproduce the gender division of labor among local social collectivities, as well as on male-female power relations in the communities.

Nawar, Isis, Saheir Nour, Mona Barakat, Madiha Taleyawi, Soinia Hassan, Mowahib Ayyaid, and Salwa Said. n.d. "Profiles of Egyptian Women." Alexandria, University of Alexandria. Mimeo, 16 pp.
The first part of this paper addresses the general status of Egyptian women, and the second focuses on the status of rural women. The presentation describes changes in the status of Egyptian women and the impact of women on national development, which is mirrored in the role of women in the labor force, at home, and in the general social and political life of the society.

Nelson, Cynthia, and Lucie Saunders. 1986. "An Exploratory Analysis of Income-Generating Strategies in Contemporary Rural Egypt." Working Paper No. 122. Cairo, American University in Cairo. Mimeo, 28 pp.
Two cases of income-generating strategies in rural Egypt are examined within the context of issues in development, particularly those that relate to women's status and power. The cases document the development of income-generating strategies through local initiation in the first case and with outside encouragement in the second. These strategies differed in the type of requirements, responsibility, and training requirements. It is argued that over the long term, having funds enables women to participate in the decision-making process in a capitalist economy.

Roemburg, Rebekka Van. 1991. "An Overview of Women in Development in the Arab Republic of Egypt." Cairo, Royal Danish Embassy (Danish International Development Agency [DANIDA] Section). Mimeo, 43 pp.
The report provides background information for the formulation of DANIDA's future strategy on women in development in Egypt. It covers the socioeconomic and legal status of women, government policies on women in development, indigenous women's organizations, and other donor activities in this field.

Seif, Janet, Nemat Shafik, Cheryl Compton, and Salwa Soliman Saleh. 1984. "Women's Access to Productive Resources: Recommendations for an AID Program Strategy." A Report to the USAID Mission in Egypt. Cairo, U.S. Agency for International Development (USAID). Mimeo, 47 pp.
The purpose of this report was to provide a review of the USAID program in Egypt with regard to the economic participation of women and to outline an approach for improving the program's success in reaching women. The assessment focused on USAID projects that provide low-income women with access to productive resources. The authors of the report reviewed the experiences of various USAID projects in both rural and urban areas to identify lessons learned in order to evaluate project implementation and future programming. In general, the team found that although USAID-Cairo has had no strategy to guide the selection of and support the efforts of women-in-development (WID), women have emerged as beneficiaries and agents of change under various USAID activities. This has contributed to a growing recognition of women's economic roles and has revealed the tremendous potential for pursuing WID goals even more vigorously.

Shalaby, M. Tarek. 1991. "Household Productivity in New Rural Settlements in Egypt: Perspectives on Kitchen Gardens." *Third World Planning Review*, 13: 237–259.
This article discusses the role of women in the generation of additional income to improve their domestic economy through production of food from kitchen gardens. The discussion is based on the findings of research and focuses on general issues regarding the new rural settlements in Egypt in household productivity. The research was carried out at the University of Nottingham and funded by the Overseas Development Administration. The case study includes information on kitchen gardens and income generation, livestock and household productivity, use of the extra income, and craft activities and income generation.

Sultan, M. Y. and Khalifa T. I., 1998, "The Role of Women In Development in the New Valley Governorate." Mimeo.
Participation of women in agricultural production (plant and livestock), in rural industries, in decision-making and other aspects were investigated in eight villages.

The results indicated the following:
- Participation in decision-making was very low.
- Participation in food industries ranged between 35% and 91% in the sample.
- The women suggested six agricultural projects and five nonagricultural projects to increase family income.

Toth, James and Pride, Purdah. 1991. "What Maintains the Gender Division of Labor in Rural Egypt?" *International Journal of Middle East Studies,* **23: 213–236.**
An examination of the gender division of labor in the Middle East is followed by an assessment of how Egyptian farm work functions on the basis of gender. Discussion focuses on why such divisions continue and why, in the last quarter of the twentieth century, supposedly clear lines of separation have become so confused. The strict boundary between men's and women's work is maintained first as a cultural distinction and then as an economic determinant. The substitution of women for men is encouraged. When absence of employment alternatives pushes men to accept 'feminine' employment, they are paid women's wages. Rural Egyptian women have clearly contributed a significant amount of labor to the production of food and exports. When economic diversification permitted unskilled male farm laborers to leave agricultural employment for migrant labor, construction jobs, and overseas work, women replaced them, although the low esteem and low wages such employment generates were transferred to them. Prior to the oil boom, employers substituted women for men in order to reduce their labor costs.

United Nations Children's Fund. 1992. "Women's Development Program: Position Paper." New York, United Nations Children's Fund (UNICEF). Mimeo, 19 pp.
This is a position paper on the activities of the UNICEF Women's Development Program, prepared for discussion by members of the Mid-Term Review Working Group. The paper gives a background of program activities since its inception in 1981, the 1989Ð1992 plan of operations, activities from 1989 to the present, major shortcomings, and the plan for the next two-and-a-half years. The overall objective of the Women's Development Program is to improve the quality of life of poor female heads of households by improving their income levels, improving their practices and level of knowledge, and increasing their use of existing services and their participation in the activities available to them.

Wickering, Deborah. 1991. "Experience and Expression: Life Among Bedouin Women in South Sinai." *Cairo Papers in Social Science,* **14: 1–70, Monograph 2.**
This monograph explores the dynamics of social relations among the Tarabiin Bedouin of the South Sinai. In particular, it asks how the Bedouin women see

themselves within the complex interpersonal relations that make up their lives. The author approaches this question from a theoretical perspective which reflects the fact that her research is a blending of several elements, including phenomenology, hermeneutics, and the sociology of knowledge. The study focuses on how members of the Tarabiin community perceive themselves, and how this experience of 'self' is expressed in their everyday work, play, and social relations. The author's participation in, and interaction within, the community and the process through which the results of this study emerged from the encounter between the author and the Tarabiin Bedouin are themes that run throughout the text.

Chapter 7

Conclusions: The Politics of Producing Knowledge in Development – Gender in Rural Production

Pnina Motzafi-Haller

This book is a product of its time. It is based on the growing realization among international development practitioners, academics and policy makers that women's contribution to agricultural production in developing countries has been understudied and underestimated. A recent FAO document encapsulates the logic of such general awareness that links gender and agriculture in the following way (emphasis in the original text):

> Both women and men play critical roles in agriculture throughout the world, producing, processing and providing the food we eat. Rural women in particular are responsible for half of the world's food production and produce between 60 and 80 percent of the food in most developing countries. *Yet, despite their contribution to global food security, women farmers are frequently underestimated and overlooked in development strategies.*
>
> Despite the fact that women are the world's principal food producers and providers, they remain 'invisible' partners in development. A lack of available gender disaggregated data means that *women's contribution to agriculture in particular is poorly understood* and their specific needs ignored in development planning.

The rationale that stood at the center of the four focal case studies documented in this book has been part of this general conviction that seems to have sent international development research cadres around the world to make visible the hitherto "invisible" role played by women in agricultural production. Read at this level, this book serves its original purpose. It provides a thorough review of the topic, placing the position of women in agricultural production in each of the four settings within a larger frame of gender relations in the respective social, educational and political national arenas. Indeed, the need to provide such a synthetic overview of gender relations in rural production is particularly urgent in the Middle-East. "Nowhere in the world has the use of over-generalizing conceptual categories gained popularity to describe the status of women as in the Middle East," notes Forouz Jowkar (1998), a Senior Researcher in the prestigious New York based Institute for Development Anthropology. Jowkar writes:

> While early writings reduced women [in the Middle East] to sexual objects at the services of men, more recent writings, drawing on the conceptual dualism of traditional/modern, created such theoretical paradigms as public and private domains and honor and shame to deal with gender hierarchy. Although some writers mentioned the power women may draw from their physical isolation, almost all of them subsumed a wide range of women's productive activities under reproductive and domestic practices. They failed to account for the labor contribution of women in such undocumented areas as petty commodity production and commerce, domestic services, seasonal agricultural labor on family farms, or herding enterprises.

This particular, "biased understanding of women's contribution to rural production systems," Jowkar suggests, is a result of orientalist Western models of explanation of gender relations in the Middle East as well as Middle Eastern officials' own misguided and uninformed interpretation of what women do and own. The conclusion is therefore that: "governments and planners can no longer afford to plan and implement agricultural policies based on stereotypes ... women's labor in the agrarian sector must be acknowledged."

Moreover, although there is solid evidence to suggest that women's participation in agricultural production had dramatically increased in the Middle East between the 1960s and the late 1980s (Delancy and Elwy, 1989, quoted in Jowkar n.d.), women's access to land, credit, loans and other formal and informal resources necessary for sustained productivity has remained extremely limited.

More than a decade after the review provided by Jowkar, our updated analyses of the place of women in the production systems in four Middle Eastern settings describes a largely unchanged reality. Women are still the weaker sector in the four societies we studied, they are rarely eligible for credit and they have few enforceable rights over land and other resources. The results of our studies are also supported by a more recent FAO study that covers nineteen countries in the Near East. The Regional Plan of Action for Women in Agriculture in the Near East (RPAWANE, 2000) was carried out between 1996 and 2001, about the same time as the work reported in this book. In lines that parallel those that stand at the base of our collaborative work, the RPAWANE 2000 produced detailed papers that record the data on women in agricultural production in each of the countries participating in the project and a final Synthesis Report.[1] Although the project is said to have produced several technical papers dealing with a range of issues, including gender and environmental sustainability, these papers were never made public in a book form.

The four-country comparative project that stands at the center of this book is similar in many ways to the two FAO studies mentioned above, and draws on a larger logic that is articulated by this and several other international development organizations (e.g. The World Bank and USAID). But it had two important unique features that are worthy of discussion here. The first is what might be called "the peace factor" and the second is "the Israeli factor."

The Peace Factor

This project involves regional partners that had obviously never collaborated on shared research projects before. The very ability to cooperate was in fact one of the most important goals of the whole process. It was known, throughout the years of struggle to keep this project going, that creating networks that link Israeli, Palestinian, Egyptian and Jordanian scholars and agricultural demonstrators and other professionals was at least as important as the outcome of our shared workshops. Put bluntly, the very process of formulating shared projects that brought together Israeli and Palestinian technical staff was as important as the efficient results these focused projects might have yielded. When other projects speak about "enhancement of networking" or of "building of institutional capacity" they seldom relate to as a complex and fragile reality as the one this project was operating in. All in all, the trials and tribulations that the larger project on agricultural development and the effort to think through ways of inserting gender awareness into this larger project are all worth their while when one considers the small contribution they all made to building cooperative bridges for a more solid peace in the region. A noble cause indeed.

The Israeli Factor

This regional project brought Israel in as one of the "partners" in the comparative frame. Israel was positioned in this project not as a "donor country" looking from the outside at its less-developed neighbors, but as an equal partner. Efforts were made to ensure that funds, membership in the central steering committee, and structure of workshops and training sessions will be carried out in a rotating fashion that will ensure the equal participation of all partners. This reality is unique. It presents a case that do not fit into the mold of other development aid projects where a number of "developing nations" are grouped together in one category and the "donor country", most often a "developed," Western nation, is outside this group, initiating, facilitating and financing the project. This more common binary position of developing vs. developed, researched vs. researching has been problematized in this case. The results were interesting both on the level of the actual on-going encounter of the various partners and in terms of the way analysis of the data could be presented and interpreted.

On the "ground floor" level, I can attest as a participant in meetings and workshops, that the experience was liberating to all concerned. The exchanges between Jewish Israeli women and Palestinian professional women, especially when it was mediated by the strong presence of Egyptian and Jordanian women was mutually enriching. Elsewhere (Motzafi-Haller, 2001) I speak at greater length about the lessons learned by the Israeli participants who came to these meetings largely ignorant about the position of gender relations in their Arab neighboring countries. Most of us had to question the orientalist myths we were all subject to that posited Israeli gender relations and Israeli scholarship about gender as more advanced, more equal than that in the Arab Middle East. In my own case, such an encounter with professional feminist women from the Arab world sent me back to my desk (and there is enough reading in English, for I do not read Arabic even if my spoken Arabic is adequate) to begin reading in earnest about the history and present circumstances of Arab feminist struggles. I had eventually attempted to integrate what I learned from such reading and encounters into my own understanding of the Israeli reality of gender relations and the knowledge we have about such reality. It will be extremely interesting to learn about the experience of our Palestinian, Egyptian and Jordanian colleagues who may care to reflect on this, for most of us, first direct encounter with professional partners across the border.

But the inclusion of the Israeli case into the comparative framework of this project presented also important challenges at the level of reporting and interpretation of results. For it was obvious from the outset that the Israeli reality of the late 1990s and early 2000s do not fit the model of a developing society with a majority of poor rural women whose contribution to agricultural production work must be documented. As the Israeli chapter presented in this book records, agriculture is a very limited sector within the largely thriving Israeli economy. So what does it say about the ability to compare these variable case studies? Does the Israeli "more developed" reality stand as a mere exception to the otherwise uniform pattern of poverty and gender inequity? I wish to answer these questions by summarizing some of the conclusions the Israeli fact-finding exercise revealed about the question of gender equity and about the politics of research and knowledge production.

The first conclusion reached by the attempt to review the position of women in Israeli society is that the myth of gender equality in Israel has to be undermined. The review of the literature showed that study after study carried out by Israeli feminist scholars over the past two decades have documented the fact that Israeli women are dramatically underrepresented in both the local and the national political arenas, that there are explicit as well as powerful implicit mechanisms that prevent the equal participation and advancement of Israeli women in the labor force, that Israeli women earn much less than Israeli men with the same qualifications and, finally, that sexist practices and institutions are still prevalent in Israeli daily reality. This very simple overall conclusion (that is, that in the "developed" economy of Israel there is no gender equality) can be used to question the very distinction drawn in the development world between Western "liberated" women (often portrayed as the "saviors" of) their less fortunate sisters in the less-developed world. The comparative perspective presented in this book thus places a mirror in front of this implicit assumption and join postcolonial feminists in their critique of the very logic of western feminism and development (cf. Chandra Mohanty's classical essay "Under Western Eyes," 1988).

A second critical conclusion emerging from the attempt to place the Israeli case within the comparative framework of the three other Middle Eastern settings has to do with the fact that there was rather a limited amount of data on rural women in Israel. Aside from the unique story of the kibbutz Jewish women, research on rural women in Israel proved to be extremely limited in scope and range. Part of the explanation to this fact is the observation that rural women in Israel are either non-Jewish or Jewish from non-European origin. Feminist research in Israel, it was shown in the chapter on Israel has tended to ignore the reality of life of these women. The research on Jewish women in the Moshav agricultural settlement also came up with the startling discovery that till this day women are not eligible to vote to the local council and their vote is only counted as wives of male members. This lack of attention to the lives of minority group women is not unique to the Israeli setting and has been evident in the other recorded setting in the Middle East. It is part of the general tendency in WID studies to focus on gender differences and ignore issues that have to do with ethnic, class and racial difference. This phenomenon has also been widely discussed in the postcolonial feminist literature (cf. Dhruvarajan and Vickers, 2002).

Finally, another interesting observation that emerged from the comparative perspective that included the Israeli case along with the other three settings in the Middle East has been the question of the amount and quality of the data recorded. Having read and reread the reviews provided by my colleagues on gender-disaggregated statistical data I came to realize that such data simply does not exist in the Israeli official record. All my efforts to extract such data from official statistics and more focused files in the Ministry of Agriculture made me aware how rich the Egyptian record is in comparison and how more detailed the Jordanian and even the fledgling Palestinian Authority's records are in comparison to the Israeli case. It was also evident that in comparison with the Egyptian as well as with the Jordanian and Palestinian cases, there was a rather limited institutional support for gender-specific concerns and interests in Israel. For example, in the Israeli Ministry of agriculture there was only one position that has any dealings with women's interests. In the other Middle Eastern settings there were whole departments and a range of gender-specific policies in addition to a range of NGOs and special research projects that dealt with gender that were initiated by international agencies like the FAO and USAID. This realization made me question the unexamined expectation that the Israeli case will be more gender-aware.

A few closing words must be said here with regards to the politics of production of knowledge that I have raised in the introduction chapter. My overall feeling (and I speak only for myself and not for the other contributors to the book, or the other participants in the project) is that the urge to produce more and more data is an escape from addressing real issues and social realities of gender inequality out-there, in the local level. It is my sense that international development organizations often construct a three-step model that justifies their involvement in a local setting. The first step consists of collecting gender-specific data which is said to be the necessary basis for the second step of policy recommendations (or the new jargon of "action-oriented recommendations"). This in turn is supposed to lead to the final goal, the third step, of changing social realities. Yet this model seems to be stuck in the first step, or, at best, in the long list of policy recommendations that have very limited effect on social reality. Such obsession with more and more data seems to go around the real question of how does one bring about social change and of course, about the question of the ability and moral justification of outside bodies to encourage such change. The fact that this book has been the only lasting product of dealing with gender in the Danida project for regional agricultural cooperation is a sad comment about the ability to introduce change. Still, and in a more hopeful closing note, the experience was significant if only for the lasting ties it enabled across borders in this war-torn region.

Note

[1]   A brief summary report on RPAWANE 2000 can be found in the FAO web site under the following address www.fao.org/Gender/Static/mideast.htm

References

Dhruvarajan, V. and Vickers, J., *Gender, Race and Nation: A Global Perspective*, Toronto: Toronto University Press, 2002.

Food and Agriculture Organization (FAO) n.d. "A 'Gender and Food Security' Network," URL: www.fao.org/Gender/Static/mideast.htm

-------- "Gender and Food Security" www.fao.org/gender/en/agri-e.htm

Jowkar, F., n.d. "Rural Middle Eastern Women," *The Circular on Desertification*, The International NGO Network on Desertification and Drought. Binghamton, New York: Institute for Development Anthropology, 1989.

Mohanty, C., "Under Western Eyes: Feminist Scholarship and Colonial Dsicourses," *Feminist Review*, 1988, No. 30: 61–88.

Motzafi-Haller, P., "Reading Arab Feminist Discourses: A Postcolonial Challenge to Israeli Feminism," *Hagar: International Social Studies Review*, 2000, 1, 2: 63–89.

Index

Adam village 127
Adar, G. 102, 109 n.4–5, 110 n.6
Adva Center 95, 96, 97, 98
Aghwar 26, 27, 29, 35
agriculture
    extension services 26, 32, 60–1, 78,
        79, 80, 84, 86, 127, 128
    feminization of 59–60, 90, 126
    and gender 165
Ajloun Governorate 26, 27, 29, 30, 35, 37
Al Al-Bayt University 20
Al-Azraq 31
Al-Hashemiya 28, 29
Al-kudauri, A.S. 28–9
Al-qussous, R.N. 29
Al-Rimawi, A.S. 33, 41
Al-Rousan, L. 7, 13–47
Al-Saraf, R.H. 27
Algeria 9
Amman 8
Appelbaum, L 111
ARIJ (Applied Research Institute
    Jerusalem) 70

Badia 26, 27, 29, 31, 35, 39
Banin, T. 104
Bar-Lev, G. 103
Bar-Yosef, R. 102
Bedouin 93, 143
    men 108
    women 108, 152, 163–4
Beer Sheva 50
Beijing, World Conference on Women
    (1995) 40
Beit Furik, olive oil production 50
Beit Hanoun 66
Bethlehem 53, 66
Blank, D. 102

BPWC (Business and Professional
    Women's Club, Jordan) 21–2
Britain 95
Brockhaus, M. 33, 34
B'Teselem 81 n.1
BZU (Birzeit University) 58, 59, 70, 75,
    79

Cairo 3, 5, 8, 117, 118, 119, 149, 155
CAPMAS (Egyptian Central Agency for
    Public Mobilization and Statistics)
    130, 146
CCAs (Community Centers, Jordan) 22
census 18, 67, 106, 144
Cheriet, B. 8–9
Cohen, A. 107
conflict
    Arab-Israeli 50, 54
    Middle East 1
    religious 33
    role 145
Crewe, E. 9

Danida (Danish International
    Development Assistance) 5, 6, 7,
    162, 170
DAWN (Development Alternatives with
    Women for a New Era) 10
Deir-Alla 27
Denmark, women, in politics 95
development
    agencies 15, 20
    agricultural 10–11, 52, 81, 86, 160,
        167
    community 22, 39, 158
    discourse 4, 9, 10
    economic 7, 57, 153
    educational 22

family 61, 151, 152
human 47, 57–8, 127
institutions 8, 9
planning 39, 76, 165
policies 8, 13, 80
and power structures 11
projects 4, 10, 29, 38, 58, 73, 79, 130,
    153, 156
rural 2, 5, 8, 29, 34, 36, 39, 61, 158, 160
socio-economic 144
strategies 165
sustainable 2, 58, 75
women's 17, 42, 131, 142, 148, 154, 158
work 2, 4, 9
writings 9

education, women 160
    see also under individual countries
Efroni, F. 94
Egypt 9, 11
    agricultural rural organizations 130–1
    agriculture, post-harvest losses 115
    CAPMAS 130
    demographic trends 116
    employment/unemployment, by
        gender 121
    feminism 141
    gender issues, awareness 115
    Gender Planning and Policies Unit 130
    household head, by gender 121–2
    life expectancy, by gender 124
    literacy 118–20
    male/female gaps, by region 119–20
    men, education 142
    MOALR 128
    PCUWA 130
    poverty 117
        and gender 122–3
    rural/urban gaps 118–19
    SFD 130
    Social Affairs Ministry 130
    WID 130
    women
        education 120, 123, 126, 141, 144, 146,
            147, 148, 151, 152, 153, 155–6, 159
        empowerment 123
        health 123
        in local councils 124

    in politics 124–5
    women in agriculture
        agricultural policy reforms, impact
            131–4
        barriers 115–16
        bibliography, annotated 141–64
        case studies 134–8
        credit, access to 127–8
        extension services/training 128
        land, access to 127
        legal rights 125–6
        new knowledge/technology 128–9
        official bodies 129–30
        role 126–7
El-Or, T. 94
El-Sanabary, N. 128, 131
El-Tobshy, Z. 6, 7, 115–39, 151, 157
Elimination of Discrimination Against
    Women, Committee (UN) 23
employment
    agricultural 144, 163
    domestic 50
    off-farm 33
    self 20, 33, 43
    women's 5, 14, 17, 90, 91, 104, 144
empowerment, women 18, 23, 35, 42,
    58, 61, 88, 89, 123
Escobar, A., *Encountering Development* 9
Espanioly, N. 97, 108

FAO 26, 39, 166, 169
    extension services 128
    gender and agriculture 165
    house gardens 71
    web site 170 n.1
    see also RPAWANE
Far East 108
farmers
    men 32, 76, 77, 84, 128, 142
    women 20, 26, 30, 31, 33, 34, 35, 40,
        43, 60, 69, 74, 75, 76, 77, 78, 79,
        80, 84, 86, 87, 128, 138, 165
feminism
    discourses 8
    Egypt 141
    in Kibbutzim 109 n.5
    and nationalism 4
    paternalist 8, 9

Western 168
feminization, of agriculture 59–60, 90, 126
Ferguson, J., *The Anti-Politics Machine*
 9, 10, 11
Fleischer, A. 104

Gaza City 66
Gaza Strip 50, 54, 55, 56, 61, 63, 65, 66,
 67, 68, 90 n.3
gender
 and agriculture 165
 awareness 4, 80, 81, 167, 169
 bias 41, 47
 blindness 41
 data 74, 76, 79, 90, 169
 discrepancy 127
 discrimination 7, 47, 58, 97
 division 28, 29, 60, 72, 91, 99, 161, 163
 equality 5, 7, 8, 54, 58, 102, 103, 106,
 168
 equity 11, 78, 81, 168
 gaps 11, 15, 58, 91, 96, 99, 116, 160
 ideology 161
 inequality 2, 69, 75, 102, 103, 169
 issues 3, 5–6, 8, 40, 41, 53, 58, 115,
 116, 152
 oppression 10
 policies, policy evaporation 58
 relations 1, 2, 40, 67, 93, 94, 108, 141,
 165, 166, 168
 role 11
 sensitivity 130, 156
 specialists 3, 6, 7
 specific 3, 5, 6, 58, 106, 107, 169
"gender mainstreaming" 40, 57, 109, 130
Germany, women, in politics 95
GFJW (General Federation of Jordanian
 Women) 22
Giacaman, R. 67
Ginat, J. 107
Green-Line 52, 107, 108
Grown, C. 9, 10
GUYS (General Union of Voluntary
 Societies, Jordan) 21

Hammami, R. 3, 7, 47–92
Harrison, E. 9
Hasan, M. 108

Hashimate University 20
Hebron 48, 53, 66
Herzog, H. 94
Himour, K. 31
housewife 59

Ibrahim, I. 108
IDF (Israel Defense Forces), Operation
 Defensive Shield 52
IFAD (International Fund for
 Agricultural Development) 13
informal economy
 Israel 56
 Jordan 17
Intifada 4, 49–50, 61, 72
Irbid 32
Islam, and women 4
Israel 11
 agriculture, in the economy 98
 Agriculture Ministry 109
 informal economy 56
 rural population, decline 100
 rural settlements 101
 women
  Arab-Israeli 97
  education 97–8
  in kibbutzim 101–3, 108–9
  in labor market 96–7
  in moshavim 103–6, 108–9
  Oriental 94
  in politics 95
  research on 93–5
 women in agriculture 98–9
  non-Jewish rural sectors 106–8
  rural tourism 104
 women's organizations 104
Izraeli, D. 94

Jareissi, R. 108
Jenin 48, 52, 53, 66
Jerash Governorate 30
Jerash Women's Society 24
Jericho 8, 53, 66
Jerusalem 53, 66, 90, 94, 106
JNCW (Jordanian National Committee
 for Women) 23
JNFW (Jordanian National Forum for
 Women) 23

JOHUD (Jordanian Hashemite Fund for
    Human Development) 22, 26
Jordan 9, 11
  Agriculture Ministry 40
  education, by gender 16
  Education Ministry 20
  Health and Health Care, Ministry 20
  informal economy 17
  Municipal, Rural Affairs and
    Environment, Ministry 20
  NGOs 21–5, 41
    Coordinating Committee 23
  Social Development, Ministry 20
  VTC 16
  women
    in administration 19
    anemia 25
    demographics 14, 15
    development, organizations 20–5
    economic participation 17–18, 19–20
    in education 15–17
    empowerment 18, 23, 35, 42
    fertility 25
    in foreign affairs 19
    in government 19
    health 25–6
    illiteracy 25, 29
    land holdings 14
    in leadership/decision making
      positions 18
    livestock ownership 13–14
    in local councils 19
    marginalization 13
    obstacles 41
    in parliament 18–19
    projects 35–9
    rural 13, 15, 25–6
    unemployment 18
  women in agriculture 26–35
    division of labor 28
    information sources 34–5
    pay 30
    projects 35–9
    recommendations 41–3
    training 29
  women in agriculture decision-making
    31–5

Jordan University of Science and
    Technology 20
Jordan Valley 27, 33, 67, 77, 91
Jordanian Committee for Women's
    NGOs 23
Jowkar, F. 166
JRF (Jordan River Foundation) 23
JWU (Jordanian Women's Union) 21

Kandiyoti, D. 4, 5, 9
Karak Governorate 27, 33, 35, 37
Katzir, Y. 106
Khan Younis 66
Kibbutzim 93, 94, 99
  feminism 109 n.5
  gender inequality 102
  women in 101–2, 108–9
Kimhi, A. 103–4
Knesset 95, 97

Lesotho 10, 11
Lewin-Epstein, N. 104, 106
Lieblich, A. 102

Ma'or, A. 94
Mar'i, M.M. 107
Mar'i, S.K. 107
Marx, E. 107
Meir, Golda 95
MENA (Middle East News Agency) 48,
    54
Middle East, conflict 1
Mizrahi Jews 105, 109 n.1
modernization 141
  economic 4
  West Bank highland farming 59
MOPIC (National Team for Combating
    Poverty, Palestine) 56, 57, 75
moshavim 93, 99, 101
  women in 103–6
Motzafi-Haller, P. 1–12, 93–114, 165–
    70
Muslim
  Israeli 107
  society 158
  women 9, 97
Mu'tah University 20

Nablus 48, 50, 53, 66, 79
Nachmias, C. 103
Nairobi 39
nationalism, and feminism 4
NEF (Near East Foundation), survey 30–1
Negev 105, 106, 108, 109
Neuman, S. 102
Nevo, N. 105
NGOs Coordinating Committee, Jordan 23
NHF (Noor Al-Hussein Foundation) 26, 41
Noor Al-Hussein Foundation 22–3
North America 26

olive oil production, Beit Furik 50

PA (Palestinian Authority) 3, 11
   Agriculture Ministry 49, 51–2
      extension/research services 60–1
   Rural Development Department 60
   Women's Division 60–1
   see also WBGS
Palestine
   unemployment 49, 50
   women
      empowerment 61, 88, 89
      in labor force 54–6
      in policy-making 57–9
      and poverty 56–7
   women in agriculture 59–73
      bibliography, annotated 90–2
      demographics 63–4
      diversification, need for 79
      education 64–5, 68–9
      employment profile 65
      extension/training services 78–9, 80
      gender awareness, need for 81
      importance 71
      in labor force 61–2
      livestock 67
      mainstreaming
         benefits 74–5, 80
         constraints 73–4
      new technologies 67
      recommendations 79–81
      regional distribution 66
      research
         data gaps 84–5
         findings 75–6

gender database 76–7
   methodology 77
   terms of reference 86
   resources, access 69–71
   task division 72–3
   training 77–8, 87–9
   wage inequality 68
   see also PA; WBGS
Palgi, M. 102
paternalism, feminism 8, 9
PBDAC (Principal Bank for
   Development and Agricultural
   Credit, Egypt) 128
PCUWA (Policy and Coordination Unit for
   Women in Agriculture, Egypt) 130
peace process 2, 4, 8, 11, 49, 167
PENGON (Palestinian Environmental
   NGOs Network) 81 n.1
PIALES (Palestinian Institute for Arid
   Land and Environmental Studies) 53
"policy evaporation" 58
post-harvesting 3, 26, 126
   losses 115, 143
Princess Basma Women's Resource
   Center 24

QAF (Queen Ai'a Fund for Social
   Development) 22, 27, 41
Qalqilya 52

Rafah 66
Ramallah 51, 52, 53, 66
Raymon 28, 29
Regional Agricultural Program 2, 3
Rosenfeld, H. 107
Rotem, A. 104
RPAWANE (Regional Plan of Action
   for Women in Agriculture in the
   Near East) 166, 170 n.1

Sadan, E. 103
Said, N. 91
Schelly-Newman, E. 106
Schwartz, M. 98
Semyonov, M. 90, 104, 106, 107
Sen, G. 9, 10
Separation Wall, agricultural loss 52–4
Sered, S. 94

SFD (Social Fund for Development, Egypt) 130
Shoked, M. 105
Solomonica, D.D. 105
South Africa 10
Soviet Union 94
Sudan 26, 161
Sweden, women, in politics 95
Syria, women, in politics 95

Talmon-Garber, Y. 102
Tamari, S. 67, 91
Tulkarim 48, 52, 53, 66, 79

UN
 CEDAW Committee 23
 Declaration of the Decade for Women 39
 Elimination of Discrimination Against
  Women Committee 23
 Office of Special Coordinator 50
UNDP (United Nations Development
  Program) 47, 54, 72
unemployment
 Palestine 49, 50
 women 14, 18, 30, 55, 104, 121
UNICEF (United Nations Children's
  Fund) 75, 163
UNIFEM (United Nations Development
  Fund for Women) 44
USAID (US Agency for International
  Development) 28, 127, 128, 162,
  166, 169

villages
 Arab 91, 93, 106, 108
 Bedouin 108
 head 135, 136, 137
 Palestinian 108
 studies 141, 142, 143, 145, 146, 147,
  148, 149, 150, 151, 152, 153, 155,
  156, 158, 159, 161, 162

Wadi Ibn Hammad 33
wage inequality 68
Wasserfall, R. 106
WBGS (West Bank and Gaza Strip) 47
 agriculture
  adverse conditions 49–54

 crops destroyed 51
 agro-economic indicators 48–9
 humanitarian crisis 50–1
WCARRD (World Conference on
  Agrarian Reform and Rural
  Development) 39
West Bank 48, 52, 54, 55, 56, 59, 63, 64,
  65, 66, 67, 68, 69
 see also WBGS
WID (Women in Development) 160,
  161, 162, 169
 establishment 130
 model 4, 5
 criticisms 6–7
women
 academicians 93
 Arab 107
 Arab Israeli 95, 97
 Ashkenazi 94, 95, 97, 99, 103, 105, 108
 Bedouin 108, 152, 163–4
 Christian 9, 97
 Druze 97
 empowerment 18, 23, 35, 42, 58, 61,
  88, 89, 123
 Ethiopian 94
 and Islam 4
 Jewish 9
 in labor market, international
  comparison 96
 Moroccan 106
 Muslim 9, 97
 organizations 20–5, 160, 162
 in politics 14, 15, 19, 22, 23, 54, 94,
  95, 124, 125, 141, 154
 poverty 20, 30, 36, 41, 57, 60, 61, 121,
  122, 147, 168
 Russian 94
 Tunisian 106
 ultra-orthodox 94
 unemployment 14, 18, 30, 55, 104, 121
 Yemenite 106
 see also under individual countries
women in agriculture, earnings 13
 see also under individual countries
"women's work" 28, 59, 67, 98
World Bank 49, 52, 56, 160, 166
World Conference on Women, Beijing
  (1995) 40

Yarmouk University 20
YMWA (Young Muslim Women's Association) 21
YWCA (Young Women's Christian Association) 21

Zamir, A. 94, 102
Zarqa Governorate 27, 29, 31
ZENID (Queen Zein Al Sharaf Institute for Development, Jordan) 23
Zionist movement 94

For Product Safety Concerns and Information please contact our
EU representative GPSR@taylorandfrancis.com Taylor & Francis
Verlag GmbH, Kaufingerstraße 24, 80331 München, Germany